**WITHDRAWN
UTSA Libraries**

Non-Standard Employment under Globalization

Other titles from IDE-JETRO:

Hiroko Uchimura (*editor*)
MAKING HEALTH SERVICES MORE ACCESSIBLE IN DEVELOPING COUNTRIES

Hiroshi Sato and Mayumi Murayama (*editors*)
GLOBALISATION, EMPLOYMENT AND MOBILITY
The South Asian Experience

Takashi Shiraishi, Tatsufumi Yamagata and Shahid Yusuf (*editors*)
POVERTY, REDUCTION AND BEYOND
Development Strategies for Low-Income Countries

Mariko Watanabe (*editor*)
RECOVERING FINANCIAL SYSTEMS
China and Asian Transition Economies

Daisuke Hiratsuka (*editor*)
EAST ASIA'S DE FACTO ECONOMIC INTEGRATION

Hisayuki Mitsuo (*editor*)
NEW DEVELOPMENTS OF THE EXCHANGE RATE REGIMES IN DEVELOPING COUNTRIES

Tadayoshi Terao and Kenji Otsuka (*editors*)
DEVELOPMENT OF ENVIRONMENTAL POLICY IN JAPAN AND ASIAN COUNTRIES

Masahisa Fujita (*editor*)
ECONOMIC INTEGRATION IN ASIA AND INDIA

Masahisa Fujita (*editor*)
REGIONAL INTEGRATION IN EAST ASIA
From the Viewpoint of Spatial Economics

Akifumi Kuchiki and Masatsugu Tsuji (*editors*)
INDUSTRIAL CLUSTERS IN ASIA
Analyses of Their Competition and Cooperation

Mayumi Murayama (*editor*)
GENDER AND DEVELOPMENT
The Japanese Experience in Comparative Perspective

Nobuhiro Okamoto and Takeo Ihara (*editors*)
SPATIAL STRUCTURE AND REGIONAL DEVELOPMENT IN CHINA
An Interregional Input–Output Approach

Akifumi Kuchiki and Masatsugu Tsuji (*editors*)
THE FLOWCHART APPROACH TO INDUSTRIAL CLUSTER POLICY

Akifumi Kuchiki and Masatsugu Tsuji (*editors*)
FROM AGGLOMERATION TO INNOVATION
Upgrading Industrial Clusters in Emerging Economies

Koichi Usami (*editor*)
NON-STANDARD EMPLOYMENT UNDER GLOBALIZATION
Flexible Work and Social Security in the Newly Industrializing Countries

Non-Standard Employment under Globalization

Flexible Work and Social Security in the Newly Industrializing Countries

Edited By
Koichi Usami

IDE-JETRO

© Institute of Developing Economies (IDE), JETRO 2010

All rights reserved. No reproduction, copy or transmission of this publication may be made without written permission.

No portion of this publication may be reproduced, copied or transmitted save with written permission or in accordance with the provisions of the Copyright, Designs and Patents Act 1988, or under the terms of any licence permitting limited copying issued by the Copyright Licensing Agency, Saffron House, 6–10 Kirby Street, London EC1N 8TS.

Any person who does any unauthorized act in relation to this publication may be liable to criminal prosecution and civil claims for damages.

The authors have asserted their rights to be identified as the authors of this work in accordance with the Copyright, Designs and Patents Act 1988.

First published 2010 by
PALGRAVE MACMILLAN

Palgrave Macmillan in the UK is an imprint of Macmillan Publishers Limited, registered in England, company number 785998, of Houndmills, Basingstoke, Hampshire RG21 6XS.

Palgrave Macmillan in the US is a division of St Martin's Press LLC, 175 Fifth Avenue, New York, NY 10010.

Palgrave Macmillan is the global academic imprint of the above companies and has companies and representatives throughout the world.

Palgrave® and Macmillan® are registered trademarks in the United States, the United Kingdom, Europe and other countries

ISBN 978–0–230–23848–0   hardback

This book is printed on paper suitable for recycling and made from fully managed and sustained forest sources. Logging, pulping and manufacturing processes are expected to conform to the environmental regulations of the country of origin.

A catalogue record for this book is available from the British Library.

A catalog record for this book is available from the Library of Congress.

10 9 8 7 6 5 4 3 2 1
19 18 17 16 15 14 13 12 11 10

Printed and bound in Great Britain by
CPI Antony Rowe, Chippenham and Eastbourne

Library
University of Texas
at San Antonio

Contents

List of Tables	vi
List of Figures	viii
Notes on the Contributors	ix

Introduction: Transformation of Employment
and Social Security in Newly Industrializing Countries:
Problems and Analytical Concepts   1
Koichi Usami

1. Labor and Social Security Reforms in Mexico:
From the Perspective of State–Labor Relationships   18
Keiko Hata

2. Re-thinking Argentina's Labor and Social Security Reform
in the 1990s: Agreement on Competitive Corporatism   47
Koichi Usami

3. The Changing Nature of Employment and the Reform
of Labor and Social Security Legislation in Post-Apartheid
South Africa   73
Kumiko Makino

4. The Impact of the Transformation of Labor Relations on
Social Security System Reform in the People's Republic
of China: The Growing Allure and Reality of Corporatism   98
Yukari Sawada

5. The Tripartite Relationship and Social Policy in Taiwan:
Searching for a New Corporatism?   142
Yasuhiro Kamimura

6. Labor and Welfare for an Advanced Economy in the
Republic of Korea: A Policy Mix of Universalism
and Neoliberalism   176
Jo-Seol Kim

Index   220

List of Tables

I.1	Unemployment rates 2003 (%)	2
I.2	Stage of welfare state in the newly industrializing countries	6
1.1	Party representation in the lower house	26
1.2	Structure of the informal sector and formal sector	33
1.3	The number of affiliated workers of the IMSS	34
2.1	Flexible labor contracts established by employment law	58
2.2	The variation in labor contracts by different type of contract in Greater Buenos Aires (November 1995–November 1996)	64
2.3	Unemployment rate and the ratio of unemployed people who received unemployment insurance from 1992 to 1998	65
4.1	Number of labor disputes accepted by arbitration committee (cases and workers involved), 1995–2005	99
4.2	Increase of employment in urban units by region (2004)	109
4.3	Job vacancies by ownership (3rd quarter, 2006)	110
4.4	Did your employer provide these social security payments and allowances?	127
4.5	Migrant women workers' replies to the question "Who do you to approach for help when you face the following problems?"	129
4.6	Replies of unemployed women with Shanghai residential registration to the question in Table 4.5	132
5.1	Company benefits and employees' welfare council benefits	153
5.2	Unionization rate, 1987–2005	155
5.3	Unions affiliated with the Taiwan Confederation of Trade Unions, 2006	159
5.4	Unionization rate by industry, 2005	160
5.5	Labor indicators for Taiwan, 1980–2006	169
6.1	Economic and social indicators	183

6.2	Development of labor and welfare policy	186
6.3	Applicability and actual coverage of social insurance (as of May 2005)	196
6.4	Performance of employment insurance	196
6.5	Revision of dismissal for managerial reasons	197
6.6	Development of provisions of retirement benefit	199
6.7	Cross-classification by status and type of employment in the supplementary survey of August 2005	201
6.8	Labor unions and labor disputes	206
6.9	Three phases in the development of tripartite negotiation	208

List of Figures

2.1	Unemployment rate in greater Buenos Aires (1980–2003)	63
2.2	Unpaid pension premium rate in the main cities	65
3.1	The NEDLAC structure	76
5.1	Organization chart of the Federation of Industries	148
5.2	Organization chart of the Labor Unions Federation	150
5.3	The ratio of employment by size of establishment in the manufacturing industries	156
5.4	Method of applying for current employment (%)	156
6.1	GDP growth rate and unemployment rate, 1960–2005	178
6.2	Mandatory establishment size for labor standards act and social security	195

Notes on the Contributors

Keiko Hata is a professor in the Faculty of Social Sciences, Waseda University, Tokyo. She specializes in the contemporary political history of Mexico, and is currently studying social policies and gender issues.

Koichi Usami is Senior Research Fellow at the Institute of Developing Economies (IDE), JETRO. He is studying social policies and the welfare state in Latin America, especially Argentina, and is interested in comparative studies of social policies among newly industrializing countries.

Kumiko Makino is Research Fellow at the Institute of Developing Economies (IDE), JETRO. Her research interests are in the fields of politics of social policy, HIV/AIDS, and civil society in South Africa.

Yasuhiro Kamimura is Associate Professor of Welfare Sociology and Comparative Social Policy at Nagoya University, Japan. He studied at the University of Tokyo, and worked both there and at Hosei University. He has published on the development of welfare states in East Asia, social attitudes toward social policy in Japan, and the relationship between social problems and social policy.

Yukari Sawada is a professor at the Tokyo University of Foreign Studies. Her study focuses on social welfare reform in South China. She is currently interested in elderly care issues in Hong Kong.

Jo-Seol Kim is a professor at the Faculty of Economics, Shinshu University, Japan. She has been studying South Korea's modern economy and social policy from both historical and political perspectives. Her study in this book deals with the remarkable contrast between the neoliberal labor reform and universal welfare since the mid-1990s.

Introduction: Transformation of Employment and Social Security in Newly Industrializing Countries: Problems and Analytical Concepts

Koichi Usami

I.1 Problems of employment and social security

In the midst of the current wave of globalization, many academic debates have been held on the flexibilization and transformation of industrial relations. In the developed countries, labor laws were amended to promote the deregulation of the labor market after the 1980s (Regini 2000). Disputes over social security reforms also occurred at the same time, spurring similar social security reforms. These phenomena were not specific to the developed countries. Disputes and reforms on transformation of employment and social security also occurred in East Asian, South African, and Latin American countries. Today, trends of high unemployment, large informal sectors, and the informalization of the formal sector can be observed in Latin America and South Africa. In East Asia, unemployment rates are relatively low (see Table I.1), but non-standard employment is not a negligible problem. In the wake of the 2008 economic crisis, employment became the issue of the hour worldwide. A wide number of scholarly discussions on these themes have taken place in the newly industrializing countries.

Taylor-Gooby observes a mismatch in developed countries between existing social security systems and the new risks posed by societal transformations (Taylor-Gooby 2004). Yet, an experimental trend is visible in Latin America, where social security reform has been proposed – and in some cases realized – in step with social change, especially in the area of industrial relations. In Korea and Taiwan, social security systems are expanding rapidly while in China, the existing social security system has required reformation due to the expanding market economy. However, expanding social security systems in the newly industrializing countries do not necessarily seem to address the risks involved in flexible work.

Table I.1 Unemployment rates, 2003 (%)

Country	Average	Male	Female	Country	Average	Male	Female
Japan	5.3	5.5	4.9	Mexico	2.1	2.1	2.3
Korea	3.4	3.6	3.1	Brazil	9.7	7.8	12.3
China*	4			Argentina	15.6	16.3	14.7
Taiwan	5	5.5	5.3	USA	6	6.3	5.7
Hong Kong	7.3	9.3	6.2	Australia	6.5	5.9	6.2
Singapore	5.4	5.5	5.3	New Zealand	4.7	4.4	5
Malaysia*	3.5	3.3	3.8	UK	4.8	5.5	4.1
Turkey*	10.3	10.9	9.4	France	9.7	8.7	10.7
South Africa	28.4	25.5	31.7	Ex West Germany	11.2	11.6	11.7

*The dates that relate to China, Malaysia, and Turkey pertain to the year 2002.
The sources have been retrieved from http://www.ilo.org/public/english/bureau/stat/portal/online.htm in April 2005.

As such, one observes a connection between the evolving industrial relations and social security reform in the newly industrializing countries after the 1980s. This book will discuss the transformation of employment and social security that occurred and the manner in which these transformations adjusted to one another. This topic can be broken down into the following three questions. First, how did trends in employment and industrial relations change in the countries that have been newly industrializing since the 1980s? When addressing this question, it is important to take into account the institutional transformation that took place, including the amendment of labor laws and *de facto* transformation such as the expansion of the informal sector. Second, how are trends in employment and social security interrelated? Third, what factors regulate their relationship? This book will answer these three questions by analyzing cases from East Asian, South African, and Latin American countries with the intent of understanding the new directions taken by the welfare states in these regions.

I.2 Previous studies on employment and social security

I.2.1 Problems of unstable employment

Many of the studies conducted on employment show that flexible, non-standard, or informal employment is one of the major problems faced by East Asia, South Africa, and Latin America. As Kim states, a general academic consensus has emerged on the fact that the industrialization and flexibilization of Korea's industrial relations after the 1990s have led to the formation of a double labor market (Kim 2006: 65–6). A study carried out by Num calls into question the instability, low income, and low social security coverage of Korean non-standard work (Nam 2006). In China, many studies pay attention to the non-standard employment caused by the privatization of state owned enterprises and large-scale labor migration from the rural to the urban areas (Sawada 2006: 152–5).

There are many cross-country analyses of employment in Latin America, and flexbilization of industrial relations is one of the important themes that they share. Marshal studied labor reforms in Argentina, Brazil, and Mexico, and concluded that Argentina experienced the most radical employment flexibilization. Brazil deregulated only a small number of labor contracts and Mexico did not deregulate at all; in fact, it experienced intense labor disputes about the issue (Marshall 2004: 10). Marshall's study scrutinized the legal framework of the labor market, whereas Martinez and Tokman considered the real situation of the labor market. They observed a decrease in wages and quality of labor conditions due to a rise in short-term labor contracts and employment without any labor contract (Martinez and Tokman 1999).

High unemployment rates and growing non-standard employment have been observed by many researchers in South Africa (Hirano 1999: 240–5). Some scholars state that globalization is the reason behind the current expansion of unemployment of unskilled workers, as the phenomenon pressures economies to deregulate labor markets in order to increase international competitiveness (Bhorat et al. 2002). Thus, many academics have observed a rise of non-standard or flexible employment and investigated the adaptation of their legal frameworks and labor market realities in East Asia, South Africa, and Latin America.

I.2.2 Studies on social security in the newly industrializing countries

In recent years, many elaborate studies have been conducted on welfare states in the newly industrializing countries. Among them are studies on the characteristics of Latin American welfare states (Usami et al. 2001) and comparative studies between Asian countries and Latin American countries (Usami 2004). Likewise, one recent book (Kim (ed.) 2006) has outlined the current academic debates over the characteristics of the Korean welfare state. Another volume, published in Japanese, compares the structure of Korea's welfare state with the Japanese model (Takekawa and Kim (ed.) 2005; Takekawa and Lee (ed.) 2006).

Although they recognize industrial relations as the major factor contributing to the formation of each social security system, these studies focus principally on welfare regimes, the characteristics of social security systems in each country, and the factors of political economy that contributed to the formation of the welfare state. Esping-Andersen's three models of welfare capitalism are frequently referenced with regard to the topic of welfare regimes in the newly industrializing countries (Esping-Andersen 1990). A variety of welfare regimes have been discussed in this work, and the factors that form specific welfare state types have been investigated.

I.2.3 Problems of social security

Where the topic of social security reform is concerned, researchers tend to focus on the problems of employment and social safety nets in Asian countries in the wake of the economic crisis of 1997. An OECD report points out that too often, insufficient social security is provided to non-standard employees as compared to full-time employees and argues the necessity of expanding unemployment insurance, job-training, and social assistance programs (OECD 2000). Kohl cites the inadequacy of weak institutions and governance as reasons for rising inequality and poverty; he advocates the flexibilization of industrial relations to cope with globalization, but calls for more academic attention to be paid to this theme (Kohl 2002). Other scholars insist that social safety nets should act as automatic stabilizers for economic fluctuations (Blomquist et al. 2002). In Latin America, which is faced by a situation of unstable employment caused by the flexibilization of industrial relations, Tokman studies the kind of security that should be implemented to counter the increasing opportunity for dismissal and calls for the establishment of a specific variety of unemployment insurance (Tokman 2003). He argues the necessity for research on the efficiency of existing pension and health systems, and proposes the creation of universal social insurance systems. In this sense, his proposal corresponds to a reality where unstable employment is increasing; one that is compatible with the research of this volume.

However, there exist a small number of studies that have been conducted on the issue of reconciling the transforming employment situation with the social security system. Huber and Stephens argue that there is a relationship between the welfare and production regimes (Huber and Stephens 2001; Hall and Soskice 2001). The authors of this volume feel that beyond the relationship between welfare and production regimes, political economy is a principal and necessary tool to analyze the connection between employment and social security. In the case of Korea, Kim analyzes social insurance in relation to employment from the viewpoint of political science. He divides Korean welfare politics post-1990 into three phases: corporatist politics, interest group politics, and civil movement politics, and insists that a new, Korean type of social contract that regulates Korea's interests will emerge (Kim, 2006: 145–51). Kamimura insists that the relationship between the state and labor unions is decisively important in the formation of welfare states in East Asia (Kamimura 2004: 37). Corporatism has also attracted attention as a tool of interest regulation in Latin America. Wiarda argued that there existed a Latin American type of corporatism with Iberian traditions (Hammergren 1977) while Zapata noted the corporative characteristics in labor unions in the course of his studies on the Latin American labor movement (Zapata 1998). Therefore, although we need to clarify the meaning of corporatism when we use it, the above studies establish that corporatism used to be considered an important vehicle for interest regulation in East Asia and Latin America.

I.2.4 Main subjects of this book

As we have seen, while deregulation of the legal framework of the labor market has been realized in some cases, an expansion of non-standard employment is widely observed in all the newly industrializing countries. On the whole, the flexibilization of industrial relations and expansion of non-standard employment have become major issues of debate in these regions. Thus, this book must focus on the manner in which labor market deregulation is realized, the kinds of non-standard employment that exist in the newly industrializing countries, and the extent to which they do so. The second analytical concern is the types of social security regimes established and the manner in which they were formed for them. The third point of focus would be the manner in which these social security regimes might be reformed in accordance with the transformation of employment.

As mentioned above, political economy presents itself as an adequate tool for addressing the above concerns. However, the term comprises many analytical methodologies that have been developed by academics in the industrialized countries. For example, Miyamoto divides the evolution of the welfare state into three stages: the formation period (1940–70), the retrenchment period (1970–90), and the reconstruction period (1990–). He insists that to be studied adequately, each stage requires a different approach: the power resources theory must be used while studying the formation period, the new institutional theory in the case of the retrenchment period, and the idea and discourse politics theories while studying the present period (Miyamoto 2006: 69–70).

Miyamoto's framework is well-suited for analyzing welfare states in the industrialized world, but it cannot be applied directly to the newly industrializing countries. While it is true that these countries formed social security systems in parallel with the industrialized countries in the period extending from 1950 to the 1970s, their coverage was nevertheless limited in comparison. Moreover, the retrenchment of social security was not observed clearly in the newly industrializing countries in the 1980s. Along with the other significant effects of the new industrialization, newly industrializing East Asian countries also witnessed the formation of welfare states and expansion of social expenditure. Public social expenditure was expanding whereas neoliberal economic reforms had been realized in Latin America during the 1990s (Table I.2). The above facts indicate that there was a clear difference in the evolutionary phases of welfare state formation between the industrialized and the newly industrializing world.

In studying the balancing of flexible labor markets and social security, this volume employs corporatism as a major tool of analysis for the following two reasons. First, many previous studies have paid attention to corporatism as a measure of interest regulation used by welfare states in the newly industrializing countries. Second, some clear characteristics of state corporatism were observed in East Asia and Latin America under the authoritarian regimes that extended from the 1950s to the 1980s. Therefore, in this book we will first consider corporatism as a regulatory mechanism. Then in instances where corporatism has disappeared or has practically ceased to function, we will consider its alternatives.

Table I.2 Stage of welfare state in the newly industrializing countries

	1950–70	1980s	1990–
Korea/Taiwan	Limited welfare	Democratization	Formation of welfare state
China	State-owned enterprises welfare	To market economy	Social insurance
South Africa	Limited welfare to the white	Alleviation of racism	Expansion to all races
Latin America	Limited welfare	Crisis/democratization	Social security reform

I.3 Principal concepts of analysis

I.3.1 Flexible, non-standard, and informal employment

This section deals with the principal analytical concepts of this book. First, we will overview the various types of employment. Following the 1980s, the subject of flexibilization and deregulation of the labor market in the industrialized countries sparked public interest. In the developed world, there is a disparity between industrial relations and employment situations caused by differences in socioeconomical structures and political situations (Regini 2000). Thelen describes the next two major transformations of employment under the phenomena resulting from globalization (Thelen 2001: 71–81). The first is the tendency of industrial relations to flexibilize due to the acceleration of market competition. The second major change is that as issues of negotiation between laborers and employers, macroeconomic policy and full employment have given way to concerns related to production.

With respect to the second item, she points out that the central negotiation systems are shifting their focus from national issues to more localized business concerns in order to flexibilize labor. As was inevitable, the influence of globalization has reached the newly industrializing countries. Like their industrialized counterparts, they must also contend with the need to improve productivity and competitiveness and deregulate labor markets. In this way, the flexibilization of industrial relations has become a key concept around which the issues of employment are presented in the newly industrializing countries.

Many scholars have framed differing definitions of the flexibilization of industrial relations. For example, Standing classifies flexibilization into five categories (Standing 2000). Regini's classification is very clear and one of the most representative. He classifies the phenomenon into the following four categories: (1) *Numerical flexibility*: adjusting the amount of labor in correspondence with fluctuations in demand and technological change; (2) *Functional flexibility*: transferring jobs easily and making workers multi-task according to fluctuations and changes in demand; (3) *Wage flexibility*: adjusting wages with ease and in correspondence with changes in the labor market and competitive circumstances; and (4) *Temporal flexibility*: employing workers with ease under different kinds of labor contract and being able to adjust the number of workers in line with fluctuations in demand (Regini 2000: 16–19).

On the other hand, some scholars classify the flexibilization of industrial relations into external and internal types. External flexibilization refers to adjusting employment in accordance with economic fluctuations, changing wages, and numbers of employees in accordance with the current economic and employment situations. Internal flexibilization implies allocating workers' activities more flexibly and having them multi-task when necessary (Esquival 1994). Regardless, these flexibilizations of industrial relations sometimes require amendment of labor laws and agreement through collective bargaining. It is important to examine the kinds of institutional changes that have spurred such flexibilization. On the other hand, it is currently widely assumed that the flexibilization occurs without any preceding institutional changes. In such cases, it is important to confirm the conditions that contribute to the promotion of such *de facto* flexibilization. These flexible industrial relations, which fall outside the legal framework, could be considered as informal work.

The informal sector is also a key concept an a discussion of employment in Latin America and South Africa. To statistically confirm the size of the informal sectors, public institutes like ECLAC (the UN Economic Commission for Latin America and the Caribbean) use the following definition: "employees of small enterprises with staffs below 5 people, family service employees, unskilled independents, or unpaid family workers" (ECLAC 2002: 6). While this definition grasps the extent of the informal sector statistically, it does not express its nature. The essence of the informal sector includes the following factors: "economic activity without legal protection, work without social security, and unstable income" (Hataya 1993: 109). If we compare informal work with flexible work, the difference is clear. Flexible work is caused by the deregulation of labor markets and is located within the legal arena. However, it is observed that many flexible positions are unstable and lack social security. In this sense, the flexibilization of industrial relations means the "informalization" of formal employment.

The term "non-standard employment" is commonly used in East Asia. Generally, standard employment implies full-time and life-time employment while non-standard employment encompasses occupations such as dispatch work, part-time work, definite-term contract work, on-call work, or contract company work (Houseman and Ogawa 2003: 4–6). In some countries, non-standard employment is generally considered to lie within the legal arena. In this sense, non-standard employment is similar in concept to flexible employment. However, sometimes it includes informal sector work in the newly industrializing countries. Like flexible and informal employment, non-standard employment also creates the problems of instability, inferior wages, and insufficient social security. Houseman and Osawa indicate that the non-standard employment situation differs greatly among the industrialized countries (Houseman and

Osawa 2003: 4–6). Thus, we need to study the concept of non-standard employment carefully on a country-by-country basis.

I.3.2 Transformation of risk structure

The concept of "new risk" proposed by Taylor-Gooby is a key factor in discussing the way in which social security confronts the transformation of employment by globalization, which is the second theme of this book. He criticizes Esping-Andersen's argument on welfare regimes on the basis that it corresponds to old, class-based risks. The social risks observed in the industrialized countries today are life risks caused by the socioeconomic transformations brought about by the transition from an industrial society to a post-industrialized one. Taylor-Gooby labels the phenomenon as society's new risk. He elaborates, "recommodification and flexibility merge alongside decommodification and stratification as key concepts for analyzing welfare reform" (Taylor-Gooby 2004: 14). His concept of "new risk" is broad, including the transformation of gender roles, but when it comes to paid work, the same concept is composed of the following three problems: the problems associated with entering the labor market; those related to maintaining stable, secure, and reasonably well-paid employment and associated social security entitlements; and problems regarding gaining adequate training in a more flexible labor market (Taylor-Gooby 2004: 19).

This book will pay attention to the kinds of risks that have emerged from the legal or de facto transformation of industrial relations and the manner in which social security systems attend to these new risks in the newly industrializing countries. Of course, one expects diversity among the above factors in the various newly industrializing countries. On the one hand, China is in the midst of industrialization, but on the other, some characteristics of post-industrial society can be observed in Korea and some Latin American countries. Thus, it is natural to assume that the new risks they face are different and need to be analyzed in the context of each country's situation. Although China is still industrializing, its mode of industrialization is undergoing a massive transformation from a socialist model to a socialist market model; likewise, China's employment situation is also changing radically. Therefore, we should also consider China within the "new risk" framework.

I.3.3 The concept of corporatism

The third theme of this book is "how to mediate social security systems with changes in employment." On this theme, Taylor-Gooby states that new risks require new interest regulations that "cross-cut old social risk constituencies in complex ways" (Taylor-Gooby 2004: 8). As mentioned above, there is a difference between the evolutionary path of welfare states in industrialized and newly industrializing countries; the new risks they face cannot be the same. The political factors that regulate them, including labor relations, must differ in the developing world. However, certain type of corporatism have existed and acted as regulatory institutions in the newly industrializing countries. Therefore, we propose corporatism as the starting point for analysis. It is natural to presume that the types of corporatism differ from country to country.

In the light of the above fact, it is important to clarify the concept of corporatism. Among the various arguments on corporatism, Schmitter's definition is the most representative and widely used. He considers corporatism to be a system of interest representation, with the following nine elements composing its units: (1) Limited number; (2) Singular; (3) Compulsory; (4) Noncompetitive; (5) Hierarchically ordered; (6) Functionally differentiated categories; (7) Recognized or licensed (if not created) by state; (8) Representational monopoly within their respective categories; and (9) Control on leadership selection and interest articulation. He then divides the concept of corporatism into two subcategories: social corporatism and state corporatism. Social corporatism occurs in democratic political regimes and involves rather the first half of the abovementioned elements. State corporatism exists in authoritarian regimes and is characterized by the second half relatively (Schmitter 1979: 20–1).

On the other hand, Lehmbruch studies the cooperation existing between labor organizations and governmental authorities under liberal corporatism (a term that corresponds to Schmitter's "social corporatism") and insists that corporatism is an institutional framework for policy formation (Lehmbruch 1979). At present, social corporatism is considered to include the institutional aspect of interest representation, as well as functional aspects such as corporative action.

As mentioned above, state corporatism existed under the authoritarian regimes in Korea, Taiwan, and Latin America. These countries democratized after the 1980s and experienced a great transformation in their industrial relations and social security systems following democratization and globalization. Thus, it is important to carefully study the process through which states evolve from state corporatism, the kinds of tripartite negotiations that are involved in this evolution, and the manner in which corporatism reconciles transformed employment structures with existing social security systems. Two of the most likely forms of post-state corporatism are social corporatism and political pluralism.

All of the authors in this book refer to some sort of corporatism, including remnants of state corporatism, attempts at social corporatism, and competitive corporatism. As proposed by Rhodes, "Competitive corporatism" takes into account the competitiveness and productivity concerning industrial relations. This method manages to consider the negative sides to market competition and implement measures to mitigate them (Rhodes, 2001).

I.4 Newly industrializing countries and findings

I.4.1 Newly industrializing countries

This book covers the newly industrializing countries of Asia, Africa, and Latin America. Korea, China, Taiwan, South Africa, Mexico, and Argentina are also analyzed. The following are among the reasons for the selection of these particular countries. First, all of these countries are industrializing economies where social problems such as unemployment and unstable work have become mainstream political issues. Some of these countries contain aspects of post-industrial societies, such as the existence of sizeable service sectors. After the 1980s, all these countries experienced some transformation in their industrial relations.

Second, these countries have developed social security systems whose coverage is not limited to a small percentage of their populations. Following their democratization in the 1980s, the East Asian countries rapidly developed social security systems while the Latin American countries began to develop the same after World War II under the policy of import-substitution industrialization and expanded coverage to formal sector workers. China's social security system grew as it evolved into a socialist regime in which the state-owned enterprises offer social security. Yet, under its transition from a socialist regime to a socialist market regime, state-owned enterprises could no longer guarantee their employees social security and thus social insurance systems were introduced in China.

Third, all of these countries have shown signs of corporatism even after the 1990s. Korea, Taiwan, and the Latin American countries experienced state corporatism under authoritarian regimes. Today, these countries maintain different kinds of corporatism as a means of reconciling the conflicting interests. In South Africa, tripartite negotiation was institutionalized as NEDLAC (National Economic Development and Labor Council) in the process of democratization. In China, a system of tripartite negotiation has been expected to emerge as a social stabilizing mechanism.

All newly industrialized countries have democratized (with the notable exception of China). Under a democratic regime, labor unions wield influence not only in social policy formation, but also with regard to the improvement of working conditions and wages through collective bargaining. However, labor union membership rates are dropping worldwide (ILO 1997: 239–40) and their influence varies considerably from country to country. Therefore, it is important to study the kinds of corporatism that have been formed and the influence they wield over social policy formation in each country. In the case of China, communist one-party dictatorship continues and labor unions are essentially semi-governmental organizations. Thus, we need to confirm the real influence of labor unions on Chinese politics.

This book is structured as follows. Chapter 1 studies the Mexican state corporatism that was formed under the PRI (Partido Revolucionario Institucional: Institutional Revolutionary Party) regime, and discusses its impact on the transformation and reform of labor and social security issues. Chapter 2 outlines the Argentine competitive corporatism that was realized in the 1990s and analyzes the flexibilization of industrial relations and social security reforms that have occurred under it. Chapter 3 discusses the corporatism formed during the democratization of South Africa. Its representativeness and efficiency in resolving social security problems are also considered. Chapter 4 examines the problems of unemployment and non-standard employment in China and analyzes the efficiency of the tripartite negotiation that the Chinese government considers to be an effective measure for resolving disputes. Chapter 5 discusses state corporatism and attempts at social corporatism and analyzes the situation of the labor market and labor–social security reforms in Taiwan. Chapter 6 analyzes the transformation of the Korean labor welfare regime between the period of developmentalism existing before 1960 and the democratic consolidation post-1987 and explores the extent of neocorporatism following the country's democratization.

I.4.2 The findings of the book

Concerning the first theme of this book – "how industrial relations and employment situations change over time" – we can divide the newly industrializing countries into the following two groups. The first includes China, Korea, and Argentina, where industrial relations became more flexible through the reform of labor laws. China suspended lifetime employment contracts through labor laws implemented in 1994, Korea established flexible labor contracts through the labor standard law passed in 1997 and permitted M&A (merger and absorption) dismissal in 1998, and Argentina introduced flexible labor contracts through labor law reforms during the 1990s. The second group includes Mexico, South Africa, and Taiwan where flexible work was expanded without the amendment of the labor laws. In the case of Mexico, there existed a sizeable informal labor sector – which is still expanding – and flexibilization was advanced through agreements between laborers and employers. In South Africa, attempts were made to protect the interests of workers through reforms in the existing labor laws and an increased use was made of flexible work – the type of labor that has commonly been used since the apartheid era. In Taiwan, the fluidity of workers has always been high and the labor market has also always been characterized by its flexibility. Therefore, with the exception of Taiwan – where the fluidity of workers can almost be taken for granted – the expansion of non-standard or flexible work has posed great problems in the countries considered above.

Regarding the second theme of this book – "how social security programs respond to expansions of non-standard or flexible employment" – we made the following findings. Some measures to alleviate the negative side-effects of non-standard or flexible employment have been implemented through the amendment of labor laws or by establishing social assistance systems in all of the countries under consideration. However, these social security systems lack effectiveness, are insufficient, or are sometimes unwilling to take new risks. The Korean social security system for non-standard workers is lacking in efficiency and a universal social assistance system complements its deficient labor laws. South Africa has expanded the labor law's nominal coverage through the Basic Conditions of Employment Act (BCEA) that provides social protection equally to standard and non-standard workers. However, the nominal coverage expansion to include non-standard workers does not seem to be functioning effectively. As the application of the BCEA to non-standard workers is limited, it is often supplemented by the universal social assistance system that aims to help the non-labor force. Argentina introduced compensatory measures such as unemployment insurance when it deregulated its labor market, but the effects of these measures have been very limited. In Mexico, social security reform is limited and has little real use as a response to the country's ballooning informal sector. Taiwan, on the other hand, has introduced universal medical insurance appropriate for existing flexible labor market conditions.

Considering the third theme of this book – "how to mediate social security systems with transformations of employment" – we observe the following three points. First, certain frameworks of corporatism did not disappear following the decline of state corporatism in Korea, Taiwan, South Africa, and Latin America. Imperfect social corporatism persists in Korea post-democratization, while nascent social corporatism is still seen in Taiwan. The Chinese government expects tripartite negotiation to solve the country's labor problems. In South Africa, a corporate institution composed of the state, laborers, employers, and the community has been formed, dealing with matters ranging from labor issues to various problems relating to development. In Mexico, frameworks of state corporatism that emerged under the PRI regime remain in force, and an agreement to increase productivity and competitiveness was signed between laborers and employers in 1992. Ironically, this residuum state corporatism functioned to maintain the existing interests of labor in Mexico. On the other hand, a competitive corporatism that prioritizes productivity and competitiveness was realized in Argentina during the 1990s.

No single type of corporatism prevails in all the cases studied; only in Korea and Argentina do corporate systems partially reconcile social security with transformations in employment. With the exception of these two cases, corporatism does not respond to the growing rift between labor transformation and existing social security systems. Specifically, an existing or newly implemented social security system for flexible work either does not function well or its coverage is too restrictive. For example, the case of Mexico shows that remnants of state corporatism hinder social security reforms. The principal reason why corporatism cannot solve the above problem is that the labor constituency under a corporate system is composed of formal sector workers. Thus, formal sector workers tend to protect existing social security policies out of self-interest, and rarely willingly help flexible or informal sector employees to improve their situation. In the case of China, this trend is also observed but is accompanied by the problematic phenomena of decreasing labor union memberships, divisions within labor unions, and lack of labor union autonomy.

From the above, it can be concluded that the existing framework of corporatism is unsuited to tackling the challenges posed by the new risks associated with flexible employment. The Korean case shows us that, unlike labor politics which requires confrontation with formal sector interests, civil society can succeed in forming a universal welfare system in the arena of welfare politics. The rare cases in which corporatism at least attempts to reconcile the flexibilization of industrial relations and social security emerge on the basis of two possible factors. The first was the case of Argentine competitive corporatism, which offered a social policy framework to alleviate the negative effects of labor market deregulation. If its agreement on social policy had proved truly effective in protecting flexible work, it would have provided one of the ideal solutions to the employment–social security mismatch resulting from the phenomenon of globalization. However, its effects were limited and such agreements based on competitive corporatism only existed in the 1990s. The other possibility is exemplified by South Africa's National Economic Development and Labor Council, which includes community groups among its members. As Makino points out in this volume, the NEDLAC is plagued by various problems, but it does show that when a corporate system makes efforts to include the community sector, it may be possible to address non-formal sector workers' issues.

References

Japanese

Hataya, Noriko. 1993. "Urban Informal Sector." In *Latin American Economy*, ed. Shoji Nishijima and Yoichi Koike. Tokyo: Shinhyoron, pp. 106–23.

Hirano, Katsumi. 1999. "An Analysis on Mass Unemployment in South Africa." In *Impacts of New South Africa*, ed. Katsumi Hirano. Chiba: Institute of Developing Economies, pp. 231–62.

Kamimura, Yasushi. 2004. "Welfare States in East Asia: A comparative Study." In *Welfare Strategy of Asian Countries*, ed. Mari Osawasa. Kyoto: Minerva, pp. 23–65.

Kim, Jo-Seol. 2006. "Employment, Transformation of Labor Policy, and Actual Problems." In *Handbook of Employment and Social Policy*, ed. Koichi Usami and Kumiko Makino. Tokyo: Institute of Developing Economies, pp. 63–85.

Kim, Yeon Myung. 2006. "Korean Welfare Politics: Characteristics and Transformation." In *The Korean Welfare State and Japanese Welfare States*, ed. Shogo Takegawa and Kim Yeon Myung Tokyo: Toshindo, pp. 128–56.

Kim, Yeon Myung, ed. 2006. *Dispute on the Korean Welfare State*. Tokyo: Ryutsu Keizai University Press.

Miyamoto, Taro. 2002. "Globalization and the New Politics of Welfare States." In *Politics of Reform in Welfare States*, ed. Taro Miyamoto. Kyoto: Minerva, pp. 1–35.

Miyamoto, Taro. 2006. "Restructuring Welfare States and the Politics of Discourse: A New Analytical Framework." In *Comparative Politics of Welfare: Institutional Transformation and Strategy of Actors*, ed. Taro Miyamoto. Tokyo: University of Waseda Press, pp. 68–88.

Nagase, Nobuko. 2004. "Vulnerabilities and Social Protection of Non-Standard Workers in Japan." *Quarterly of Social Security Research* 40, no. 2: 116–26.

Nam, Jaeryang. 2006. "The Situation of Non-Standard Employment in Korea." Paper presented to the workshop organized by Japan Institute for Labour Policy and Training, Korean Labor Institute, and CALSS.

Sawada, Yukari. 2006. "Employment and Social Policy in China." In *Handbook of Employment and Social Policy*, ed. Koichi Usami and Kumiko Makino. Tokyo: Institute of Developing Economies, pp. 151–68.

Takegawa, Shogo, and Kim Yeon Myung, eds. 2005. *The Korean Welfare State and Japanese Welfare States*. Tokyo: Toshindo.

Tkegawa, Shogo, and Lee Hye-Kyung, eds. 2006. *The Welfare Regimes in Japan and Korea: Social Security, Gender, and the Labor Market*. Tokyo: University of Tokyo Press.

Usami, Koichi, ed. 2001. *The Welfare Sates in Latin America*. Chiba: Institute of Developing Economies.

English and Spanish

Beck, Ulrich, Anthony Giddens and Scott Lash. 1994. *Reflexive Modernization: Politics, Traditional and Aesthetics in the Modern Social Order*. Cambridge: Polity Press.

Bhorat, Haroon, Paul Lundall and Sandrine Rospabe. 2002. "The South African Labor Market in a Globalizing World: Economic and Legislative Considerations." ILO Employment Paper no. 2002/32. Geneva: International Labour Organization.

Blomquist, John, Juan Pablo Cordoba, Marijn Verhoeven, Patricia Moser and Cecer Bouillon. 2002. "Social Safety Nets in Response to Crisis: Lessons and Guidelines from Asia and Latin America." In *Towards Asia's Sustainable Development: The Role of Social Protection*, ed. OECD. Paris: Organisation for Economic Co-operation and Development, pp. 297–382.

Economic Commission for Latin America and the Caribbean (ECLAC). 2002. *Social Panorama of Latin America 2000–2001*. New York: ECLAC.

Esping-Andersen, Gøsta. 1990. *The Three Worlds of Welfare Capitalism*. Cambridge: Polity Press.

Esquival, Valeria. 1994. "¿La flexibilización laboral como generadora de empleo?" *ERGO* 1, no. 1: 36–9.

Hall, Peter A., and David Soskice. 2001. "An Introduction to Varieties of Capitalism." In *Varieties of Capitalism: The Institutional Foundations of Comparative Advantage*, ed. Peter A. Hall and David Soskice. Oxford: Oxford University Press, pp. 1–68.

International Labour Organization (ILO). 1997. *World Labor Report 1997–98*. Geneva: ILO.

Lehmbruch, Gerhard. 1979. "Liberal Corporatism and Political Party." In *Trends toward Corporatist Intermediation*, ed. Philippe C. Schmitter and Gerhard Lehmbruch. London: SAGE Publications, pp. 53–61.

Hammergren, Linn A. 1977. "Corporatism in Latin American Politics: A Reexamination of the Unique Tradition." *Comparative Politics* 9, no. 4: 443–61.

Houseman, Susan, and Machiko Osawa eds. 2003. *Nonstandard Work in Developed Economies: Causes and Consequences*. Kalamazoo, MI: Upiohn Institute.

Huber, Evelyne and John D. Stephens. 2001. *Development and Crisis of the Welfare State*. Chicago and London: The University of Chicago Press.

Kohl, Richard. 2002. "Globalization and Inequality in Southeast Asia." In *Towards Asia's Sustainable Development: The Role of Social Protection*, ed. OECD. Paris: Organisation for Economic Co-operation and Development, pp. 23–47.

Marshall, Adriana. 2004. "Labor market policies and regulations in Argentina, Brazil and Mexico: programs and Impacts" Geneva: International Labour Organization.

Martínez, Daniel, and Víctor Tokman. 1999. "Efectos de las reformas laborales: Entre el empleo y la desprotección." In *Flexibilización en el margen: La reforma del contrato de trabajo*, ed. Daniel Martínez and Víctor Tokman. Ginebara: Oficina Internacional del Trabajo, pp. 11–37.

Organisation for Economic Co-operation and Development (OECD) 2000. *Pushing Ahead with Reform in Korea: Labor Market and Social Safety Net Policies*, Paris: OECD.

Regini, Marino. 2000. "The Dilemmas of Labour Market Regulation." In *Why Deregulate Labour Markets?*, ed. Gøsta Esping Andersen and Marino Regini. Oxford: Oxford University Press, pp. 11–29.

Rhodes, Martin. 2001. "The Political Economy of Social Pacts: Competitive Corporatism and European Welfare Reform." In *The New Politics of the Welfare Sate*, ed. Paul Pierson. Oxford: Oxford University Press, pp. 165–94.

Schmitter, Philippe C. and Gerhard Lehmbruch (eds). 1979. *Trends toward Corporatist Intermediation*. London: SAGE Publications.

Standing, Guy. 2000. "Globalization and Flexibility: Dancing around Pensions." Geneva: International Labour Organization.

Taylor-Gooby, Peter. 2004. "New Risks and Social Change." In *New Risks, New Welfare: The Transformation of the European Welfare State*, ed. Peter Taylor-Gooby. Oxford: Oxford University Press, pp. 1–28.

Thelen, Kathleen. 2001. "Varieties of Labor Politics in the Developed Democracy." In *Varieties of Capitalism: The Institutional Foundation of Comparative Advantage*, ed. Peter A. Hall and David Soskice. Oxford: Oxford University Press, pp. 71–103.

Tokman, Víctor E. 2003. *Hacia una visión integrada para enfrentar la inestabilidad y el riesgo*. Santiago: Comisión Económica para América Latina y el Caribe.

Usami, Koichi. 2004. "Introduction: Comparative Study of Social Security Systems in Asia and Latin America — A Contribution to the Study of Emerging Welfare States." *Developing Economies* 42, no. 2: 125–45.

Zapata, Francisco. 1998. "Trade Unions and Corporatist System in Mexico." In *What Kind of Democracy?*, ed. Philip D. Oxhorn and Graciela Ducatenzeiler. University Park, PA: Pennsylvania University Press, pp. 151–67.

1
Labor and Social Security Reforms in Mexico: From the Perspective of State–Labor Relationships

Keiko Hata

Introduction

With the financial crisis of 1982, Mexico's development strategy shifted from a policy of state-guided import-substitution industrialization (ISI) to a market economy. First structural adjustment programs were implemented, and later other measures – such as the liberalization of trade and capital and the privatization of state-run companies – were implemented. During the administrations of Salinas, Zedillo and Fox, which are dealt with in this chapter, reforms in labor relations and the social security system were also attempted in order to adapt them to globalization. As these reforms would have a great impact on organized labor as a whole, the opposition they met from the labor movement was stronger than that to the privatization of state-run companies, trade liberalization and tax system reform (Madrid 2003: 60–6). Despite labor's opposition, the private sector workers' pension system was privatized, and labor relations gradually became more flexible – although the Labor Law was not revised. This flexibility led to job instability which meant an increase in layoffs and more non-regular/irregular employment. Despite this situation, Mexico has yet to implement measures, such as the introduction of unemployment insurance, in order to meet the risks of job insecurity.

In this chapter I will examine Mexico's labor and social security reforms in terms of the effect that they have had on state–labor relationships and the restructuring of labor organizations.

1.1 State–labor relationships under the PRI system

It was possible to carry out labor reforms in Mexico without revising the relevant laws and by imposing unilateral risk on workers precisely because they were implemented under the Institutional Revolutionary Party (PRI) system. The PRI system can be regarded generally as corporatism. According to Philippe C. Schmitter,

> Corporatism can be defined as a system of interest representation in which the constituent units are organized into a limited number of singular, compulsory, noncompetitive, hierarchically ordered and functionally differentiated categories, recognized or licensed (if not created) by the state and granted a deliberate representational monopoly within their respective categories in exchange for observing certain controls on their selection of leaders and articulation of demands and supports.

And Howard J. Wiarda points out the following three characteristics of corporatism: (1) a strong directing state; (2) restrictions on interest-group freedom and activity; (3) incorporation of interest groups into and as part of the state system, responsible both for representing members' interests in and to the state and for helping the state administer and carry out policies (Adams 2004: 61–2).

Corporatism is classified into state corporatism, in which the state has a strong controlling power, and social corporatism, which is based on the spontaneous characteristics of social groups. Mexico fits into the former where corporatism is essentially an exchange relationship consisting of state control over occupational groups and the regulation of benefits among these groups, with the realization of benefits for occupational groups determined by their support and subordination to the government.

The main occupational groups in Mexico are labor, peasants, public employees and teachers' organizations (all of these groups were included within the PRI), and nonpartisan business groups.

The labor sector of the PRI comprises the Confederation of Mexican Workers (CTM), inaugurated in 1936, and the unions in key industries such as oil, railways and electric power. The popular sector is made up of the Federation of Public Service Workers (FSTSE) and the National Teachers Union (SNTE). In 1966 the Labor Congress (CT) was organized in order to eliminate opposition elements within the labor groups. It consists of PRI-aligned groups[1] and has always been led by the CTM. Most labor groups were under the control of the PRI and independent organizations were a minority, representing less than 10 percent of the number of unions and union members in 1979 (Burgess 2003: 76). However, there are two points that should be mentioned in this regard. First, in the labor sector there have been several national-level organizations apart from the CTM, which made possible the segmentation of the labor movement during the Salinas administration. Second, the bargaining power of the popular sector has been stronger than that of the labor sector. Moreover, the recent neoliberal measures have weakened the labor movement, particularly in the export sector, while the FSTSE and SNTE have risen to supremacy.

Unlike the above groups, the business groups were not aligned with the PRI and were independent to a certain extent, but through public and private channels, they were within the PRI system. These business groups included the National Confederation of Chambers of Commerce (CONCANACO), the Confederation of Industrial Chambers (CONCAMIN), the National Chamber of the Manufacturing Industry (CANACINTRA), the Mexican Employers' Confederation (COPARMEX), the Mexican Council of Businessmen (CMHN), and the Business Coordinating Council (CCE).[2] In the second half of the 1930s, enterprises capitalized above a certain amount were required to join CONCANACO, CONCAMIN or CANACINTRA. This indicates that these three groups are semi-public bodies, different in nature from other voluntary organizations. During the discussions about the revision of labor legislation and during the tripartite negotiations carried out starting in the 1980s, the CCE and COPARMEX played principal roles.

In collaboration with the government, labor groups and business groups formed tripartite organizations, such as the National Minimum Wage Commission (CNSM) and the Labor Conciliation and Arbitration Boards (JCAs), where the government (Ministry of Labor and Social Security – STPS) acted as arbitrator. In these bodies, the CTM accounted for the majority of labor representation. After World War II, it was an urgent task for the government and business, which together were promoting import substitution industrialization, to control radical labor movements and obstruct the formation of independent labor unions. The CTM and other labor unions aligned with the PRI played a part in this task. In return, they were guaranteed employment and wage increases, and benefited from health insurance for workers affiliated with labor unions, social security such as pensions, and the housing fund for workers (National Workers' Housing Fund Institute (INFONAVIT)). The CTM still holds the right to represent labor at the Mexican Institute of Social Security (IMSS) and at INFONAVIT, and even today the housing fund in particular is an important resource for the CTM (Burgess 2003: 76–8). Being under the influence of the political system, bodies like the CT and CTM became known as *official unionism* or *corporate unionism*. The privileges of the CTM were guaranteed in exchange for support of and relative submission to the government. In addition, the activities of all unions, including those affiliated with the CTM, were strictly controlled by the Labor Ministry (STPS) and the JCAs.

The honeymoon relationship between the PRI and the labor organizations changed following the adoption of liberalization policies in the 1980s. As there was a reduction in the functions of the state, an adequate distribution of profits became more difficult, which called into question the rigidity of labor thereby threatening the vested interests of labor organizations. Furthermore, a new center of labor power was born in 1992 when the Federation of Public Goods and Services Unions (FESEBES) achieved official recognition. As a labor organization in the neoliberal period, FESEBES later became the leader of the independent labor movement promoting "new unionism" based on cooperation with management. In 1997 it was dissolved and became the National Workers' Union (UNT). The Mexican Telephone Workers' Union, the Workers' Union of the Mexican National Autonomous University and the National Social Security Workers' Union (SNTSS) constitute the backbone of the UNT.

All previous research on the PRI system agrees that from the time of the De la Madrid administration (1982–88), neoliberal economic measures were implemented which weakened the power of labor, and the main labor organizations such as the CTM turned to cooperating with the government. If corporatism is regarded as an exchange relationship between the state (government) and interest groups, i.e., control and profit distribution by the former and support and obedience by the latter, what has the CTM obtained by supporting and obeying the government? Furthermore, with economic liberalization, has Mexico's corporatism continued, disappeared or transfigured? In the following section, I will focus principally on the relationship between the government and the CTM, and examine what type of relationship was formed between them during the liberalizing reform process of the labor and social security systems.

1.2 The debate over labor law revision

1.2.1 Attempts to revise labor law and the points at issue

According to Article 123 of the Mexican Constitution, enacted in 1917, workers are given guarantees, such as the right to an eight-hour working day, the right to form labor organizations and the right to strike. At the time of enactment, these were progressive provisions, even when considered worldwide. In 1931 the Federal Labor Law (LFT) was enacted and still remains in force after a revision in 1970. The gap between legislation and reality is wide, and workers' rights have not always been protected. However, as economic liberalization demanded further deregulation of the legal framework, the pressure from management groups and international bodies for revising it strengthened.

Salinas showed an interest in labor legislation revision before assuming the presidency. However, the first bill calling for revision was drawn up in 1989 by COPARMEX, a management organization. They regarded the growth of productivity and competitive power as the main issues, and saw the following points as essential: flexibility in working hours and terms of contract, the introduction of payment according to ability, the reduction of technical skill training requirements, support for the expansion of employment in small and medium-sized businesses, the decentralization of labor legislation, and labor–management dialogue and cooperation. Although the Commission for the Revision of the Federal Labor Law, a tripartite body under the Labor Ministry was formed at that time, these points were never opened to public debate. This may be explained by the following facts: the Commission for the Revision of the Federal Labor Law lacked a clear policy; the CTM was against the revision while FESEBES agreed to it, so labor's position on the issue was split; the government was in the middle of the North American Free Trade Agreement (NAFTA) negotiations and was concerned that the debate about labor legislation revision might produce uneasiness in labor organizations which might have affected the NAFTA negotiations (Zapata 2006: 88–91).

The Zedillo administration, which took office in the middle of the 1994 financial crisis, had to implement emergency measures to avoid a prolongation of the crisis. It had to have the cooperation of labor organizations to restore stability to the economy. Consequently, the government, by its own account, did not take any steps toward revising labor legislation. However, the debate on revision was resumed following the OECD's recommendation concerning the "need to reform labor legislation and the social security system in order to improve market functionality".

The National Action Party (PAN), a center-right opposition party, set the renewed effort in motion, submitting a reform bill to the upper house of the congress in 1995. Strongly reflecting the demands of business, the bill called for employment and productivity to be the general principle for the determination of labor rights, fixed-term employment and the expansion of contracts with foreign workers, the establishment of an independent labor court instead of the Conciliation and Arbitration Boards (JCAs), a reduction in the weekly working time from 48 to 40 hours, a simplification of the procedures for the official recognition of labor organizations, a recognition of the right to enter into collective contracts for delegates of individual workers and enterprise committees, and an elimination of the privileges of labor unions. The aim of the bill was to curb the power of the government and the PRI-aligned labor unions over labor issues, and deregulate labor relations. The PRI-aligned labor unions opposed these measures, and the PRI president also showed his support for the CTM and CT.

The Democratic Revolutionary Party (PRD), a center-left opposition party, did not deny the need for legislation revision per se, but opposed the PAN bill which impaired the benefits of workers (Aguilar and Vargas 2006: 111–14). In 1998, while conceding to some of the demands of business, such as productivity-oriented measures and strike restrictions, the PRD prepared its own revision bill which added some provisions to existing workers' rights, such as establishing an independent labor court system and simplifying the recognition procedures for labor unions and contracts. However, both the PRI and the PAN objected to it (Alexander and La Botz 2003).

The position of the labor organizations was mixed. The CTM opposed fixed-term and trial employment, and insisted on the continuation of the Labor Conciliation and Arbitration Boards (JCAs), the continuation of collective contracts, and along with ability the addition of seniority to the promotion system. FESEBES (the UNT from 1997) insisted on the establishment of an independent arbitration body and free union rights for workers, which meant that its position was basically close to that of the PAN and the business organizations. But it argued that a revision bill should be based on an agreement of the labor union leaders. Therefore, it rejected a reform bill submitted by a political party (Aguilar and Vargas 2006: 115–16). In essence, though for different reasons, both the CTM and UNT opposed the reform bills proposed at this time.

During the Salinas and Zedillo administrations, the initiative for labor legislation revision was taken by business organizations and the PAN. Meanwhile the PRI government shelved any revision bill in order to garner the support of labor bodies for its preferential policies such as NAFTA. In effect, the dispute over legislation revision was a PRI tool to control and win over labor rather than a measure to be implemented for economic purposes.

When the PAN defeated the PRI in the 2000 July presidential election, there was a revival of the debate over the revision of labor legislation. The PAN favored the entrepreneur and had been active from the start in supporting legislation revision. Furthermore, Carlos Abascal, the ex-president of COPARMEX, took office as Minister of Labor. He formed the Central Decision Panel, which was made up of the principal labor and business groups. Representing labor were the PRI-aligned CT (which included CROC – the Revolutionary Confederation of Workers and Peasants and CROM – the Mexican Regional Confederation of Workers) and the independent group UNT. Participating for business were COPARMEX, CONCAMIN and CONCANACO (Aguilar and Vargas 2006: 142–6, 188–92).

The PAN's revision bill was submitted to the lower house of congress in December 2002. The main points called for: changing the term "patron" to "employer"; introducing employment systems such as technical skill training contracts at the beginning of employment, trial employment contracts and fixed-term labor contracts in order to promote employment flexibility; increasing requirements for the establishment of labor organizations to enable greater control over labor union activities; setting up restrictions on collective contracts so as to protect employers' rights; and establishing mandatory normal, direct and secret voting procedures for union leader elections (jil 2005; STPS 2002). The above points, which were to the benefit of business, clearly indicate that this commission was led by the business groups and the Labor Ministry, and the participation of labor organizations was only formal. Midway through the discussions, the UNT left the tripartite conferences after being asked to do so. This was probably the result of a disagreement between the UNT, which rejected corporatism, and the commission, which sought to conciliate the labor representatives.

In 2000, with the support of the PRD, the UNT drew up its own reform bill. This bill included provisions for the modernization of the labor model to respond to the globalization of production systems, an improvement of the labor legislation system, democracy within labor unions, the freedom to establish unions, the strengthening of unions' independence, the dissolution of corporatism and elimination of corruption, and labor flexibility based on agreements with unions (Alexander and La Botz 2003). However, this reform bill was never even considered by the government.

Regarding labor's appraisal of the PAN reform bill, the UNT was in favor of reform but was opposed to the particular proposals. In the CT and CTM some affiliated unions approved the bill,[3] but dissenting voices were stronger. The CTM disapproved of the provisions aimed at democratizing the unions and guaranteeing free secret elections. This was because in PRI-aligned labor unions, boss control and non-democratic practices continued, and democratization would inevitably threaten the position of the leader.[4] There was also the Mexican Workers Front (FSM), an independent labor organization that opposed the PAN bill. However, given the fact that there were voices in the PRI-aligned labor organizations supporting the revision bill, the revision of the labor law might have been approved had it been supported by the PRI. However, considering the opposition of labor and the influence on the 2003 midterm elections scheduled for summer, the Fox administration gave up legislative revision (Zapata 2006: 92–5, 101; Aguilar and Vargas 2006: 193–7).

1.2.2 Primary factors preventing the approval of revision

Given that administrations in recent years, regardless of political party, have recognized the need for labor deregulation and the revision of labor legislation, why has reform not been implemented in Mexico? According to Zapata, it was due to the political crisis and the conclusion of NAFTA during the Salinas administration, the economic crisis during the Zedillo administration and the political vulnerability of the Fox administration (Zapata 2006). In other words, in order to deal with priority policy issues, legislation revision which could agitate labor was evaded. The Fox administration in particular formed closer ties with the PRI-aligned labor leaders in order to avoid confrontation with labor organizations. One can conclude that by not submitting the 2000 UNT–PRD reform bill for debate, by removing the UNT from the Central Decision Panel and by pigeonholing the revision bill of 2002 after insufficient discussion in the lower house, the Fox administration prioritized the maintaining of the social order guaranteed by a cooperative union movement rather than modifying the relationship with labor and causing confusion (Zapata 2006: 100–2).

While Zapata's analysis is convincing, another factor influencing the debate was the fact that this period represented a great turning point in Mexican party politics and the labor movement. Following the formation of the center-left PRD and the expansion of both PRD and PAN power, Mexican politics from the end of the 1980s changed from PRI one-party control to tripolar political competition. This has been shown not only in the votes of the presidential elections, but also in the number of parliamentary seats of the lower house as well (Table 1.1). In 1988 the PRI could not achieve the number of parliamentary seats for the

Table 1.1 Party representation in the lower house

	1988	1991	1994	1997	2000	2003	2006
PRI	260	320	300	239	209	224	106
PAN	102	89	119	121	223*	151	206
PRD			71	125	68*	97	127
Other	48	41	10	15	2	28	61
Total	400	500	500	500	500	500	500

Sources: Silvent [2002,86,99,118,125], IFE[http://www.ife.gob.mx].
* Party Alliances are included.

two-thirds needed for constitution revision; in 1997 it did not achieve a majority. Since then no political party has been able to achieve a simple majority. This indicates that since 1997 the congress has had veto power over the executive, and the need to negotiate in the congress has increased its importance. During the preceding era of strong PRI control over the congress, the latter's approval was pro forma and post-factum as negotiations were all concluded before congressional debate.

At the same time, the implementation of economic liberalization measures weakened the labor movement as a whole, while independent organizations such as the UNT increased in power. The era when the CT and CTM had monopolized the labor movement came to an end. The reorganization of the movement received further impetus from the double-sided labor policies of the Salinas administration. In order to adapt the labor system to a market economy, a union movement suited to the demands of the new economy became necessary, a movement different from the PRI-aligned unions which had been a hotbed for corruption in the defense of vested union interests. However, reform could not be accomplished without the support of the PRI-aligned labor unions. While recognizing on the one hand the CTM's privileged position as a labor representative, Salinas at times adopted oppressing measures[5] against it, and approached other labor organizations, in this way upsetting the CTM. Among the PRI-aligned labor organizations, he approached the Revolutionary Confederation of Workers and Peasants (CROC), and among the independent organizations, he gave tacit support to FESEBES.

Outmanoeuvred by skillful sectoral labor policy, the CTM abandoned its resistance, and from the late 1980s supported the government's measures and endeavored to defend its vested interests. These included such rights as collective bargaining, social security, and representation at state councils such as the Minimum Wage Commission, the

Labor Conciliation and Arbitration Boards and also in both houses of congress. Seats in the congress in particular constituted a reward from the PRI to individual labor leaders. At least from 1988 to the first half of 1997 the CTM had occupied between 45 and 51 parliamentary seats in both houses. This fact indicates that the exchange relationship between the government and labor leaders was still functioning. However, the number of parliamentary seats held by it fell to 36 in the 1997 election and no more than 15 in the 2000 election, causing a great decrease in the overall representation of labor organizations (Aguilar and Vargas 2006: 200–1).

The reorganization of labor bodies is also reflected in the number of affiliated members. Such members in the CTM numbered 926,500 in 1997, 896,900 in 2000, and then fell by half to 454,000 in 2003. On the other hand, the number of independent labor unions increased from 67 in 1986, to 373 in 1997, and 469 in 2000, while the number of their affiliate members also grew from 52,500 in 1986, to 248,800 in 1993, 282,300 in 1997, and 1,101,000 in 2000, reaching a size that exceeded the CTM. However, the overall number of union members in Mexico showed a downward trend, falling from 4,700,000 in 2000 to 3,730,000 in 2003. The unionization rate within the total workforce decreased from 11.9 percent in 2000 to 9.1 percent in 2003 (Aguilar and Vargas 2006: 203–5).

The UNT is the core of Mexico's independent labor movement, advocating a new unionism based on cooperation with business and aims at alternative policy proposals such as political independence and democracy within unions. It is critical of the subordination and non-democratic nature of the PRI-aligned labor unions. Another independent organization is the Mexican Workers Front (FSM) which is made up of labor groups such as the Mexican Electricity Workers Union (SME), the Independent Union of Workers of the Metropolitan Autonomous University (SITUAM) and the National Confederation of Labor (CNT). The FSM opposes the government's economic labor policies (especially the privatization of electric power), and is critical of the CTM and UNT. There are also radical labor unions critical to the establishment, notably the May First Inter-union Coordination Group (CIPM) and the National Workers Assembly (ANT).

The fact that the debate over labor law revision took place at a time when the PRI, the overwhelmingly dominant political party, and its aligned labor unions lost power as a result of the advance of pluralism in both the political and labor spheres complicated the points at issue and made it more difficult to implement the reform of labor legislation.

The main points at issue included the advantages and disadvantages of labor deregulation, democratization within the unions, the abolition of the Labor Conciliation and Arbitration Boards and the establishment of a labor court, restrictions on government participation in labor-related issues, and the strengthening of labor union initiatives.

1.2.3 State–labor relationship in the debate on legislation revision

The changes in the relationship between the state and labor during the debate over legislation revision included the decrease in the power of the government, whether the PRI or PAN, the multipolarization of labor bodies, and, above all, the expansion of the mismatch of interests between the state and labor. The government, through labor deregulation, aimed at constructing a relationship with labor that could withstand globalization. The business community also agreed to this, but it wanted the government to make fewer interventions in labor matters, whereas the government wanted to maintain a controlling interest. At the same time there were differences between the labor bodies over deregulation. In principle, both the CTM and the UNT approved it, but they differed in the way workers should participate. The groups most suited to globalization were those based on new labor ethics, such as the UNT. However, the independent labor unions disliked partisanship and government control, and because they sustained the independence and initiative of the labor organizations, the government could not expect their full support and loyalty. Having to carry out policy in the midst of a three-party rivalry, the underpinnings of the government lacked stability, so the government needed any support it could get from labor. At the same time, the CTM, while not acknowledging labor's change of relationships with the government and its weakened position, no longer had enough power to confront the government and could no longer avoid supporting the government and accepting its benefits.

In this way a gap also appeared between the government and the CTM and UNT in respect of policy orientation and expected roles and abilities. Nevertheless, this did not bring an end to the corporatist-style relationship between the government and the CTM. The loyalty of the latter persisted in exchange for the realization of benefits from the former. However, these benefits no longer meant wage rises or steady employment; they now referred to the right to representation at commissions and congress, access to social security and the retention of collective bargaining rights. These rights, however, are being reduced gradually. Arguably another concession to the CTM was the fact that discussions about labor law revision were repeatedly promoted, then held up and sidetracked. Though it is possible here to see an exchange relationship of support for benefit realization, the CTM was just protecting the legacy of the past, and it did not mean that the government could rely fully on the CTM. This government–CTM relationship had a short-term objective based on a realistic judgment. It was a relationship that had to be termed fictitious corporatism.

Sooner or later, through the pressure of business organizations and international organizations such as the World Bank and the OECD, labor legislation revision would probably be decided, but as the de facto liberalization of labor advanced, legislation revision became less essential. As the actual change preceded the law, the government could use the dispute over Labor Law revision as a negotiation tool vis-à-vis the labor organizations.

1.3 Labor reform and employment liberalization

1.3.1 Suppression of the labor movement and acceptance of a new labor culture

Murillo points out that during the Salinas administration, the Labor Ministry and the Labor Conciliation and Arbitration Boards, in spite of the spirit of labor laws, approved collective contracts which reduced fringe benefits and the rights of labor unions (Murillo 2001: 104–5). De la Garza argues that in Mexico labor organizations which became part of the political mechanism were controlled by the state through the registration and approval of collective contracts, and that negotiations and practices based on unwritten rules were more important than the legislation system in the state–labor relationship (De la Garza Toledo 2004: 104–6).

At state-run companies, union resistance was broken with an iron fist during the privatization process. If an enterprise declared itself bankrupt, it was not necessary to pay redundancy benefits, and therefore labor unions that found themselves under this threat gave way to the management. Moreover, if a strike was judged illegal, a company was allowed to lay off workers, could call for the intervention of the police and military, and could demand that workers return to the workplace within 48 hours. During the Salinas administration, labor organizations were divided in their stance, and labor leaders who resisted were replaced and even arrested (Murillo 2001: 171–3). The existing legal and institutional mechanisms to control the labor movement, i.e., the surviving corporatism system bequeathed from the past PRI structure and found mainly in multinational enterprises and privatized enterprises, made it possible to implement measures, such as modifying collective contracts, reducing full-time employment while increasing temporary employment, adjusting the workforce through a shift in the system, and implementing mass layoffs. In carrying out these measures, the compliance of the CTM with government policy became decisive. This can be seen in the fact that the number of strikes during the Zedillo administration fell to less than half of the number during the Salinas administration.[6] In the 1990s an attempt was made to have workers accept new labor standards instead of resorting to "iron fist" measures.

Salinas emphasized that the participation of workers in the economic reorganization process and agreement between the production sectors were indispensable for the implementation of a national development program aimed at economic recovery, price stabilization, employment expansion and wage guarantees (Federal Executive Power 1989: 68). This agreement was modeled on the Economic Solidarity Pact (PSE) reached in 1987 among labor organizations, business organizations and the government in order to control inflation. Under the PSE the government devaluated the peso, implemented austerity measures, curbed wage hikes, and promoted trade liberalization. As a result, during the agreement period, with inflation soaring to 85 percent, wages only increased by 23 percent, which meant a great decrease in real wages. Despite the cost that this agreement implied for the labor sector, the CTM complied with the 1989 Pact for Stabilization and Economic Growth because it considered that the agreement would effectively protect its representation rights even if the participation in decision making was not guaranteed by it (Aguilar and Vargas 2006: 44-7).

In 1992 two new agreements came into effect – the National Agreement for the Promotion of Quality and Productivity (ANEPC) in May and the Agreement for Stability, Competitiveness and Employment in October. These differed from the economic agreements that focused on inflation control. They were labor–business agreements dealing with neoliberal principles such as productivity and competitiveness. ANEPC called for the modernization of management customs, the creation of ability development schemes, and the strengthening of labor–management relations in order to overcome confrontation. Also in 1992 the CTM concluded an agreement with the Nacional Financiera (National Financing Corporation) on a productivity program that included real wage hikes based on the improved productivity of plants, the integration of family businesses, and the skill training for workers (Aguilar and Vargas 2006: 48). Although this helped wage levels to recover during the second half of the Salinas administration, with the financial crisis at the end of 1994, real wages fell once again.

During the first half of 1995, the CTM concluded agreements with business organizations such as CANACINTRA and COPARMEX in respect of labor standards. Although the debate about labor law revision became heated, the CTM made these agreements because it feared that it might be removed from the negotiations. At the beginning, the government had not participated in them, but at the request of the business sector and the CTM, in 1996 the Labor Ministry summoned the principal players and held workshops which reached an agreement on a New Labor Culture. The new standards rejected the idea of class structure and class conflict, and upheld the concept of an enterprise as a collective unit based on solidarity, legitimate remuneration and employment with skills developed in line with productivity, improved competitiveness and globalization.[7]

Such agreements urged workers to accept a more flexible and productivity-oriented working style, but they also brought about a new risk structure with employment instability. However, the CTM, rather than considering the cost implied by forcing workers to accept these conditions, preferred to maintain its own position as a negotiation partner representing the labor sector in dealings with the government and business organizations, and so it accepted these kinds of agreements. One of the factors that made labor reform possible in Mexico without any revision of legislation is the conclusion of these types of economic and work ethics agreements which not only imposed great restrictions on the labor movement, but also brought the labor sector into line with the fundamental policies of the government and the business sector. These agreements were realized through consultation between the government and the main interest groups, a tradition of corporatism, and the CTM's tenacity and anxiety over its own rights, interests and its position as a representative of the labor sector in the PRI system. But work ethics that made competitiveness and productivity the absolute standard did not bring about improved employment or wages.

1.3.2 Labor flexibility and new risks

In the 1980s the Mexican economy was restructured and diversified from an oil-based economy to one incorporating an export-oriented industrial structure focusing on manufacturing which achieved a 7.3 percent increase in labor productivity in the 1994–99 period (3.0 percent of the total economy). This was due to measures such as the introduction of technology, improvements in the quality of workers through skill training, and an intensification of work. During the same period the working hours per worker also increased by 23.4 percent (Dussel Peters 2004: 125, 131). However, this was not reflected in wage levels; after peaking in 1993 and 1994, there was a decline in real average wages in the manufacturing sector. But even the peak average wages in 1994 represented no more than about 85 percent of the average in the second half of the 1970s (Dávila Capella 1997: 302).

Although 1,300,000 new workers entered the Mexican labor market annually during the 1990s, only an average of 600,000 jobs were created, and jobs with social insurance accounted for less than 450,000 workers. Thus, 850,000 persons resorted to looking for jobs in the informal sector (Dussel Peters 2004: 126). The informal sector accounted for 40 percent of the working population, and most of these workers were outside the social security system. The formal sector shrank due to the privatization of the public sector and the reduction of public employees, and since there was insufficient employment creation in the private sector, the scale of the informal sector remained almost unchanged; in recent years it has even grown slightly (Table 1.2).

The unemployment rate was extremely low, around 2–3 percent, excluding 1995 and 1996. But this did not mean that stable employment opportunities were guaranteed, because Mexico has a loose definition of unemployment. Moreover, because there is no unemployment insurance, people cannot afford to spend time searching for jobs, so most of them find work in the vast informal economy, and this reduces the unemployment rate. Although the rate is generally high among people with a poor educational background, the ratio of high school and university graduates to the total unemployed population in Mexico is comparatively high. It stood at 18.5 percent in 1991, before rising successively to 24.2 percent in 1995, 36.3 percent in 2000, and 40.9 percent in 2004 (INEGI). These figures suggest that from the 1990s, employment opportunities in the formal sector for high school and university graduates decreased.

A consideration of the number of workers affiliated with the Mexican Institute of Social Security (IMSS) can show us the actual situation of labor flexibility. As shown in Table 1.3, the number of workers in the private formal sector has trended upward in the past decade or so, except during the financial crisis between 1995 and 1996, and the period of economic stagnation between 2001 and 2003. However, the ratio of formal employment (permanently insured workers) decreased while that for temporary employment (temporarily insured workers)[8] rose.

Table 1.2 Structure of the informal sector and formal sector (%)

	Informal sector*									Formal sector					
		Self-employed			Domestic Services	Micro enterprises**						Private enterprises***			Self-employed
	Total	Sub-total	Self-employed	Unpaid		Sub-total	Employer	Employee	Total	Public sector	Sub-total	Employers	Employees	
1990	38.8	19.4	14.7	4.7	4.5	14.9	3.5	11.5	61.2	19.2	40.3	1.0	39.3	1.6
1995	43.4	21.1	15.3	5.8	5.2	17.1	3.6	13.5	56.6	16.1	38.5	1.2	37.3	2.0
2000	39.4	18.6	14.7	3.8	3.6	17.2	3.6	13.6	60.6	14.5	44.2	1.2	43.0	1.9
2004	42.8	20.4	15.9	4.5	4.3	18.2	3.8	14.3	57.2	13.7	41.3	1.0	42.1	2.2
2005	42.6	20.0	16.1	3.9	4.6	18.1	4.1	14.0	57.4	14.6	40.6	1.0	39.6	2.2

Source: OIT Panorama Laboral 2006 [http://www.oit.org.pe].
* lawyers and specialists are excluded.
** not more than 5 employees.
*** more than 6 employees.

Table 1.3 The number of affiliated workers of the IMSS

	Total number of affiliated workers	% of permanently insured workers	% of temporarily insured workers	Difference compared with previous year		
				Affiliated workers	Permanently insured workers	Temporarily insured workers
1994	10,070,955	87.4	12.6	−611,200	−301,617	−309,584
1995	9,459,755	89.9	10.1	239,803	313,569	−73,765
1996	9,699,558	90.9	9.1	744,847	76,367	−18,822
1997	10,444,405	91.7	8.3	816,590	469,266	347,324
1998	11,260,996	89.2	10.8	645,330	347,244	298,086
1999	11,906,326	87.3	12.7	700,427	518,176	182,251
2000	12,606,753	86.6	13.4	−65,817	−56,046	9,771
2001	12,540,936	86.6	13.4	−10,527	−131,791	2,652
2002	12,435,666	86.2	13.8	−56,059	−70,339	14,281
2003	12,379,607	86.1	13.9	159,736	123,824	35,912
2004	12,539,343	86.0	14.0	387,294	186,391	200,903
2005	12,926,637	84.8	15.2	743,403	284,005	459,397
2006*	13,670,040	82.3	17.7			

Source: STPS [http://www.stps.gob.mx] (2006.11).
* the average from January to October.

According to Regini's classification, this is a numerical flexibility of employment, i.e., an adjustment of the number of workers in response to technological innovation demands.[9]

Mexico experienced recession and recovery during the periods 1995–97 and 2001–04, but there was a contrast in the way employment adjustment was implemented during each period. In the 1995 crisis, formal and temporary employment were both substantially reduced, but in 1996 and 1997 when Mexico started to show signs of recovery, temporary employment was further reduced while formal employment expanded. However, during the period 2001–2003, formal employment was reduced and exceeded by temporary employment except in 2004, and as a result new employment shifted to temporary employment. Though temporary employment contracts are unstable and last 30 days at the most, they belong to the formal sector, so social security benefits are guaranteed. However, if re-employment is not possible, the insurance premium becomes a heavy burden, as 1,250 weeks of contributions are needed to qualify for retirement benefits, making it difficult for those qualified as insured to comply with this requirement. Employment flexibility also started adding restrictions to the access to social security.

In this way, employment – even in the formal sector – became unstable. Furthermore, the tendency for wages not to reflect the improvement in labor productivity and extended working hours can be considered a risk that the worker must face anew. In the next section, I will examine how social security reforms did or did not respond to these new risks and needs.

1.4 Current situation and assessment of social security reform

1.4.1 IMSS reform

Dion points out two possible changes in the social security system under globalization: (1) a reduction of management's social security burden is required in order to strengthen competitiveness; (2) an expansion of the social security system is needed to respond to the increasing unemployment risk. However, in Latin America, due to the pressure of international competition and the weakening of the labor movement, a reduction of social security expenditure was demanded (Dion 2006: 53–6).

In Mexico, reform was concentrated on the IMSS pension sector. The aim was to avoid the bankruptcy of the pension system and to strengthen domestic savings through privatization. The main pillars of the Mexican social security system are the IMSS, which covers workers in the private sector, and the Institute of Social Security for Federal State Workers (ISSSTE), which covers workers in the national public sector.[10] Originally the reform plan was scheduled to include both systems, but because of the strong resistance of teaching and public sector unions, the reform of the ISSSTE was abandoned.

After the CT and CTM strongly resisted the basic reforms of the system, the Salinas administration, feeling concerned about the influence on NAFTA negotiations, postponed pension reform and presented a new proposal in its stead: the Retirement Savings System (SAR). The SAR was proposed as a complement to pensions with contributions from employers and the Workers' Housing Fund Institute (INFONAVIT) which is also funded by employers' contributions. Administration of the SAR was to be entrusted to a private financial institution. Labor organizations agreed to the establishment of the SAR because it did not involve contributions from workers. Moreover, discussions on labor law revision were taking place at that time (Burgess 2003: 84–7; Bertranou 1998: 94–101), and labor conceded to establishing the SAR out of fear that the government might decide to go forward with legislation revision.

In its "National Development Plan for 1995–2000", the Zedillo administration criticized the rigidity of the labor market, and made it clear that the government intended to move forward with deregulation and promoting greater labor flexibility. One of the points at issues was the high non-wage costs (such as social security) in Mexico (Federal Executive Power 1995: 150–9).

Another concern of the Zedillo administration was the crisis produced by the large-scale outflow of foreign capital. The government strongly recognized the need to strengthen domestic capital to prevent a recurrence, and speeded up the privatization of pensions. The Social Security Law was revised in 1995, the pension section of the IMSS was privatized in 1997, and the government's "pay-as-you-go" pension scheme was replaced by a private system of individually funded retirement accounts. In addition, in order to stop the financial diversion of funds to the medical system, which kept on expanding and had become the primary factor for the pension fund deficit,[11] the pension system was separated from the medical system. Labor bodies such as the CTM and CROM supported the reform because it avoided the collapse of the pension scheme, even though it meant an extension of the contribution period and the acceptance of larger costs to be paid by workers.

Another factor for labor's support was the fact that the reform did not include the Workers' Housing Fund Institute (INFONAVIT).

During the Fox administration, reform was restricted to the approval of technical corrections such as the overseas operations of part of the IMSS reserve fund, and ISSSTE fund reform could not be launched because of the resistance from labor unions.

The outcome of pension reform can be summarized as follows. The establishment of the SAR and the privatization of the pension system contributed to an activation of the domestic capital market, something that was being demanded by both the government and business. The modification of the contribution ratio (the federal government's from 4 percent to 39 percent, that for enterprises from 76 percent to 52 percent and that for workers from 20 percent to 9 percent), in particular the decrease in the ratio contributed by enterprises, was favorable to the business sector which was under pressure to strengthen its competitiveness. For workers one of the biggest benefits was avoiding the bankruptcy of the pension system. Moreover, the shift from the "pay-as-you-go" pension scheme to a private system of individually funded retirement accounts, and also the allowance of optional affiliation for self-employed workers and the informal sector with IMSS Medical Insurance, meant a reform suited to the changes in the labor market, such as changes of workplace, increases in the worker turnover and decreases in formal employment. However, the substantial extension of the contribution period (500 weeks to 1,250 weeks) became a huge burden even for formal employees, so it was a more difficult requisite for short-term employees and for women who tended to interrupt their jobs.

1.4.2 State–labor relationship in pension reform

One aspect that should be noted in relation to IMSS reform was the fact that the CTM proposals were rejected entirely by the Salinas administration. As the risk of layoffs intensified in the privatized former state-run companies and the export sector, the CTM proposed to establish a national unemployment fund which would be funded by business. However, this proposal was given no consideration. Regarding the SAR, the CTM demanded that it should be administered by the Workers' Bank (Banco Obrero) and that labor should participate in fund distribution. These demands were also rejected (Bertranou 1998: 94–6). However, in the reform of IMSS by the Zedillo administration, the CTM took an attitude of approaching the government and business, and opposing the National Social Insurance Workers' Union (SNTSS). The CTM had the right of representation in the tripartite body, the Technical Council of the IMSS, and it was dissatisfied by the excessive demands of the SNTSS and the low quality of the services provided by the IMSS. Furthermore, the SNTSS seceded from the PRI, and in November 1997 it participated in the launch of the National Workers Union (UNT) to develop an independent labor movement as a principal organization. This strengthened the rivalry between the CTM and SNTSS (Dion 2006: 68).

So why did the SNTSS finally accept the reform? The main factor was that Zedillo had abandoned the reform of the medical sector. Originally, the government had conceived of a reform which included the privatization of not only the pension system but also medical services (Dion 2006: 66–7). But when the IMSS labor union resisted some items included in the government proposal, especially the freedom of entrepreneurs to contract institutions other than the IMSS, Zedillo made a concession to the union by immediately withdrawing this point from the proposal (González Rosetti 2004: 77–8, 82). In the second half of the 1990s, the SNTSS was a mighty organization with 250,000 members. The government judged that rather than being in confrontation with the union over medical reform, which would have a minor effect on the macro economy, it was better to go ahead first with pension reform.

In 2004 the SNTSS again opposed both the authorities and the Technical Council of the IMSS concerning collective bargaining contracts. With its strong negotiating power, the IMSS labor union had privileged pension payment conditions in its collective contracts. As this was considered to be a factor in the deterioration of IMSS finances, there was an effort to revise the Social Security Insurance Law in order to limit the creation of new jobs and the payment of retirement allowances. However, although the framework for workers' contributions was modified, the conditions for receiving pensions were deferred, and the creation of large-scale employment was also approved (Dion 2006: 71–3).

In this way the SNTSS was able to defend benefits for its affiliates. The National Teachers Union (SNTE) and the Federation of Public Service Workers (FSTSE) were likewise able to obstruct a planned ISSSTE pension reform. These were unions belonging to the popular sector of the PRI, and they already had strong independence and negotiation power compared with the more subordinate labor sector. Furthermore, as education and social security do not receive the pressure of international competition, they are sectors that hardly became a target of employment reduction or privatization, and this meant the preservation and even the relative strengthening of their power. On the other hand, the CTM, whose power was being weakened, was not concerned so much with whether workers benefited, but rather with whether INFONAVIT reform and labor law revision would be postponed, and whether its own rights and interests were guaranteed.

1.4.3 Compensation for new risks and needs

As mentioned above, the purpose of IMSS pension reform was to strengthen the domestic financial market, and it was not aimed at responding to the new risks which came with employment instability. The reform also allowed workers in the informal sector to participate optionally in IMSS medical insurance which can be seen as a transformation toward a system more suited to a more flexible labor environment. But the intended objective was to incorporate those in the informal sector who had the capacity to pay insurance premiums in order to maintain the system and not to include the whole sector. Thus risk compensation was not a consideration, and one of the factors for this can be found in the labor movement.

By the 1990s the Mexican labor movement found itself in an inferior position vis-à-vis business, and in the 1990s the movement became multipolarized with the rise of independent movements and new organizations. Within this new environment the CTM and UNT were the two greatest organizations. Bipolarization or multipolarization complicates issues at debates and the axis of confrontation,[12] and makes it difficult to implement joint strategies. In this situation, it was the CTM that maintained the closest relationship with the government and had the right of representation in government bodies and congress. However, the interests of the CTM were in protecting the rights that its leaders enjoyed, rather than the problems the workers were facing. On the other hand, the UNT insisted on the independence of the union movement, but it basically shared the neoliberal views of the government and business. Furthermore, since the majority of its affiliated labor unions had strong bargaining power and hardly felt the impact of globalization, there was a high possibility of solving individual problems through collective contracts. In this situation it was difficult for the labor movement to visualize the risks that caused unstable employment. Furthermore, the informal sector acted as a buffer for unstable employment which lowered the probability of it becoming a social problem.

However, this does not mean that no measures were taken against risks. Since the mid-1990s, the vocational training program has been expanded, as part of a set of measures that were expected not only to improve competitive power, but also to contribute to employment stabilization. During the Zedillo administration, opportunities for vocational training were offered through programs such as the National Service for Employment, Study and Training (SNECA), the Training Grants Program for the Unemployed (PROBECAT) and the Integral Quality and Modernization Program (CIMO) which is oriented toward employed workers. SNECA had two main aims: on the one hand it gave job seekers the opportunity to acquire labor market information and the opportunity to acquire abilities and skills; on the other hand it supported enterprises in recruitment by acting as a link in the demand and supply of employment. PROBECAT was a study system offering scholarships at a rate equivalent to the minimum wage. According to a government report, 710,000 people were employed under SNECA during 1995–99, and 520,000 persons annually received training under PROBECAT (Federal Executive Power 2000: 437–42).

It is clear that these kinds of programs are important for accessing the labor market and stable employment; however, their effects will probably be limited. This is because globalization opens the Mexican economy to the influences of overseas markets, and to deal with this volatility, it becomes necessary to adopt an unstable employment system that allows easy employment adjustment. Furthermore, the existence of a large-scale informal sector lowers the possibility that increased unstable employment will become a social problem, which in turn lowers the possibility that the government will expand costly employment stabilization programs. Therefore, public programs are implemented as a protection policy aimed at giving less skilled or unemployed persons basic technical skills and relieving social dissatisfaction. It is presumed that genuine technical skill acquisition is to be carried out through the programs conducted by companies.

Conclusion

In this chapter I have examined labor and social security reform in Mexico in correlation with the relationship between the government and labor and the restructuring of the labor movement. It is clear from the examination that labor flexibility became a *fait accompli* through the modification of collective contracts and the acceptance by labor organizations of the new neoliberal work ethics, but the reform owed much to the corporatist system constructed under the PRI regime. The oppressive measures used by the government during the 1980s to control the labor movement, and the consensus reached through tripartite agreements during the 1990s, which restricted CTM activities, were based on the traditional practices of old-style PRI corporatism.

With the shift to neoliberal strategies, there was a divergence between the interests of the government and the CTM, with the latter resisting the reforming efforts of the former. However, the two sides made the pragmatic and realistic choice of sustaining the relationship because the government needed labor's support to implement policies, and the CTM, by cooperating with the government, sought to protect, even if only a little, its long-held acquired rights.

Though there were no new benefits that the CTM could obtain from this relationship, and its acquired rights were gradually reduced, it was able to retain the right of representation in bodies such as the tripartite commission and the congress, and the labor unions' right to bargain collectively were decisive for the CTM's survival. In effect, this exchange relationship was what can be called fictitious corporatism which only sought immediate results and could not produce anything new. In this sense, the postponement of labor law revision can be interpreted as a favorable government consideration towards the CTM, i.e., a passive offering of benefit to the CTM.

The labor group closest to the economic policy of the Salinas, Zedillo and Fox administrations was not the CTM, but the independent UNT. However, the UNT insisted on independence and non-alignment with any party, and demanded the end of the corporatist relationship between the government and the labor bodies. Therefore the government could not demand the total and unconditional support from the UNT, nor could it accept the broad independence of the labor movement. At the same time, the CTM saw the UNT as a threat to its own predominance. It would seem that this threat and the gap between the government and the UNT pushed the government and the CTM closer.

It was also shown that almost no measures were taken to deal with the new risk structure that arose from labor flexibility. Corporatism, which functioned to control labor and gain the support of workers, became indifferent and even helpless to the new risks and needs, such as employment instability and unfair wage levels. Moreover, the UNT showed no signs of tackling with the new issues confronting labor. While the multipolarization of the labor movement is desirable for individual benefit realization, it tends to complicate cooperation with other organizations. In order to update risk compensation, there is the need for a labor movement that represents and benefits temporary workers, and there is the need to construct a new tripartite relationship unencumbered by the legacy of PRI corporatism.

Notes

1. Along with the CTM, other institutions affiliated with the CT include: CROM, CROC, FSTSE, SNTE and the Sole Union of Workers of the Government of the Federal District (SUTGDF) (Alexander and La Botz 2003).
2. COPARMEX was inaugurated in 1929, and currently has 36,000 members (http://www.coparmex.org.mx). CCE, the top management organization, was established in 1976 with the purpose of promoting free enterprise activities; its member organizations, such as CONCAMIN, CONCANACO, COPARMEX, the Association of Mexican Banks (ABM), CMHN, the Mexican Association of Insurance Institutions (AMIS) and the National Council for Agriculture and Animal Husbandry (CAN), represent Mexico's major domestic industries.
3. On May 1 (Labor Day) 2003, the railroad labor union leaders of CROC approved the labor law revision, while the mining labor union leaders stated their opposition to any amendment to the labor law (Aguilar and Vargas 2006: 194).
4. In Mexico, the union boss is called *charro* and the boss's control is called *charrismo*. Non-democratic boss control is evident in the fact that Fidel Velazquez ruled as secretary-general of the CTM from 1940 to 1997. His successor, L. Rodriguez Alcaine, from the Mexican Electricity Workers Union, who served three terms as congressman, and two terms as senator, was 78 years of age when assuming the secretariat (Musacchio 2002: 356), and passed away in 2005. The 78-year-old J. Gamboa Pascoe, from the Federal District Labor Union, was elected as his successor.
5. Immediately after assuming the presidency, Salinas dispatched troops against the Oil Labor Union, which had turned its support to the opposition party in the 1988 election, and forcefully arrested the leaders after a shooting; he made his confrontational attitude clear to the opposition labor union leaders.
6. Concerning the number of strikes, there was a decrease from 573 incidents during the De la Madrid administration, to 407 during the Salinas administration and 192 during the Zedillo administration (La Botz 2004). Although the right to strike is guaranteed in Mexico, the Labor Conciliation and Arbitration Boards, a body composed of representatives from the government, labor and business, restricted its exercise, so the decrease in the number of strikes does not indicate that the dissatisfaction of the workers also decreased. In 1993 there were 7,531 strike calls, but only 148 strikes were actually carried out; in 1995 there were 7,509 calls and 93 carried out, and in 2000, 8,282 calls, but only 22 strikes executed. As these figures show, it is clear that rather than taking drastic actions and confronting the government and business, labor chose to take a conciliatory attitude. (Aguilar and Vargas 2006: 105–6).
7. The workshops counted on the participation of organizations from the business sector (CCE, CONCAMIN and COPARMEX), labor bodies (CTM, CROC, CROM and the Bank Workers Association and other CT-affiliate organizations), and the Federal Government. The essence of the agreement reached for the "new labor culture" was as follows.
    (i) Foster between workers and management "the revaluation of remuneration for work, assigning it the dignity it deserves as a means to satisfy the material, social and cultural needs of each wage earner and his/her family".

(ii) Promote the creation of jobs and preserve existing ones "through the rational use of the available resources and through the development in the enterprise of better forecasting capacities and adaptation to changes.
(iii) Provide fair remuneration levels that "foster the development of productivity and competitiveness and reward the individual and the collective efforts made by the enterprise".
(iv) Encourage the training of workers and entrepreneurs as a permanent and systematic process throughout working life.
(v) Strengthen dialogue and agreement "as appropriate methods to make labor–management relationships develop in a harmonic atmosphere" (Aguilar and Vargas 2006: 102–3).
8. Short-term employment refers to employment over 12 days without interruption, or working for the same employer over a two-month period with interruptions, but including 30 effective working days (Federal Executive Power 2000).
9. Regini classifies labor flexibility into four types: (1) numerical flexibility: the numbers of workers employed can be adapted to meet fluctuations in demand, (2) functional flexibility: the tasks carried out by employees can be adapted to changes in demand, (3) wage flexibility: management is free to alter wages and wage system in response to changing labor market or competitive conditions, and (4) temporal flexibility: the adjustment of the amount of labor utilized in accordance with cyclical or seasonal shifts in demand (Regini 2000: 16–17).
10. The Mexican social insurance system has as two main institutions, the IMSS inaugurated in 1943 which deals with the private sector union workers, and the ISSSTE inaugurated in 1963 which deals with the national public employees. However, there are independent social insurance systems for the military and key industries such as the Mexican Oil Corporation (PEMEX) and the Federal Electric Power Commission (CFE). The affiliates of these systems account for 60 percent of the population. The majority of workers in the informal sector and peasants have no social insurance. Apart from the fact that the payment of insurance premiums is economically difficult for these sectors, under the PRI structure the social security system itself functioned as a guarantee of benefits to unionized workers who in return for such benefits would give their political support to the party.
11. The deterioration of the IMSS pension's finances was due to: (1) careless management which also included the diversion of funds to the medical sector; (2) the decrease in value of funds due to inflation and the economic crisis of the 1980s; (3) the fact that affiliate members reached retirement age. Moreover, the aging of the Mexican population has advanced more rapidly than expected, which is also a concern.
12. The axis of confrontation in the labor movement is that between the official labor movements (such as the CT and CTM) and the independent labor movements (such as the UNT). The latter criticize issues such as corporatism (partisanship) and the lack of democracy within the unions of the former. But the UNT had been an ally of the Democratic Revolutionary Party (PRD), so it cannot claim to be completely free from partisanship.

While the CT, CTM and UNT all support the neoliberal measures of the government, the UNT advocates, together with the business organizations, the new labor culture of labor–management cooperation. However the unions of the independent movement, such as the FSM and CIPM, oppose the neoliberal measures. The FSM in particular has refused electric power privatization.

References

Adams, Paul S. 2004. "Corporatism in Latin America and Europe." In *Authoritarianism and Corporatism in Latin America – Revisited*, ed. Howard J. Wiarda. Gainesville: University Press of Florida, pp. 58–87.
Aguilar García, Javier, and Reyna Vargas Guzmán. 2006. *La CTM en el periodo de la globalización: Del sexenio de Carlos Salinas al gobierno de Vicente Fox*. México, D.F.: Universidad Autónoma del Estado de México.
Alexander, Robin, and Dan La Botz. 2003. "Mexico's Labor Law Reform." *Mexican Labor News and Analysis* 8, no. 4.
Angeles Pozas, María. 1996. "Flexible Production and Labor Policy: Paradoxes in the Restructuring of Mexican Industry." In *Changing Structure of Mexico*, ed. Laura Randall. New York: M.E. Sharpe, pp. 137–44.
Bertranou, Julián. 1998. "Mexico: The Politics of the System for Retirement Pensions." In *Do Options Exist?*, ed. Maria Amparo Cruz-Saco and Carmelo Mesa-Lago. Pittsburgh: University of Pittsburgh Press, pp. 85–108.
Burgess, Katrina. 2003. "Mexican Labor at a Crossroads." In *Mexico's Politics and Society in Transition*, ed. Joseph S. Tulchin and Andrew D. Selee. Boulder: Lynne Rienner, pp. 73–107.
CEPAL (Comisión Económica para América Latina y el Caribe). 2000 *Estudio Económico de América Latina y el Caribe 1999–2000*. Santiago de Chile: CEPAL. http://www.eclac.cl.
CEPAL (Comisión Económica para América Latina y el Caribe). *Panorama social de América Latina*. Santiago de Chile: CEPAL. http://www.eclac.cl.
CEPAL (Comisión Económica para América Latina y el Caribe). *Estudio Económico de América Latina y el Caribe 2000–2001*. Santiago de Chile: CEPAL. http://www.eclac.cl.
CEPAL (Comisión Económica para América Latina y el Caribe). *Panorama social de América Latina*. Santiago de Chile: CEPAL. http://www.eclac.cl.
CEPAL (Comisión Económica para América Latina y el Caribe). *Estudio Económico de América Latina y el Caribe 2004–2005*. Santiago de Chile: CEPAL. http://www.eclac.cl.
Dávila Capalleja, Enrique Rafael. 1997. "Mexico: The Evolution and Reform of the Labor Market." In *Labor Market in Latin America*, ed. Sebastian Edwards and Nora Claudia Lustig. Washington, DC: Brookings Institute, pp. 292–327.
De la Garza Toledo, Enrique. 2004. "Manufacturing Neoliberalism: Industrial Relations, Trade Union Corporatism and Politics." In *Mexico in Transition: Neoliberal Globalism, the State and Civil Society*, ed. Gerardo Otero. London and New York: Zed Press, pp. 104–20.
Dion, Michelle. 2006. "Globalización, democatización y reforma del sistema de seguridad social en México, 1988–2005." *Foro Internacional* 46, no. 1: 51–80.

Dussel Peters, Enrique. 2004. "Who Reaps the Productivity Growth in Mexico? Convergence or Polarization in Manufacturing Real Wages, 1988–99." In *Mexico in Transition: Neoliberal Globalism, the State and Civil Society*, ed. Gerardo Otero. London and New York: Zed Press, pp. 104–20.
Federal Executive Power. 1995. "Plan Nacional de Desarrollo 1995–2000." http://www.presidencia.gob.mx.
Federal Executive Power. 2000. "El sexto informe de gobierno de Ernesto Zedillo." http://www.presidencia.gob.mx.
Federal Executive Power. 2001. "Plan Nacional de Desarrollo 2001–2006." http://www.presidencia.gob.mx.
Federal Executive Power. 2004. "El cuarto informe de gobierno de Vicente Fox." http://www.presidencia.gob.mx.
Federal Executive Power. 2006. "El sexto informe de gobierno de Vicente Fox." http://www.presidencia.gob.mx.
González Rosetti, Alejandra. 2004. "Change Teams and Vested Interests: Social Security Health Reform in Mexico." In *Crucial Needs, Weak Incentives: Social Sector Reform, Democratization in Latin America*, ed. Robert Kaufman and Joan M. Nelson. Washington, DC: Woodrow Wilson Center, pp. 65–92.
Grayson, George W. 2004. "Mexico's Semicorporatist Regime." In *Authoritarianism and Corporatism in Latin America – Revisited*, ed. H.J. Wiarda. Gainesville: University Press of Florida, pp. 242–55.
IFE (Instituto Federal Electoral). http://www.ife.gob.mx.
INEGI (Instituto Nacional de Estádistica Geofrafía e Informática). http://www.inegi.gob.mx.
Jil (Japan Institute for Labor Policy and Training). 2003. "Mekishiko" [Mexico]. *Kaigai Rodo Jiho* [International Labor Information], no. 336. http//www.jil.go.jp (accessed February 1, 2006).
Jil (Japan Institute for Labor Policy and Training). 2005. "Kaigai rodo joho: Mekishiko renpo rodo ho kaisei no ugoki" [International labor information: Labor law reform in Mexico]. http://www.jil.go.jp (accessed February 2006).
La Botz, Dan. 1997. "Mexican Labor Year in Review: NAFTA Three Years Later." *Mexican Labor News and Analysis* 2, no. 1, January 7.
La Botz, Dan. 1998. "Mexico's Labor Year in Review: 1997." *Mexican Labor News and Analysis* 3, no. 1, January 2.
La Botz, Dan. 1999. "Mexico's Labor Year in Review: Amidst Continuing Decline of Official Unions, UNT Emerges as Alternative Pole." *Mexican Labor News and Analysis* 4, no. 1, January 1.
La Botz, Dan. 2000. "Mexican Labor Year in Review: 1999." *Mexican Labor News and Analysis* 5, no. 1, January 16.
La Botz, Dan. 2001. "Mexico's Labor Year in Review: 2000 The End of the System, the Beginning of the Future." *Mexican Labor News and Analysis* 6, no. 1, January.
La Botz, Dan. 2002. "Mexico's Labor Year in Review: 2001 Political Disappointment, Economic Crisis, and Their Turn to Struggle." *Mexican Labor News and Analysis* 7, no. 1, January.
La Botz, Dan. 2003. "Mexico's Labor Year in Review: 2002 Year of Frustration." *Mexican Labor News and Analysis* 8, no. 1, January 15.
La Botz, Dan. 2004. "Mexican Labor Year in Review." *Mexican Labor News and Analysi* 3, no. 1, January 2.

La Botz, Dan. 2005. "Mexico's Labor Year in Review: 2004 Labor Starting Fast, Stepping Forward." *Mexican Labor News and Analysis* 10, no. 1, January.
La Botz, Dan. 2006. "Mexican Labor Year in Review: 2005." *Mexican Labor News and Analysis* 11, no. 1, January.
Ley Federal del Trabajo, 13th edn. 2006. México, D.F.: Ediciones Luciana.
Madrid, Raúl L. 2003. "Labouring against Neoliberalism: Unions and Patters of Reform in Latin America." *Journal of Latin America Studies*, no. 35: 53–88.
Middlebrook, Kevin L. 1995. *The Paradox of Revolution: Labor, the State and Authoritarianism in Mexico*. Baltimore: Johns Hopkins University Press.
Murillo, Maria Victoria. 2001. *Labour Unions, Partisan Coalitions and Markets Reform in Latin America*. Cambridge: Cambridge University Press.
Musacchino, Humberto. 2002. *Quién es quién en la política mexicana*. México, D.F.: Plaza Janes.
OIT. 2006. "Panorama Laboral 2006." http://www.oit.org.pe.
Prud'homme, Jean-François. 1998. "Interest Representation and the Party System in Mexico." In *What Kind of Democracy? What Kind of Market?*, ed. Philip D.Oxhorn and Graciela Ducatenzeiler. University Park, PA: Pennsylvania State University, pp. 169–92.
Regini, Marino. 2000. "The Dilemmas of Labour Market Regulation." In *Why Deregulate Labour Market?*, ed. Gøsta Esping-Andersen and Marino Regini. Oxford: Oxford University Press, pp. 11–29.
Román, Richard and Edur Velasco Arregui. 2001. "Neoliberalism, Labor Market Transformation and Working-Class Responses." *Latin American Perspectives* 28, no. 4: 52–71.
Román, Richard and Edur Velasco Arregui. 2006. "The State, the Bourgeoisie and the Unions: The Recycling of Mexico's System of Labour Control." *Latin American Perspectives* 33, no. 2: 95–103.
Silvent, Carlos. 2002. *Partidos políticos y procesos electorales en México*. México. D.F.: Facultad de Ciencias Políticas y Sociales, UNAM, M.A. Porrúa.
Solís Soberón, Fernando, and F. Alejandro Villagómez (eds). *La seguridad social en México*. México, DF: CIDE, CONSAR, Fondo de Cultura Económica.
STPS (Secretaría de Trabajo y Previsión Social). 2002. "Propuesta de modificación de la Ley Federal del Trabajo, titulos primero a septimo." http://www.stps.gob.mx.
STPS (Secretaría de Trabajo y Previsión Pública). http://www.stps.gob.mx.
Teichman, Judith A. 2001. *The Politics of Freeing Markets in Latin America: Chile, Argentina and Mexico*. Chapel Hill and London: University of North Carolina Press.
Zapata, Francisco. 1996. "Mexican Labor in a Context of Political and Economic Crisis." In *Changing Structure of Mexico*, ed. Laura Randall. New York: M.E. Sharpe, pp. 127–36.
Zapata, Francisco. 1998. "Trade Unions and the Corporatist System in Mexico." In *What Kind of Democracy? What Kind of Market?*, ed. Philip D. Oxhorn and Graciela Ducatenzeiler. University Park: Pennsylvania State University, pp. 151–67.
Zapata, Francisco. 2006. "La negociación de las reformas y la ley federal del trabajo (1989–2005)." *Foro Internacional* 46, no. 1: 81–102.

2
Re-thinking Argentina's Labor and Social Security Reform in the 1990s: Agreement on Competitive Corporatism

Koichi Usami

Introduction

During the 1980s, the so-called "lost decade," Argentina experienced an economic crisis of unprecedented proportions. This contrasted with the nature of her transition from an authoritarian regime to a democracy in 1983. Carlos Menem, from the Peronist Party, was elected president in 1989 at a time when the country's inflation rate had reached almost 5,000 percent. To restore the economy, he adopted neoliberal economic policies and carried out social reforms, including the deregulation of the labor market. These policies were adopted to cope with an increase in market competition brought about by the processes of globalization and to combat high levels of unemployment through increasing the flexibility of the labor market. Social security reforms were required to deal with the transformation in industrial relations, the high rate of unemployment, and a huge financial deficit.

Neoliberal reform was dramatic in the economy, but with regard to the social arena, tripartite negotiations occurred between the state, labor and employers before reforms were introduced, and certain measures were taken to mitigate the effects of the market-oriented social policies. This chapter will pay attention to these negotiations and the agreements in the area of social policy reform. We assume the formation of a certain type of corporatism in a situation of increased market competition and that labor and social security reforms were achieved through agreement. The aim of this chapter is to prove this hypothesis.

2.1 Political economy around neoliberal reform

Many scholars have commented on the unique characteristics of the democracy under which neoliberal reforms were introduced during the 1990s in Latin America. O'Donnell termed it delegative democracy which consists of "constituting, through clean elections, a majority that empowers one to become, for a given number of years, the embodiment and interpreter of the high interests of the nation" and to be given an authority independent of other organizations (O'Donnell 1999: 164). The Menem administration in Argentina is a representative example of this type of democracy, as is the Fujimori administration in Peru.

Panizza criticized the concept of delegative democracy on the grounds that it focuses only on the peculiarity of a neopopulist style of leader. He insisted on the need to understand the context within which such leaders acted. He pointed to the formation of an alliance between the Peronists' traditional support groups, on the one hand, and the group which encouraged neoliberal reforms, on the other, and claimed that this alliance was behind the success of the neoliberal reforms (Panizza 2001: 164–6). Levitsky paid attention to the institution, especially to the flexibility of the Peronist Party. He argued that the flexible organization of the Peronist Party made it possible for the party to change from one that was labor-based to one that was clientelist. To establish this political clientelism, the Menem administration used various kinds of government resources. This is how it was able to achieve its neoliberal reforms (Levitsky 2003).

Panizza and Levitsky looked beyond the peculiar character of the Menem administration to identify institutional factors behind the success of the government's neoliberal reforms. The study of welfare states in developed countries, and new institutionalist theories, such as path dependency, were applied in an analysis of the retrenchment of the welfare state (Pierson 1994, 2001: 414–19). However, we know that in Argentina, negotiations between the state, labor and industry all continued to negotiate social reforms, even in the 1990s. Labor and social reforms were also realized after the three reached certain agreements. As we can clearly detect these tripartite and corporatist negotiations and agreements, we need, in the case of Argentina, to examine them when analyzing labor and social security reform.

When analyzing labor and social security reforms in this way, we need to reconsider the concept of corporatism. Schmitter's definition is widely accepted. According to him, corporatism is a system of representation in which the constituent units are organized into a limited number of singular, compulsory, non-competitive, hierarchically ordered and functionally differentiated categories, recognized or licensed (if not created) by state and granted a deliberate representational monopoly within their respective categories in exchange for observation of certain controls on their selection of leaders and articulation of demands and support. (Schmitter 1979: 13)

The concept of corporatism can be divided into the following two sub-concepts: state corporatism and social corporatism (Schmitter 1979: 20–2) as the introduction of this book explains. I have argued that the formation of the Argentine welfare state under the Perón government is related to state corporatism (Usami 2001).

During the 1990s the situation in respect of tripartite negotiation in Latin America changed radically. With the increase in international and domestic competition in the market, tripartite negotiations about the issues became increasingly common. We assume that competitiveness and productivity must have been considered in the agreements reached in this manner. This type of negotiation may be different from that of the social or state corporatism that was mentioned by Schmitter. To analyze this new type of corporatism, which looks at competitiveness and productivity in the context of globalization, we will draw upon the concept of "competitive corporatism", developed by Rhodes.

Grote and Schmitter identified the resurrection of corporatism on macro-issues at the national level during the 1990s in western European countries (Grote and Schmitter 2003). Rhodes observed that it began to be more difficult to solve the problems of employment and social security during globalization. Referring to Southern Europe, the Netherlands and Ireland, he insists that this does not entail a decline in the influence of corporative processes on socioeconomic reforms (Rhodes 2001: 176). He named this new type of tripartite negotiation "competitive corporatism". The structures of competitive corporatism are less routine, the partners weaker institutionally, exit costs lower, and the presence of the state is much more strongly felt (Rhodes 2001: 177). The new social pacts involved new coalitions over the nature of distribution and productivity. The former required policies such as the "redesign of social security systems to prevent implicit or explicit disentitlement in relation to two particular groups: women workers and those not in permanent employment", and the latter includes the policies like "a shift away from legislated or rule-governed labour market regulation to negotiated labour market regulation" (Rhodes 1998: 180–1).

So what produces this new type of corporatism? Labor unions seem weaker these days, but Rhodes says that it is unions who have the networks in the workplace and are embedded organizationally. These unions can thus form social pacts, because they can place restrictions and allocate resources on social issues. "Restrictions" here means a union veto on certain policies, while "resources" means support for certain policies. It is also necessary to point out that the absence of well-organized unions makes it difficult for employers to handle fragmented workers (Rhodes 1998: 195–6).

2.2 The Menem Administration and competitive corporatism

2.2.1 Neoliberal reform by the Menem Administration

In 1989, Carlos Menem of the Peronist Party won the presidential election, forming his government in the midst of an unprecedented economic crisis. In this situation, the most urgent political aim of the Menem administration was to restore the collapsed economy. Although labor unions constituted the largest organized support group for the Peronist Party, the Menem government adopted neoliberal policies to stabilize the economy.

Neoliberal economic reforms were introduced extensively when Domingo Cavallo, who had no previous political connections with the Peronist Party, became Minister of the Economy in 1991. He simplified the customs system and dramatically lowered the level of tariffs. Almost all state-owned enterprises were privatized, which meant that the state did not compensate for these entities' losses, while it was also able to obtain special revenues from their sale. At the same time, this privatization, through debt equity swaps, helped solve the problem of Argentina's massive external debt.

Through these policies, the Argentine economy was liberalized and the fiscal deficit reduced, and this slowed down the inflation rate. As a result of these neoliberal economic reforms, measures to protect industry, which were installed under import substitution policies, were abolished, and many industries were exposed to severe market competition. This meant that many formal sector workers suffered from both a loss of job and wages security.

The legal framework to promote neoliberal economic reform was the National Reform Law and the Economic Emergency Law, which were passed by Congress in 1989. The former stipulated the deregulation of the domestic market and promoted privatization, while the latter stipulated the abolition of laws to protect industry, which were at the core of the import substitution industrialization (ISI) economic model. The second also aimed to reform the pension and medical insurance systems. To achieve neoliberal economic reform, it is well known that the Menem administration used emergency presidential decrees when necessary: President Menem promulgated 336 presidential decrees between July 1989 and April 1994 (Rubio and Goretti 1996: 451). This style of Menem's formed the background to O'Donnell's view on delegative democracy theory (O'Donnell 1997). However, in respect of labor and social security reform, sometimes the government intended to carry out reforms through presidential decrees but could not do so because of labor union opposition. In these circumstances, the Menem administration tended to achieve its goals through tripartite negotiations.

2.2.2 The major component of new corporatism

Now we can identify the major components of the new corporatism in the Menem administration. First, as the leading labor union organization, there is the General Confederation of Labor (CGT: Confederación General de Trabajo) which until now has been the major support group for the Peronist Party. The CGT is the only national center of labor unions that is certified by the Ministry of Labor to be a legal entity as a labor union. Labor unions opposed to the Menem government, such as the teachers' unions and the government employees' unions formed a major new organization, the Center of Argentine Workers (CTA: Central de los Trabajadores Argentinos). They have relations with unemployed and poor people's social movements, but are not legal labor entities like the CGT.

In the 1989 presidential elections the CGT divided into two groups. One group supported Carlos Menem as the presidential candidate of the Peronist Party, and the other supported Antonio Cafiero, the governor of the province of Buenos Aires. This division continued until their unification in 1992 under the leadership of the pro-Menem unions, a development that enhanced the CGT's power to negotiate, so the Menem administration changed its style of policy making from one that was characterized by delegative democracy to one that was based on negotiation, at least in respect of social policy.

Nevertheless, many indicators still show a decline in the labor unions' political power. Many scholars point out that the division of the CGT reduced its political influence (Senén González and Bosoer 1999: 29–31; Levitsky 2004). Levitsky also referred to the decline in the number of national congress deputies from labor unions, which fell from 29 in 1983 to just three in 2001 (Levitsky 2004: 20). Marshall also referred to the fall in the union's organizational rate from 49 percent in 1990 to 42 percent in 2001 (Marshall and Groisman 2005: 12).

Second, we can identify the presence of eight major industrial organizations during the period of the Menem administration: (1) ADEBA: The Association of Banks of Argentina (Asociación de Bancos de la Argentina); (2) ABRA: The Association of Banks of the Republic of Argentina (Asociación de Bancos de la República Argentina); (3) The Stock Exchange of Buenos Aires (Bolsa de Comercio de Buenos Aires); (4) The Argentine Chamber of Commerce (Cámara Argentina de Comercio); (5) The Argentine Rural Society (Sociedad Rural Argentina); (6) The UIA: Argentine Industrial Union (Unión Industrial Argentina); (7) The Argentine Chamber of Construction (Cámara Argentina de la Construcción); and (8) The Argentine Union of Construction (Unión Argentina de la Construcción).

Of these, the UIA, ADEBA, and Sociedad Rural were the three major industrial organizations. The UIA, especially, founded in 1887, has, in practice, represented manufacturing, so it was used to represent the opinions of industry in the tripartite negotiations. Unlike the CGT, the UIA has not maintained a formal partnership with traditional political parties, such as the Radical Civic Union (Unión Cívica Radical) or the Peronist Party.

Third, in terms of the state, technocrats who were political appointees and had no political relations with the Peronist Party were the people who actually realized the neoliberal reforms. Domingo Cavallo was judged solely on his merits and he was invited to join the cabinet as Minister of the Economy. He executed the main neoliberal economic reforms in the Menem administration from 1991 to 1994, when he resigned. He held a PhD from Harvard University and had no political background with the Peronist Party.[1] Another representative, José Armando Caro Figueroa, was another technocrat who worked as Labor Minister and carried out labor and social security reforms between 1994 and 1997. He was a labor lawyer and worked in the government of the Radical Party in Argentina and in the Ministry of Labor in Spain. After these experiences, he was brought into the Menem government as a specialist on labor reforms (Caro Figueroa 1997). There were numerous other technocrats who worked in the Menem administration to achieve neoliberal reforms. However, they did not have political bases or relations with industrial and labor organizations, such as the CGT. So we need to research how they could carry out their policies with no political base or relationship with such organizations.

2.2.3 Competitive corporatism in Argentina

This section will review the kinds of negotiations and agreements that were reached during this period. At the beginning of the Menem administration, anti-government labor unions protested against the Menem government which was intending to push for neoliberal economic reform. Nevertheless, President Menem did call for the formation of a tripartite agreement as early as December 1989.[2] Tripartite negotiations had frequently been held before this, especially on labor and social security reform. Usually it was the administration who called for these negotiations, so such corporatism can be characterized as being carried out under the leadership of the state.[3]

In relation to labor reform, the state, the Group of Eight representing industry as mentioned above, and the pro-Menem labor unions began to negotiate over legislating on "employment law" in a way that would help make industrial relations more flexible. Although they could not agree on the details, they formed a consensus to pass legislation in Congress.[4]

In terms of social security reform, the two major objectives of the Menem government were medical insurance reform and pension reform, but pension reform took precedence over medical insurance reform. A new director of the social security department in the Ministry of Labor was appointed as someone who intended to promote pension reform, and 20 members of staff from that department were hired with subsidies from the World Bank in January 1991 (Coelho 2002: 51). In June 1992, President Menem addressed the need for pension reform in a television address.[5] At that time, changes to the pension system bill were being presented to the Lower House. These intended to reform the existing "pay-as-you-go" pension system into basically a two-pillar system, composed of a common basic "pay-as-you-go" pension for all and a mandatory capitalization system for employees under 45 years of age (Isuani and San Martino 1993: 47–50).

Pensioners' organizations opposed this proposal immediately and took to the streets to express their opposition.[6] The reason for the pensioners' opposition was clear. They feared that the existing "pay-as-you-go" system under which they received pensions would be unsustainable with the introduction of capitalization, because the premiums existing workers would pay would go into their own accounts and the state would have to compensate and provide monies to fund current pensions. But the organization rate of the pensioners was low, around 10 percent according to their own figures, and they were divided into minor organizations, so their influence on policy formation may have been insignificant (Alonso 1998: 613–14). The unified national center of labor unions also opposed the pension reform.[7] However, the UIA justified the government's new policy by saying that the existing pension system was bankrupt, and it agreed to the government's proposals.[8]

Under these circumstances, tripartite negotiations began on pension reform on the initiative of the Minister of the Economy, Domingo Cavallo, in an advisory committee on production, investment, and growth (Consejo de producción, inversión y crecimiento). In these negotiations, the government, in May 1992, accepted the demands of the labor unions, which required that the union be able to manage their own private pension companies, and stipulated the foundation of a supervisory body on the privatized pension system.[9] The deciding votes in the Lower House were cast by the deputies from the labor unions, and the other deputies who sympathized with them, so the final amendment approved by the Lower House stated that an employee could select as a second pillar either the "pay-as-you-go" system or the capitalization system.

Labor unions, however, also recognized the problems in the existing "pay-as-you-go" system,[10] so they did not strongly oppose pension reform per se. Thus, the focus of the negotiation was on how to combine the capitalization system, which was more market-oriented, with the "pay-as-you-go" system, which guaranteed existing pensioners' living standards. The pension reform at the end of 1992 must therefore be regarded as a compromise between the demands of the unions and those of the technocrats who wanted to achieve market-oriented reform in the social arena.

The most notable agreement reached through tripartite negotiation during the Menem administration was the "Framework-Agreement on Employment, Productivity, and Social Equity" (*Acuerdo marco para el empleo, la productividad y la equidad social*), which was signed at the presidential residence. Caro Figueroa, the Minister of Labor, promoted this agreement from the beginning of July and it was signed on July 25, 1994. This agreement consisted of 17 clauses, but can be summarized in the following six points (Ministerio de Trabajo 1994): (1) Promote flexible industrial relations to create employment, and, at the same time, introduce compensatory policies for the problems caused by flexibility, such as the re-employment of the jobless and medical programs for the unemployed; (2) Promote access to information on management and participation in management by the labor unions; (3) Decide the ratio of social security contributions to family assignation between labor and the employers, and privatize industrial accident insurance; (4) Recognize the importance of collective bargaining and introduce policies against illegal employment or corporate bankruptcy; (5) Review industrial relations to increase competitiveness and productivity according to changes in circumstances, reform collective bargaining, and regulate immigration during globalization; and (6) Set up a committee and an agenda to realize this agreement.

Based on this agreement, in 1995 many laws were established. The most important was the Labor Liberalization law, which permitted, for the first time, part-time labor contracts in order to promote flexibility in industrial relations. At the same time, this law aimed to increase the employment of women, disabled persons, and the elderly. Other laws passed in 1995 included the Small and Medium-Sized Companies Law, which was established to promote these companies, the Industrial Accident Law, which included private insurance, the Bankruptcy Law, which regulated asset management and collective bargaining when a company went bankrupt. In 1996, Congress passed two laws. One stipulated compulsory arbitration in labor disputes and the other reformed the family assignation (Giordano and Torres 1997: 236–44; Ediciones del País 2006).

These laws, based upon the tripartite agreement of 1994, are compromises between labor, the state, and industry. On the one hand, labor unions accepted institutional reforms to increase competitiveness and productivity in accordance with transformations in the market. On the other hand, the state and enterprises compensated for the new risks brought about by these institutional reforms. In this sense, the style of this agreement is in line with competitive corporatism.

The following three characteristics are found in this agreement. First, it certainly contributed to increased competitiveness and productivity, but it offered weak compensatory policies to mitigate the negative effects of the reforms. Second, the ideal type of negotiation, according to competitive corporatism, is de-centralized. However, in Argentina, there were centralized negotiations, instead of negotiations on the issues, in which the state, the national center of labor and companies all participated. Third, competitive corporatism in Argentina continued for only seven years under the Menem administration. It began with a provisional agreement on employment law in 1990, reached its peak with the Framework-Agreement on Employment, Productivity, and Social Equity in 1994, and collapsed with the resignation of the Labor Minister, Caro Figueroa, in 1997.

2.2.4 What created Argentine competitive corporatism?

Although many scholars point to a decrease in the influence of the labor unions, we should ask the question: why were tripartite negotiations and agreements signed in Argentina? First, it is important to understand Argentina's labor union and collective bargaining laws. Both only permit a labor union that is a legal labor entity as certified by the guidelines of the Ministry of Labor to sign a collective bargaining agreement (Fernandez Madrid and Caubet 1996: 274–6), and only the CGT has such a certification as the national center of labor unions. This legal framework, instead of changes in external circumstances, contributed to the continuation of the corporatist type of tripartite negotiation in Argentina.

Second, the behavior of the three actors also contributed to the formation of corporatist negotiations. Labor unions opposed the neoliberal reforms of the Menem government from the outset, because they thought these reforms would reduce wage levels and damage working conditions. Though the unions opposed the reforms, they had different positions on them. Some unions intended to participate in the negotiations to reduce the disadvantages arising from the reforms.[11] The key point concerning government participation in the negotiations is that the people who realized the reforms were politically appointed technocrats. They had no relation with labor unions and no political background. The Labor Minister Caro Figuroa himself testified that he felt this weakness of not having a political background. So he needed to participate in the tripartite negotiations and persuade the unions and industry to realize social reforms.[12] The person in charge of social policy at the UIA also said it was desirable to participate in the tripartite negotiations on labor and social security reforms.[13] So all three actors thought it necessary to negotiate labor and social security reforms in a situation of socioeconomic transformation, such as globalization and increased market competition.

Murillo also analyzed the achievements of corporatism by the government and labor unions in her analysis of the neoliberal economic reforms in the 1990s. She applied institutionalist rational choice theory to the interaction between the labor unions and the union-based political parties. Given the objective of union leaders to maintain their position, when there was no competition among political parties concerning the unions or among the unions concerning the political party in power, corporative action between the union and the government could be achieved. After the unification of the CGT in 1992, there was corporative action and the unions obtained certain concessions (Murillo 2000: 148–9). However, although her argument can explain corporate actions between the government and the unions during the Menem administration after 1992, it is necessary to explain why these actions were market-oriented. For this, again need to consider the effects of globalization and the decline in union influence.

2.3 Labor and social security reforms

2.3.1 Flexibility in industrial relations

In this section, we will discuss the contents of the labor and social security reforms in the agreements based on competitive corporatism in Argentina. The liberalization policies of the Menem administration produced more intense domestic and external market competition. Industry demanded labor policy reforms in line with this situation. The president of the social policy department at the UIA, Funes de Rioja, insisted that the deregulation of the labor market was required to reduce labor costs and create new industrial technology in the new economic situation.[14] The Menem government also stated the need for the deregulation of the labor market because it increased jobs (Senén González and Bosoer 1999: 51; Caro Figueroa 1993: 30–47). Under these circumstances, employment and labor liberalization laws were enacted in 1991 and 1995 respectively.

The three principal changes which labor liberalization law stipulated in 1995 are as follows: (1) Prolonging the period of the probation contract from three months to six months by collective agreement; (2) Stipulation of the part-time labor contract; and (3) Stipulation of a definite-term contract from three months to two years for women, disabled persons, and veterans of the Malvinas War. The government's original plan for this law intended to decentralize negotiations on working hours, paid vacations, and layoffs, but these were deleted in the final plan after strong opposition from the unions (Ferrario 1994).

Employment law established four new definite-term labor contracts with exemptions or reductions in social insurance contributions (see Table 2.1). This flexibility in industrial relations was expected to reduce the level of labor costs, making it possible for young people and the unemployed to enter the labor market, and offering opportunities for young people to obtain job skills. Employment law also established compensation for unregistered workers and integrated legislation so that workers with definite-term contracts had to register their contracts

Table 2.1 Flexible labor contracts established by employment law

New labor contract	Targeted person	Period	Social security
Definite-term labor contract to promote employment	Registered unemployed and unemployed people through administrative reform	From six months to 18 months	50 percent reduction in pension, family allowance and unemployment insurance contributions by the employer
Definite labor contract for the establishment of a new business	Employment for new production lines	From six months to 24 months within four years of the establishment of a business	50 percent reduction in pension, family allowance and unemployment insurance contributions by the employer
Probation contract for young people	Young people under 24 years old who experienced job training	One-year certification of acquirement of a skill	Exemption from pension and family allowance contributions by the employer
Definite labor contract for the acquirement of a skill	Young people under 24 years old who have not experienced job training	From four months to two years. Wages to be paid out of unemployment insurance	Exemption from pension and family allowance contributions by the employer

Source: Font, 1997.

and join the social security system. In this way, it was anticipated that there would be a reduction in the number of workers without labor contracts and a guarantee of social insurance for them. At the same time, this law created a comprehensive unemployment insurance system in Argentina for the first time. In this sense, this law aimed at a deregulation of the labor market as well as protection for workers with a flexible labor contract.

This deregulation of the labor laws introduced flexible industrial relations, such as a definite-term labor contract, the prolongation of the probation period, and part-time contracts which appear to be suitable in a situation of increased competition. On the one hand, the persons targeted by these laws are limited to socially vulnerable people, such as young people and unemployed persons, and on the other hand, these laws established an unemployment insurance system and stipulated that young people could obtain skills through these new job contracts, so that the negative side of the deregulation of the labor market would be mitigated by these measures. In this sense, these two laws for the deregulation of the labor market were formed along the lines of an agreement arising out of the idea of competitive corporatism. As far as wages are concerned, it was decided, by presidential decree 1334/91 enacted in 1991, to base wages on increases in productivity. Thus, productivity and competitiveness more directly affected the issue of wages.

2.3.2 Social security reforms

This section will discuss the contents of the social security reforms. The principal social security reforms during the Menem administration were the establishment of unemployment insurance by employment law, pension reform, and medical insurance reform. First, we will look at pension reform in Argentina. As described in section 2.2, a compromise was achieved in the Advisory Committee on Production, Investment and Development under the Ministry of Economy in 1992. The new pension system consisted of the following three pillars: (1) a basic, common "pay-as-you-go" pension for all; (2) a compensatory "pay-as-you-go" pension for certain people, the contributor can choose between (3) an additional "pay-as-you-go" pension, or (4) a capitalization system from a private company.

We can see that the advantage of pension privatization is to foster a capital market and to contribute to economic development (Banco Mundial 1994: 242). At the same time, pension privatization makes clear the relationship between contributions paid and pensions received so one can expect a reduction in non-payments. In this way, the private pension system was to increase the coverage of the pension system. What is more, all contributors to the private pension system would have their own accounts held by a private company and this was appropriate for the new labor market situation where a worker's chances to change jobs would increase. On the other hand, a "pay-as-you-go" system guarantees existing pensioners' interests. To sum up, the new pension system which combined a "pay-as-you-go" system and a private system can be classified as an agreement in line with competitive corporatism.

On the other hand, in terms of medical insurance reforms, a compromise based on competitive corporatism could not be reached. The existing social medical insurance system originated in the government of Perón (1946–55) and was expanded in 1970 when the Onganía military government obliged employed workers to participate in the medical insurance system and allowed labor unions to manage their own medical insurance. After 1970, social medical insurance expanded in Argentina, but it began to be criticized for its inefficiency and bad service. Also, its management by the unions was criticized for their opaque accounts processing. Panadeiros proposed a reform plan which intended to introduce market mechanisms to social medical insurance to improve its service and efficiency. She suggested a free choice in medical insurance by contributors to increase competition (Panadeiros 1991: 13–27).

The government reform, announced in January 1992, was created by technocrats at the Ministry of Health and Economy. It proposed a free choice in medical insurance, including that of a private medical insurance company.[15] The introduction of free choice was expected to increase the level of efficiency through competition and to cut the relationship between contributors and their jobs. In this sense, the proposal of a free choice in social medical insurance is convenient for the new flexible labor market situation.

Labor unions voiced strong opposition to the proposal of a free choice in social medical insurance. The general secretary of the pro-government CGT, Raúl Amín, insisted that the medical insurance managed by labour unions must achieve financial stability through their own efforts, and labor unions must continue the management of their medical insurance.[16] The General Secretary of the anti-government CGT, Saúl Ubaldini, also insisted that it was necessary to maintain the current system.[17] One labor union leader stated that labor unions were concerned about the background to the free choice proposal in which some of its advocates might think that some of the unions' power came from their management of medical insurance, and this is why it was better to change the situation.[18]

The conflict between the advocates of free choice and the labor unions continued for a while, then in May 1997 the Minister of Labor, Caro Figueroa, and representatives of the unified CGT reached an agreement in which private medical insurance companies would be excluded from the free choice in social medical insurance reform.[19] The UIA rejected this agreement and criticized it.[20] This agreement was in line with labor union demands, which included a reduction in the levels unstable employment and the maintenance of the existing centralized negotiation system. Here we can see the decline of competitive corporatism in Argentina, which we will discuss later in more detail.

2.4 Results of the reforms

2.4.1 Significance of labor and social security reform

This section will analyze the significance of labor and social security reform based on agreements reached through competitive corporatism in Argentina, especially with concern to its institutional aspects and results. The key point of competitive corporatism is that labor unions will cooperate to increase productivity and competitiveness in an increasingly competitive market, and enterprises and the state will compensate for the new risks that arise from deregulation. First, we will see how this agreement and the policies based on this agreement contributed to an increase in productivity and competitiveness.

With regard to the deregulation of the labor market, we need to pay attention to the kind of flexibility that has been achieved. Many scholars give various definitions of flexibility in industrial relations, but it is convenient to use Regini's classification, which seems to be very clear. He classified flexibility in industrial relations into four categories: (1) *Quantitative flexibility*: adjusting the amount of labor in correspondence with fluctuations in demand and technological change; (2) *Organizational flexibility*: transferring jobs easily and making workers multi-task according to fluctuations and changes in demand; (3) *Wage flexibility*: adjusting wages with ease and in correspondence with changes in the labor market and competitive circumstances; and, (4) *Temporal flexibility*: employing workers with ease under different kinds of labor contract and being able to adjust the number of workers in line with fluctuations in demand (Esping-Andersen and Regini 2000).

The main deregulation of the labor market during the Menem administration was the establishment of the definite-term contract, the prolongation of the term of probation, and the establishment of the part-time contact. These corresponded to what Regini has labeled quantitative flexibility, wage flexibility, and temporal flexibility. These types of flexibility are defined as being "external." They react to both increased domestic and external competition in the market and also the processes of globalization. On the other hand, organizational flexibility could not be achieved during the Menem government, contrary to the desires of both government and industry. For this to have happened, negotiations would have had to have been decentralized, but this was prevented by strong union opposition.

We now need to see what social security institutions were established to attend to the risks generated by this transformation in industrial relations. As shown in the introduction to this book, Taylor-Gooby has indicated three new risks for paid work in the post-industrial world: (1) problems entering the labor market; (2) problems in maintaining stable, secure and reasonable paid employment, together with associated social security entitlements; and, (3) problems in gaining adequate training in a more flexible labor market (Taylor-Gooby 2004: 19). In Argentina, there existed problems for young people entering the labor market and problems for informal sector workers entering the formal labor market. What is more, the deregulation of the labor market caused problems of instability arising from the new flexible working environment. How that instability is dealt with by the social security system must now be examined. We will also look carefully at whether workers with flexible labor contracts had a chance to improve their skills. In this sense, the problems Taylor-Gooby has pointed out existed in Argentina.

The laws establishing a flexible work system were aimed at young people, unemployed people, women, and the disabled and were intended to get them to enter the labor market, but definite-term contracts or the prolonged probation term worsened job security, so labor unions criticized these flexible contracts and called them *"contrato basura"* (contract sweepings). If a worker on a flexible contract could obtain skills during their working term, and then could obtain stable employment, the problems would not get worse. But the reality in Argentina is that two different kinds of labor markets have formed in the formal sector. This is made very clear by Labor Minister Caro Figueroa's next words. He stated that the intention behind making the labor market more flexible was to create a second labor market for young and unemployed people without having an impact upon the existing formal labor market.[21]

We will now move on to consider whether or not the social security systems which were established along with the flexibility in industrial relations precisely matched the new risks. The establishment of a comprehensive unemployment insurance in Argentina through employment law was a measure to address a situation where there was an increase in the possibility of unemployment and job insecurity, but the probation contract is exempted from unemployment insurance and pension contributions, so workers were not covered by unemployment insurance and the levels of their future pensions were affected. Employment law also intended to reduce the number of non-contract workers through an integrated system of registration for labor contracts and social security, but, as will be seen in the next section, the number of informal workers has never fallen. The partial privatization of pensions was expected to increase pension coverage through the establishment of a clear relationship between contributions and future pensions. Also, private pensions are considered appropriate in a flexible labor market, but here again this goal could not be achieved, as will be seen in the next section.

2.4.2 The employment situation

In this section, we will gain a more precise picture of how deregulation affected the labor market. First, the unemployment rate in Greater Buenos Aires increased from 6.3 percent in 1991 to 20.5 percent in 1995, when the Mexican economic crisis was affecting all Latin American economies. After 1995, the unemployment rate fluctuated around 15 percent while the rate of growth in the GDP was relatively high until 1998 (see Figure 2.1). This unemployment rate is higher than the average for the 1980s, which was labeled "the lost decade." In considering these points, the 1990s can be characterized as a period of "growth without employment."

Two of the main factors that lie behind this increase in unemployment during the 1990s are: (i) an increase in women's participation in the labor market; and (ii) the massive number of dismissals that resulted from the privatization of state-owned enterprises. We now need to see whether the deregulation of the labor market under the Menem administration contributed to an increase in employment and to a solution of the problems of unemployment. The unemployment rate remained high after the deregulation of the labor market. It fell from 20 percent in 1995 to around 15 percent in the following years. However, this reduction can

Figure 2.1 Unemployment rate in greater Buenos Aires (1980–2003)
Sources: INDEC (2001, 2003).

Table 2.2 The variation in labor contracts by different type of contract in Greater Buenos Aires (November 1995–November 1996)

Type of labor contract	Index
Indefinite-term contract	94.4
Definite-term contract	178.9
Probation contract	386.5
Agency contract	68.1
Total employment	101.2

Source: La Nación, January 8, 1997. November 1995 = 100.

be explained by the economic recovery after the crisis and it is not clear whether deregulation made any contribution to the recovery.

We now turn to the effect of two deregulation laws on the increase in employment. Table 2.2 shows the variation in labor contracts by type for one year from November 1995 when the two deregulation laws were in effect. It is true that the level of total employment increased a little, but indefinite-term contracts decreased and flexible contracts increased at a very rapid rate (see Table 2.2). The decrease in agency contracts can be attributed to a decrease in the need for them because of the establishment of flexible labor contracts. Table 2.2 suggests that the decline in indefinite-term contracts was compensated for by an increase in flexible labor contracts. In this sense, flexibility in industrial relations fulfils one of the conditions for an increase in competitiveness and productivity. At the same time, this deregulation reduced the amount of "formal work" and destabilized the employment situation as a whole.

Employment law in 1991 not only deregulated the labor market, it was also intended to protect the entitlement of workers on flexible contracts to social security, as stated above. Figure 2.2 shows the percentage of workers with pension premiums from 1990 to 2003. If a worker has unpaid pension contributions, it means that they are not covered by social insurance. In this sense, they are essentially informal sector workers. This shows that employment law could not reduce the size of the informal sector.

2.4.3   Evaluation of social security reform

This section will examine whether social security reform covers the new risks brought about by the transformation in industrial relations. Employment law established comprehensive unemployment insurance in Argentina for the first time. The establishment of unemployment insurance was a key element of competitive corporatism in Argentina, and it was expected to compensate for the negative effects of the deregulation of the labor market.

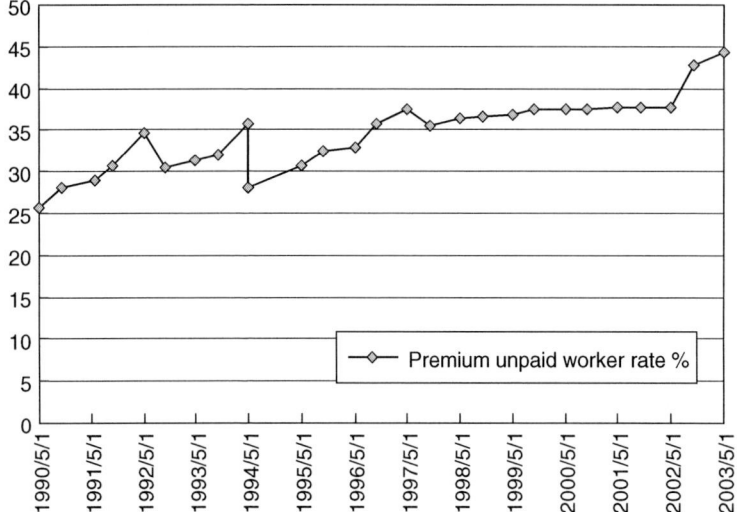

Figure 2.2 Unpaid pension premium rate in the main cities
Source: Retrieved from http://www.trabajo.gov.ar/ on November 11, 2006.

Table 2.3 Unemployment rate and the ratio of unemployed people who received unemployment insurance from 1992 to 1998

Year	1992	1993	1994	1995	1996	1997	1998
Unemployed people who received insurance	12,808	73,376	98,516	122,349	128,673	95,379	90,712
Unemployment rate (%)	7.0	9.3	12.1	16.6	17.3	13.3	12.4

Sources: INDEC (1999: 296; 1997: 294). Retrieved from http://www.indec.mecon.gov.ar/, on November 14, 2006.

The point is whether this new institution for the new risk was successful. The number of unemployed people in 1992 was estimated at around 920,000, and only 1.4 percent of them – around 12,800 persons – received unemployment insurance (see Table 2.3). This had increased to only 3 percent in 2004, 13 years after the establishment of unemployment insurance. This means that the unemployment insurance established by employment law could not guarantee the living standards of those dismissed during the 1990s (INDEC: 1997: 181; Ministerio de Trabajo 2006: 252).

The reasons why the proportion of unemployed people who were covered by unemployment insurance was so low must be attributed to the conditions concerning their benefits. Unemployment insurance is targeted at workers who have formal labor contracts, so it is not focused on informal sector workers, who do not possess such contracts. Workers are required to pay premiums for at least three months during the year before their dismissal, and the terms under which they can receive benefits differ according to how long contributions have been paid – on a scale from four months to one year. In this way, the long-term unemployed are also excluded from unemployment insurance. Furthermore, workers on probation contracts and definite-term contracts are also excluded from this insurance. Therefore, the new unemployment insurance system does not actually work as an institution that protects the majority of those dismissed in the 1990s.

Under the Employment Foundation that was established by employment law there were 13 programs for unemployed and poor people. These include: subsidy programs to small and medium-sized enterprises which hire the unemployed persons; employment schemes on public works in the community, which targets the heads of indigent families; employment in the community service of the female heads of low-income families; subsidies to small and medium-sized enterprises to increase their number of employees; and subsidies to unskilled workers to improve their skills. The beneficiaries of these programs numbered 745,000 persons in 1996 (Ministerio de Trabajo 1997: 107–12). In this sense, these non-contributory social programs were more important in mitigating the effects of the massive unemployment of the 1990s. Although the 1996 unemployment rate, at 17.3 percent, was so high that these measures could only reach around half of those unemployed.

One reason for the introduction of the private sector into the pension system was to clarify the relationship between contributions paid and benefits so as to reduce the level of non-payments. A personal account also seemed to be appropriate for a deregulated labor market where workers have more opportunities to change jobs. However, it is hard to say whether pension coverage increased as expected. Only 45.03 percent of those joining the private pension system paid their contributions in June 1999 (Superintendencia 1999: 58). As far as social security reform is concerned, it is difficult to confirm that it worked to compensate for the negative effects of the deregulation of the labor market as anticipated by those involved in the agreement that was reached on the grounds of competitive corporatism.

2.4.4 The end of competitive corporatism in Argentina

Competitive corporatism in Argentina reached its peak with the Framework-Agreement in 1994, but this tendency was reversed after 1997. The problem of Menem's second re-election was the main reason for this reversal. Memen was elected under the constitution of 1853, which fixes a six-year presidential term and prohibits consecutive re-election. He amended this constitution, and the new constitution of 1994 reduces the six-year term to four and permits a one-time consecutive re-election. Menem was re-elected under this amendment in the election of 1995. However, he then went for a second re-election and began his presidential campaign in 1997. The logic for this was that the second term was to be counted as a first term under the amended constitution, so it was not unconstitutional to re-elect the existing president. The governor of Buenos Aires Province, Eduardo Duharde, who wanted to be the presidential candidate of the Peronist Party, strongly resisted this maneuver and the conflict between the two men became very apparent.

For his next re-election, Menem needed labor union support to build his political base in the Peronist Party. Caro Figueroa stated that he felt a decline in the president's desire for labor and social security reform as well as in Menem's political support for him, so he decided to resign.[22] Menem named his aide, Erman González, to succeed Figueroa. González and the CGT established a new agreement in which González accepted the CGT's previous demands. This agreement included the abolition of major flexible labor contracts, which the unions opposed, maintained a clause in the labor law which stipulated the continuing validity of collective bargaining agreements until there is a new agreement, and maintained the centralized collective bargaining system.[23]

Industry strongly opposed this reversal in the trend of labor reform and proposed their own reforms.[24] However, the new labor "reform law" of 1998 abolished the main flexible labor contracts which employment law and labor liberalization law had established, and the union demands mentioned above became law. In this way, President Menem met union demands in order to gain their support, and industry left the tripartite agreement. As a result, the Menem administration dropped the idea of labor deregulation and the old system returned. Thus a new agreement based on the idea of competitive corporatism was never reached. We may therefore say that competitive corporatism in Argentina ended here.

The emergence of an influential political rival to Menem within the Peronist Party strengthened the unions' political influence and Menem had to change his stance toward the unions. As Murillo has stated, opposition to reform could succeed when there was no competition among the labor unions around a political party and there was competition among the political parties around the unions (Murillo 2000: 151–2). When the Menem administration promoted neoliberal reforms, the Peronist Party was very strong and Menem had no rival in the party, but Menem's attempt to seek a second re-election reversed the political situation and two Peronist Party politicians were fighting to obtaining the CGT's support. This is the type of situation where, according to Murillo, reform cannot be achieved.

Final remarks

Economic liberalization made great advances with the Menem administration's neoliberal policies during the 1990s. Reductions in labor costs were required by industry when there was an increase in domestic and external competition in the market. On the other hand, massive numbers of unemployed people were a common sight, the deregulation of the labor market was discussed from the point of view of an increase in employment. At the same time, disputes over social security reform became a core issue for the Menem administration. It is important to recognize that economic liberalization was realized by technocrats who were political appointees through presidential decrees, but labor and social security reforms were realized through tripartite collective negotiation although each particular project was originally drafted by the technocrats. Also, such agreements were enacted in Congress after certain agreements were reached.

The most important agreement was the Framework-Agreement on Employment, Productivity, and Social Equity, which was signed in 1994. In this agreement, the labor unions cooperated to increase productivity and competitiveness, and accepted the deregulation of the labor market after considering the changes in the market, whereas industry tried to compensate for the negative effects of the deregulated labor market and to maintain social equity. These agreements, including the Framework-Agreement, possessed almost the same concept of competitive corporatism that Rhodes has insisted upon. Pension reform in 1993 could also be considered to be a result of this type of corporatism. The characteristics of the agreement based on competitive corporatism in Argentina set the pursuit of productivity and competitiveness above those of compensation and social equity. There was, for example, a high unemployment rate, especially for women, an increase in the number of workers with unpaid pension premiums, an expansion of the informal sector, and a low level of coverage for unemployment insurance.

Competitive corporatism in Argentina was dismantled as the result of political factors after 1997 and the main labor deregulation contracts were abolished in 1998. However, during the period of the De la Rua coalition government, the successor in 2000 to the Menem administration. Labor reform law deregulated the clause which stipulated the continuing validity of a collective bargaining agreement until a new agreement is reached, and it decentralized collective negotiations (Stefanescu et al. 2000). This coalition government collapsed in the economic crisis of 2001 and the deregulation of the validity of collective bargaining agreements was changed back to the old system by the Peronist government of Kirchner in 2004. As a result, the current labor market consists of two long-existing sectors: a formal sector, which is covered by labor law and social security, and an informal sector, which is not covered. The benefits of social security reform also do not reach the informal sector. In this situation, non-contributory social assistance is becoming more important in mitigating the problems of unemployment and poverty.

Panizza and Levitsky have cited the transformation of the Peronist party as being behind the neoliberal reforms of the 1990s, but it is also important to notice the existence of tripartite negotiations on social policy. This chapter has shown how each element in this tripartite negotiation needed a place where their demands would be discussed and could in part be realized. The formation and collapse of competitive corporatism in Argentina can be explained by examining institutions and the behavior of the actors. After the collapse of this competitive type of corporatism, tripartite negotiations did not disappear. They continue. A future object of research will be to analyze what kind of collective negotiations are being held, what kinds of agreements will be reached, and how those agreements can be realized.

Notes

1. Retrieved from http://www.cavallo.com.ar on October 30, 2006.
2. *El Bimestre*, November–December 1980, p. 40.
3. Interview with Funes de Rioja, president of the department of social policy of the UIA, held on September 19, 2006.
4. *La Nación*, August 2 and 9, 1990.
5. *La Nación*, July 3, 1992.
6. *La Nación*, June 3 and 4, 1992.
7. *La Nación*, May 2, 1992.

8. Interview with Funes de Rioja, president of the Department of Social Policy of the UIA, held on September 19, 2006.
9. *La Nación*, November 27, 1992.
10. Interview with Rubén Cortina, one of the leaders of the Union of Commercial Workers, held on September 25, 2006.
11. Ibid.
12. Interview with Caro Figueroa, Minister of Labor, on September 25, 2006.
13. Interview with Funes de Rioja, president of the Department of Social Policy of the UIA, held on September 19, 2006.
14. Interview with Daniel Funes de Rioja, 1994, *ERGO*, vol. 1 no. 1, p. 26.
15. *La Nación*, January 3, 1992.
16. *La Nación*, January 15, 1992.
17. *La Nación*, January 21, 1992.
18. Interview with Rubén Cortina, one of the leaders of the Union of Commercial Workers held on September 25, 2006.
19. *Clarín*, May 9 and 10, 1997.
20. *Clarín*, May 13, 1997.
21. Interview with Caro Figueroa, Minister of Labor, September 25, 2006.
22. Interview with Caro Figuero, Minister of Labor, September 25, 2006.
23. *La Nación*, March 12, 1998.
24. *Clarín*, April 24, 1998.

References

Alonso, Guillermo V. 1998. "Democracia y reformas: Las tensiones entre decretismo y deliberación. El caso de la reforma provisional argentina." *Desarrollo Económico* 38, no. 150: 595–626.

Banco Mundial. 1994. *Envejecimiento sin crisis*. Washington, DC: Banco Mundial.

Caro Figueroa, José Armando. 1993. *La flexibilización laboral*. Buenos Aires: Editorial Biblos.

Caro Figueroa, José Armando. 1997. *Modernización laboral*. Buenos Aires: Fundación de trabajo.

Coelho, Vera Schattan P. 2002. "El poder ejecutivo y la reforma de la seguridad social: los casos de la Argentina, Brasil y Uruguay." *Desarrollo Económico* 42, no. 165: 45–62.

Esping-Andersen, Gøsta, and Mariano Regini. 2000. *Why Deregulate Labour Markets?* Oxford: Oxford University Press.

Ferrario, Adriana. 1994. "Proyectando una reforma," *ERGO* 1, no. 1: 22–5.

Fernández Madrid, Juan Carlos, and Amanda Beatriz Caubet. 1996. *Leyes fundamentales del trabajo: sus reglamentos y anotaciones completarias*. Buenos Aires: Joaquín Fernández Madrid, Editor.

Font, Miguel Angel. 1997. *Compendio de leyes laborales*. Buenos Aires: Editorial Estudio.

Giordano, Osvaldo and Alejandra Torres. 1997. "En el contexto de reformas estructurales, Argentina 1989/1996." *El empleo en la Argentina: El rol de las instituciones laborales*, Buenos Aires: FIEL. http://www.fiel.org/ (accessed July 21, 2007).

Grote, Jürgen and Philippe Schmitter. 2003. "The Renaissance of National Corporatism." In Fans van Waarden and Gerhard Lehmbruch eds. *Renegotiating the Welfare State*, London: Routledge, pp. 279–302.
INDEC. 1997. *Statistical Yearbook of the Argentine Republic 1999*. Buenos Aires: INDEC.
INDEC. 1999. *Statistical Yearbook of the Argentine Republic 1999*, Buenos Aires: INDEC.
INDEC. 2001. *Encuesta permanente de hogares, Gran Buenos Aires, mayo de 2001*. Buenos Aires: INDEC.
INDEC. 2003. *Mercado de trabajo: Principales indicadores de los aglomerados del Gran Buenos Aires, mayo 2003*. Buenos Aires: INDEC.
Isuani, Ernesto Aldo, and Jorge A. San Martino. 1993. *La reforma previsional argentina: opciones y riesgos*. Buenos Aires: CIEPP.
Levitsky, Steven. 2003. *Transforming Labor-Based Parties in Latin America: Argentine Peronism in Comparative Perspective*. Cambridge: Cambridge University Press.
Levitsky, Steven. 2004. "Del sindicalismo al clientelismo: La transformación de los vínculos partido-sindicato en el peronismo, 1983–1999." *Desarrollo Económico* 44, no. 173: 3–32.
Marshall, Adriana and Fernando Groisman. 2005. "Sindicalización en la Argentina." In *Nuevos escenarios en el mundo del trabajo: rupturas y continuidades*, Buenos Aires: ASET.
Ministerio de Trabajo and Seguridad Social. 1994. *Acuerdo marco para el empleo, la productividad y la equidad social*. Buenos Aires: Ministerio de Trabajo y Seguridad Social.
Ministerio de Trabajo and Seguridad Social. 2006. *Instituciones del mundo del trabajo (I)*. Buenos Aires: Ministerio de Trabajo y Seguridad Social.
Murillo, Victoria M. 2000. "From Populism to Neoliberalism, Labor Unions and Market Reforms in Latin America." *World Politics*, no. 52: 135–74.
O'Donnell, Guillermo. 1999. *Counterpoints*. Notre Dame, IN: University of Notre Dame Press.
Panadeiros, Mónica. 1991. *El sistema de obras sociales en la Argentina: Diagnóstico y propuesta de reforma*. Buenos Aires: FIEL.
Panizza, Francisco. 2001. "Más allá de la democracia delegativa." In *Política e instituciones en las nuevas democracias latinoamericanas*, ed. Isidro Cheresky and Inés Pousadela. Buenos Aires: Paidós.
Pierson, Paul. 1994. *Dismantling the Welfare State?* Cambridge: Cambridge University Press.
Pierson, Paul. 2001. "Coping with Permanent Austerity: Welfare State Restructuring in Affluent Democracies." In *The New Politics of the Welfare State*, ed. Paul Pierson. Oxford: Oxford University Press.
Rhodes, Martin. 1998. "Globalization, Labour Market and welfare States: A Future of 'Competitive Corporatism'." In *The Future of European Welfare: A New Social Contract?*, eds Martin Rhodes and Yves Mény. London: Macmillan, pp. 178–203.
Rhodes, Martin. 2001, "The Political Economy of Social Pacts: Competitive Corporatism and European Welfare Reform." In *The New Politics of the Welfare Sate*, ed. Paul Pierson. Oxford: Oxford University Press, pp. 165–94.
Rubio, Delia Ferreira, and Matteo Goretti. 1996. "Cuando el presidente gobierna solo: Menem y los decretos de necesidad y urgencia hasta la reforma constitucional." *Desarrollo Económico* 36, no. 141: 443–74.

Schmitter, Philippe C. 1979. "Still the Century of Corporatism?" In *Trends toward Corporatist Intermediation*, ed. Philippe C. Schmitter and Gerhard Lehmbruch. Beverly Hills and London: SAGE Publications.

Senén González, Santiago and Fabián Bosoer. 1999. *El sindicalismo en tiempos de Menem*. Buenos Aires: Ediciones Corregidor.

Stefanescu, Raul B., Marcelo Daniel Rolon and Mariano Oscar Muñoz. 2000. *La reforma laboral, ley 25,250 comentada*. Buenos Aires: Editorial Atlántida.

Superintendencia de A.F.J.P. 1999. *Memoria trimestral*, no. 20. Buenos Aires: Superintendencia de A.F.J.P.

Taylor-Gooby, Peter. 2004. "New Risks and Social Change." In *New Risks, New Welfare: The Transformation of the European Welfare State*, ed. Peter Taylor-Gooby. Oxford: Oxford University Press.

Usami, Koichi. 2001. "Formation of the Argentine Welfare State: Social Security Policy under the Peronist Government" (in Japanese). *Ajia Keizai* 42, no. 3: 2–29.

3
The Changing Nature of Employment and the Reform of Labor and Social Security Legislation in Post-Apartheid South Africa[1]

Kumiko Makino

The struggle against apartheid in South Africa reached its peak in the 1980s, as increasing numbers of people were mobilized through trade unions, religious organizations, residents' associations (called "civics"), and other civil society organizations across the country. The mobilization for the struggle spread so widely that the National Party government was no longer able to use force to suppress the movement. The criticism of apartheid from the international community was also heightened, and economic sanctions against South Africa were implemented by major countries from the mid-1980s, severely affecting the South African economy and making the cost of maintenance of the apartheid system prohibitively high. As a result, the government made a decision to initiate negotiations with the anti-apartheid forces, released Nelson Mandela, and lifted the ban on the African National Congress (ANC) and other liberation movements in 1990. Following prolonged negotiations, the first non-racial general elections were held in 1994, and the transition from an apartheid regime to democracy was realized.

The labor movement played a significant role in the anti-apartheid struggle in the 1980s as well as in the negotiation process of the early 1990s (Adler and Webster 2000). The role of the Congress of South African Trade Unions (COSATU), the biggest labor organization, established in the mid-1980s, was particularly important in this process. Although it was not a direct ally of the ANC in the 1980s, COSATU supported the Freedom Charter, and its activism concerned not only "bread-and-butter" issues but also political liberation. After the removal of the ban on the ANC, COSATU allied itself formally with the ANC and the South African Communist Party (SACP). These three organizations form the tripartite alliance through which the ANC has won four overwhelming general election victories since 1994. In the labor law reforms of the post-apartheid era, COSATU has succeeded in winning significant protection of workers through exploiting its political influence in the new government.

At the same time there has been some destabilization of employment. Since the beginning of the political transition, South Africa has been rapidly integrated into the global economy, and there has been strong pressure on the South African labor market in the direction of flexibilization and deregulation. As was typically seen for African mineworkers who worked on a contract basis, flexible and insecure employment has been practiced for a long time in South Africa. In addition to the classical type of non-standard employment, there is a growing trend toward outsourcing employment, avoiding direct employment relations by utilizing labor brokers and "independent contractors" (Bezuidenhout et al. 2004; Kenny and Webster 1999; Theron and Godfrey 2000; Theron et al. 2005; Webster and Von Holdt 2005). Social protection for workers in non-standard employment is significantly worse than that offered to workers in standard employment, due to the insecure nature of employment as well as the lack of social security arrangements associated with employment such as medical schemes and retirement provisions.

This chapter tries to understand these changes that are taking place simultaneously in opposite directions in the context of the characteristics of labor and social security legislation in South Africa, as well as the nature of labor and social security reforms after democratization. Our focus is on the corporatist nature of labor policy making as the factor influencing the course of reforms. Specifically, we will focus on the process of the reforms of labor and social security legislation which have been carried forward through consensus making between the government, business and labor representatives at the National Economic Development and Labour Council (NEDLAC). Regarding the definition of corporatism, the two most well-known conceptualizations are that of Schmitter (1979[1984]), who defined corporatism as a system of interest representation and intermediation, and that of Lehmbruch (1979[1984]), who saw corporatism as an institutional pattern of policy formation; we will follow the latter definition and understand corporatism as a process of policy making and implementation where large interest groups cooperate with each other and with public authorities.

NEDLAC was established in 1995 as a platform for "social dialogue" between the representatives of government, business, labor and community. As of 2008, organized business is represented by the Business Unity South Africa (BUSA), and organized labor by the three main labor federations in South Africa: COSATU, the National Council of Trade Unions (NACTU), and the Federation of Unions of South Africa (FEDUSA). It is a unique feature of NEDLAC that, in addition to the conventional tripartite partners, it includes the community constituency, which is represented by national organizations of civics, youth, women, disabled people, NGOs and so on. The role of the community constituency, however, is limited because it takes part in only the Development Chamber out of the four chambers of NEDLAC: Development, Trade and Industry, Public Finance and Monetary Policy, and Labour Market (Figure 3.1).

According to the NEDLAC Act, NEDLAC considers and seeks to reach consensus about "all proposed labour legislation relating to labour market policy before it is introduced in Parliament" as well as "all significant changes to social and economic policy before it is implemented or introduced in Parliament" (Section 5). In fact, not all significant socioeconomic policy changes have been considered at NEDLAC before being introduced, as is demonstrated by the process of the introduction in 1996 of an important macroeconomic strategy, Growth, Employment and Redistribution (GEAR), in which NEDLAC played no role. However, in respect of labor legislation, for which discussions by NEDLAC are mandatory before submission to Parliament, policy making has been based on consensus reached between government, business, and labor.[2] The contents of labor law reform in the post-apartheid era therefore reflect points of compromise between organized business and labor, balancing the flexibility of the labor market, which is preferable for business, and the protection of workers' rights, which is the core demand of labor. The balance taken, however, has been between the interests of organized workers and their employers, and not a result of the process where "all key stakeholders in the South African society and economy" are ensured effective participation in the formulation of policy, as was envisioned when NEDLAC was established.[3] In a society like South Africa, where the unemployment rate is extremely high and the unionization rate of workers in non-standard employment is low, the representativeness of organized labor participating in corporatist mechanisms becomes problematic (Buhlungu 2006; Webster 2006). What is important for the theme of this chapter is that organized labor and business do have a corporatist means for their interests to be reflected

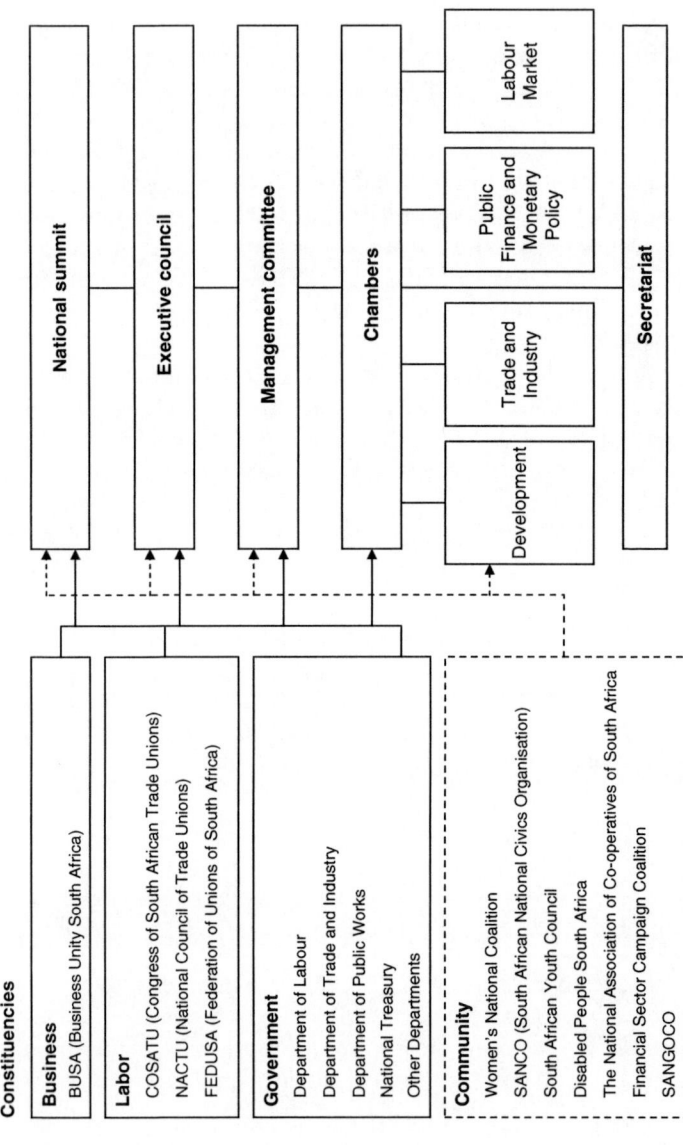

Figure 3.1 The NEDLAC structure
Source: NEDLAC (2008: 2–3).

in policies, while unemployed and unorganized workers have no such means. Corporatism has been criticized in South Africa for its undemocratic nature due to the centralization of power in a small number of elites as well as the risk of marginalizing unorganized vulnerable people (Von Holdt 1993). It was against this backdrop that the community constituency was included in NEDLAC to increase its inclusivity. However, as stated above, the community constituency participates only in the Development Chamber, and does not engage in labor policy making.

Our central argument is that the apparently contradictory changes – labor policy reform in the direction of better protection of workers' rights, and the increase in flexible and insecure employment – can be explained consistently by the corporatist labor policy-making process which has been practiced notwithstanding the problem of representativeness. The remainder of this chapter will demonstrate our argument by examining how the working conditions and social security of workers in non-standard employment have been dealt with in the series of labor and social security reforms in the post-apartheid period. This chapter is structured as follows. Section 3.1 will summarize the major arguments concerning the South African labor market and the increase of non-standard employment (flexibilization and informalization). Section 3.2 will describe the outlines of South African labor and social security legislation and show how workers in non-standard employment are positioned within them. Section 3.3 examines the process of labor and social security reforms in the post-apartheid period and argues that, although the protection of workers' rights has been generally strengthened, the significance of reforms for workers in non-standard employment has been limited. Finally, we will conclude by examining the factors that have led to the delay of reforms concerning workers in non-standard employment.

3.1 Characteristics of the South African labor market and the transformation of employment relations

The South African labor market is regarded by some commentators as rigid and by others as flexible. It is regarded as rigid if the focus is on high wages resulting from strong trade unionism and the centralized collective bargaining system (Moll 1996), yet it is seen as flexible in terms of the presence of comparatively high rates of non-standard employment (Standing et al. 1996). Diagnosis and prescriptions for problems with the labor market differ depending on which aspects are focused on; some would argue the rigidity of the labor market is the cause of the high unemployment rate and thus flexibilization of the labor market is necessary for job creation, yet others would argue it is the poor working conditions of workers in non-standard employment that is problematic and that the policy challenge for the government is how to strengthen and widen the levels of worker protection. The former argument is supported by organized business while the latter is supported by labor, and the dispute is as ideological as it is factual.

According to official statistics, South Africa's unemployment rate in the third quarter of 2008 was 23.1 percent, with 4,122,000 people unemployed. This figure does not include discouraged work-seekers, the number of which is estimated to exceed one million. Moreover, another two million are estimated to be underemployed, i.e. work less than 35 hours in the reference week but are willing and available to work longer hours. The unemployment rate differs significantly according to race and gender, with the highest being for African women (30.9 percent) and the lowest for white men (3.6 percent) (Statistics South Africa 2008). Since unemployment is closely related to poverty (Bhorat et al. 2001), the extremely high unemployment rate has attracted the attention of many scholars. Job creation and poverty alleviation are top priorities for the South African government, which has set a goal of halving unemployment and poverty by 2014 in its policy document, Accelerated and Shared Growth Initiative for South Africa (ASGISA), published in 2006.

There are various analyses of the factors that lie behind the high unemployment rate in South Africa. Bhorat points out that the absolute number of those in employment is increasing yet the unemployment rate rises because the pace of new participation in the labor market outstrips the increase in employment (Bhorat 2004; Bhorat and Oosthuizen 2006). From political and institutional points of view, strong trade unionism and labor market regulations have been blamed for pushing up wage levels and thus for the high unemployment rate. What is characteristic of the labor market regulations in South Africa is the collective bargaining system; basic working conditions such as minimum wages and social security are determined by bargaining councils (previously called industrial councils), which are permanent collective bargaining institutions established by employer and employee organizations in a specific industry, and the agreements made there bind not only the members of bargaining councils but also those parties in the same industry who do not participate in the negotiations. It has been argued that such a centralized bargaining system has the effect of pushing up wages and has hindered job creation, especially in small and medium-sized enterprises (Moll 1996). At the same time, however, there are objections to arguments that claim the rigidity of the labor market is the main reason for the high unemployment rate, focusing instead on problems of industrial structure and its low capacity for employment absorption (Hirsch 2005: 174–84; Hirano 1999; Rodrik 2006).

Another dimension of the labor market emerges if we go beyond the dichotomy of employed and unemployed, and pay more attention to various ways of working. The policy challenge of the reduction of unemployment and job creation is mainly about the quantity of employment; meanwhile the problem of non-standard employment, which is the theme of this chapter, is more concerned with the quality of employment. So far, in the ANC government's discourse, the problem of the quality of employment has been largely ignored compared to that of quantity (Barchiesi 2008). However, the issue of quality of employment is important because non-standard employment is increasing in South Africa, as elsewhere in the world, against the backdrop of globalization.

This change, however, is difficult to pin down using statistics. Official figures regarding non-standard employment, such as terms of employment (permanent or not), became available only after 2000 when Statistics South Africa started to publish LFS, and even after the introduction of LFS, there were criticisms that the questionnaires were not adequate to grasp the reality of employment conditions and tended to underestimate the scale of non-standard employment. For instance, the estimated number of temporary workers according to LFS March 2003 was 167,486, which is less than half of the estimate made by an association of labor brokers, the Confederation of Associations of Private Employment Sector (CAPES) (Theron el al. 2005: 9–11). There was another major revision of labor statistics in 2008, with the Quarterly Labour Force Survey (QLFS) being introduced and LFS discontinued.

Therefore, there is a limit to how far the real scale of non-standard employment can be grasped through statistical data, yet there is a consensus among the government, labor, and business sectors that the non-standardization of employment is progressing. At the Growth and Development Summit in 2003, NEDLAC constituencies agreed that engagement would be required as to "measures to promote decent work and to address the problem of casualisation" (NEDLAC 2003: 29), after which the "changing nature of work and atypical forms of employment" became one of the items on the agenda at the Labour Market Chamber of NEDLAC.

In respect of the informal sector, although it is an accepted notion that the South African informal sector is relatively small compared to other countries at a similar economic level (Kingdon and Knight 2004), it has been pointed out that recently the informalization of employment is progressing in parallel to the flexibilization of employment (Valodia 2001). Casale et al. (2004), who analyzed the trend of the informal sector from 1995 to 2003, while agreeing with Bhorat's finding that the absolute number in employment is on the rise, points out that more than 60 percent of the employment increase in the period was in the informal sector. Bezuidenhout et al. (2004) summarizes the phenomenon of the non-standardization of employment in South Africa as a combined effect of casualization (increase in temporary and part-time employment), externalization (outsourcing, subcontracting, and utilization of labor brokers) and the informalization of employment, which suggests that flexibilization and informalization are not two different phenomena, but are deeply related to each other, drastically changing the quality of employment in South Africa. When we refer to workers in non-standard employment in this chapter, we mean not only workers in the formal sector who do not work full-time on a permanent basis, but also include externalized workers and workers in the informal sector.

Diagnosis and prescriptions for the problems of the South African labor market inevitably differ depending on whether our focus is on the quantity or the quality of employment. For those who claim that the labor market regulations are the principal cause of the high unemployment rate, deregulating the labor market is desirable for job creation, lowering of the unemployment rate, and poverty reduction. Such a diagnosis has been proposed repeatedly by the business sector. The typical example is "Growth for All", a document published by the South African Foundation in 1996, which asserted that "the South African labour market is one of the most rigid in the world" and that the high wages for unionized workers are sustained by the "Continental-type industrial relations systems" which prevent the creation of low-wage jobs. Therefore, the document argued for a two-tier labor market in which, in addition to the existing high-wage capital-intensive sector, a free entry flexible wage sector with minimum labor standards would be allowed (South African Foundation 1996: vii).

As a counterargument, the labor constituency of NEDLAC published "Social Equity and Job Creation," which asserted that it was retrenchment and overhasty trade liberalization that were the causes of increased unemployment, and argued for more protection of workers' rights, as well as job creation and redistribution through budgetary measures (COSATU et al. 1996). Such an argument against deregulating the labor market by trade unions has often been criticized as based on the self-interest of organized workers. For instance, Seekings and Nattrass (2005) depict the situation where the interests of organized workers and the unorganized unemployed are different and the former has managed to protect and promote their interests at the expense of the latter. According to Seekings and Nattrass, the line which separates "insiders" and "outsiders" has changed since the end of the 1970s, from race (whites as insiders and blacks as outsiders) to class (those with jobs as insiders and whose without jobs as outsiders). With democratization, all racial discrimination in legislation was eliminated, yet this did not mean the coming of an egalitarian society. Some blacks were now included in the insiders, yet the majority of blacks were left excluded, and the unequal nature of society remains the same.

The picture Seekings and Nattrass present is rather dichotomist in its way of categorizing participants in the labor market into insiders and outsiders; those who have jobs being insiders and those who do not being outsiders. They depict insiders typically as organized workers who enjoy relatively high wages and stable employment, and not workers in non-standard employment. This is not unreasonable considering that their focus of analysis is more on historical rather than contemporary aspects of inequality and unemployment; i.e. the characteristics of the "distributional regime" which was shaped under apartheid but maintains its influence even now. "Distributional regime" is a concept originated by Seekings and Nattrass. Based on Esping-Andersen's concept of "welfare regime," they construct the concept of "distributional regime" as consisting of economic policy (growth path strategies), labor market institutions, and redistribution through taxation and cash transfer, and argue that the "distributional regime" shapes the distributional outcome of the society. Their concept put more emphasis on the influence of labor market institutions on distributional outcome than that of Esping-Andersen's. Although their analysis is mostly historical, they devote one chapter to the post-apartheid distributional regime and argue that the interests of organized labor, especially COSATU, are more easily reflected in policies, while those of unorganized unemployed and the poor are not. As a result, labor market deregulation does not progress and therefore job creation is hindered (Seekings and Nattrass 2005).

Nonetheless, if we focus on the increase of non-standard employment, a somewhat different picture emerges. Von Holdt and Webster (2005) argue that, as a result of work restructuring against the backdrop of globalization, the post-apartheid South African labor market can be categorized into three zones, which they term respectively core, non-core, and periphery. Included in the "core" zone are full-time workers in the formal sector, similar to the "insiders" of Seekings and Nattrass; the "non-core" zone, which lies just outside of the "core" zone, includes outsourced, temporary, part-time, and domestic workers; workers in the informal sector and the unemployed are in the "periphery" zone, which is at the outer edge. The increase in non-standard employment is understood in this schema as an expansion of the "non-core" zone (shrinkage of the "core" zone) and marginalization of employment (a shift of employment from "core" to "non-core" and from "non-core" to "periphery"). From this schema, what is depicted as problematic is the difference in terms of workers' rights and protection depending on the location of the zone. While workers in the "core" zone enjoy stable employment and relatively high wages, the jobs of "non-core" workers are generally unstable and low-waged, and, although their rights as workers have improved on paper through the series of labor law reforms, they seldom enjoy practical protection of their rights. The increase in "non-core" workers in turn threatens the working conditions of "core" workers (Von Holdt and Webster 2005: 29). In such an understanding, the goal to be sought is an expansion of protection and rights which "core" workers are enjoying to "non-core" and "periphery" workers and a reduction in the difference in levels of protection between the zones, rather than a deregulation of labor market and a further erosion of the "core" zone. This is basically in line with the position of organized labor.

In sum, organized business asserts that the current labor market regulation hinders job creation, while organized labor argues for more protection of workers. As stated above, the difference between the two is almost ideological and agreement is never reached. This chapter does not intend to integrate or find a compromise between these different positions; our interest is in how non-standard employment has increased, and how and to what extent labor and social security reform for workers in non-standard employment has progressed against the backdrop of the contradictory positions of organized business and labor.

3.2 Non-standard employment in labor and social security legislation

This section outlines the current South African labor and social security legislation and how workers in non-standard employment are dealt with within the legislation, as preparation for the next section, which examines post-apartheid labor and social security reform with a focus on workers in non-standard employment. Generally speaking, although there are some exceptions, workers in non-standard employment and standard employment are treated equally. However, the effectiveness of regulations differs, and the actual level of rights and protection which workers in non-standard employment enjoy is significantly inferior to that for workers in standard employment.

3.2.1 Non-standard employment and labor legislation

The two principal South African labor laws are the Labour Relations Act (LRA) and the Basic Conditions of Employment Act (BCEA). LRA is concerned with labor relations in general, including the rights of trade unions, collective bargaining, strikes and lockouts, unfair labor practices, and procedures for labor disputes, and regulates the collective bargaining institutions called bargaining councils (BC), in which registered trade unions and employers' organizations negotiate for basic working conditions for a specific industry. If the trade unions and employers' organizations which are members of a BC are sufficiently representative of the sector, collective agreements at the BC bind non-parties within the same sector. The history of LRA dates back to 1924 when the centralized collective bargaining system through industrial councils (IC) was introduced by the Industrial Conciliation Act. Despite the change in name, the functions of IC and BC are basically the same.

There is no unified minimum wage in South Africa, sectoral minimum wages being set by BC agreements. BCEA establishes unified minimum standards as to working time, payment for overtime work, paid leave and so on, yet most of the standards can be varied downwards if there are BC agreements. For sectors not covered by BCs, the Minister of Labour can determine the basic conditions of employment such as minimum wage, working time, paid leave, and conditions of termination of employment. So far such sectoral determinations have been made, for instance, for domestic workers, farm workers, and contract cleaning.

BCEA and LRA are in principle applied equally to workers in standard employment and non-standard employment, except that certain regulations of BCEA, such as those on working time, are not applied to employees who work for an employer for less than 24 hours a month. BC agreements and sectoral determinations by the Labour Minister are also applied equally. However, as we will see in more detail in the next section, there are problems of effectiveness of labor regulations, especially for those in non-standard employment.

3.2.2 Non-standard employment and social security

The social security system in South Africa is characterized by its dual character; on the one hand, private retirement provisions (pension funds and provident funds) and medical schemes are well developed; on the other, there is a large-scale public cash transfer system through means-tested social grants for the elderly, disabled people, and for children. The South African medical system is also dualistic and divided sharply into public and private sectors. The medical standards of private hospitals are quite high though treatment is costly; free treatment is available for poor people at public health facilities, yet these are generally understaffed and waiting times tend to be quite long.

As for compulsory statutory insurance, there are Unemployment Insurance and Compensation for Occupational Injuries and Diseases. All employees have to be registered for the Unemployment Insurance Fund (UIF), with the exception of those who work for an employer for less than 24 hours a month, learners (apprentices), public servants, foreigners working on contract, workers receiving a state old age pension, and workers who earn only commission. If workers are injured, disabled, killed, or become ill, they receive compensation from the Compensation Fund, except for workers who are totally or partially disabled for less than three days, domestic workers, anyone receiving military training, members of the South African National Defence Force or South African Police Service, any worker guilty of wilful misconduct, unless they are seriously disabled or killed, anyone employed outside South Africa for 12 or more continuous months, and workers working mainly outside South Africa and only temporarily employed in the country. While both employers and employees contribute to the UIF, contributions to the Compensation Fund are made only by employers. Although not compulsory, provisions for private pensions and medical schemes for employees are in general included in BC agreements.

There are about nine million members of retirement funds, and the coverage rate for formal sector employees is estimated to be in the region of 60 percent (National Treasury 2007). Participation levels for medical schemes are lower because some employees (especially if their wage is not high) choose not to be enrolled in medical schemes due to the high cost and the perceived low benefit.[4] There are significant differences in the coverage of retirement provisions and medical schemes for workers in standard and non-standard employment in the formal sector. It is reported that temporary workers are often not registered for the UIF and the Compensation Fund, in spite of it being compulsory for employers to do so (Department of Labour 2006: 6.11). Furthermore, there is no social security associated with employment for independent contractors and workers in the informal sector. Therefore, most workers in non-standard employment end up being dependent on the public social security system.

3.3 Labor and social security reform and non-standard employment

3.3.1 Strengthening of workers' rights and protection through labor law reform

After democratization, the South African government pursued a policy of economic liberalization, as symbolized by the introduction in 1996 of the new macroeconomic strategy, GEAR. As a point of departure, GEAR noted the necessity for greater labor market flexibility for transformation toward a competitive economy that could yield economic growth of 6 percent per annum. At the same time, however, it was noted that the extension of basic rights to a broader pool of the workforce should be done in parallel with flexibilization of the labor market to facilitate employment creation (Department of Finance 1996: 1.3, 2.3). The core task of labor market reform has been to strike a delicate balance between flexibilization and workers' protection, which can be summed up in the phrase "regulated flexibility" (Department of Labour 1996). Since the starting point for the labor market reform was apartheid legislation, strengthening workers' rights and protection, rather than flexibilization, has progressed more in the process of reform as a whole.

In the apartheid era, African workers were excluded from the definition of "employee" and prohibited from forming trade unions and participating in collective bargaining. This was changed by amendments to labor legislation after the Wiehahn Commission report at the end of the 1970s, which recommended that Africans should be allowed to register trade unions, leading to an intensification of labor movement activity in the 1980s. However, politicized trade unions which had strong links with anti-apartheid movements were harshly oppressed, and many trade union leaders were arrested and detained. The right to strike without fear of being dismissed was only established by the introduction of the new LRA in 1995 (Bendix 2004: 83).

The LRA was among the important items of legislation which were enacted soon after democratization, and one of the first items that NEDLAC dealt with (NEDLAC 2005: 34). There were many points of issue which labor and business disputed, yet as a whole, the Act reflected more of the demands of labor than those of business (Baskin and Satgar 1996; COSATU Parliamentary Office 2000: 21–7). In the background of such speedy enactment of LRA was the fact that the representatives of government, labor, and business had agreed as early as 1990 to the principle that a new LRA would be drafted upon extensive consultation and with the consensus of labor and business.[5] Policy making based upon consensus seeking among stakeholders was not practiced before the democratic transition; under the apartheid regime, black people were excluded from political power, and, even among whites, there was an increasing centralization of power to the executive branch of the government and marginalization of the parliament during the political crisis of the 1980s. The apartheid government did listen to the opinions of white interest groups, yet decision making in the late-apartheid period was characterized by secrecy and authoritarianism, and consensus among stakeholders was not sought even for important policy changes (Houston et al. 2001).

COSATU, which was formed in the mid-1980s with mostly black members, moved for the formation of a corporatist forum once the negotiation for transition started in 1990, so that the government at the time would not change important socioeconomic policies unilaterally before the transition took place (Habib 1997; Webster and Adler 1999; Maree 1993). It was the labor movement that took the initiative, yet organized business also found some merit in the proposals for the sake of stabilization of labor relations against the backdrop of potential racial tensions at workplaces where employers were mostly white and employees were mostly black (Friedman and Shaw 2000). Against such a background, the National Economic Forum and the restructured National Manpower Commission were formed during the negotiation process, based on which NEDLAC was formed after the transition took place.

In the process of the establishment of the new LRA, there were some minor amendments during the parliamentary committee, yet the amendments were not substantial and the NEDLAC agreements were respected. As stated above, it is obligatory for NEDLAC to consider and seek to reach consensuses about all proposed labor legislation before it is introduced into the Parliament. Agreements reached at NEDLAC do not have legal binding force, yet there is an unwritten rule that Parliament respects the agreements and does not make significant amendments. This is a salient feature of labor policy making in South Africa, and all the new labor legislation and amendments after democratization have basically followed the same process; i.e., firstly, the government prepares draft bills, and, secondly, the representatives of organized business and labor discuss and reach consensus and compromise in the Labour Market Chamber of NEDLAC or at other forums,[6] and lastly the bill is introduced in the Parliament, which passes the bill into law without major amendments.

More developments followed the new LRA for strengthening workers' rights and protection. The new constitution, which was enacted in 1996, established workers' rights to form and join trade unions, to strike, and to engage in collective bargaining, which are rights that everyone should enjoy without exception as they are part of the Bill of Rights. The new BCEA in 1997 set the minimum working conditions for all kinds of workers, including domestic workers and farm workers, who were excluded from the previous BCEA. With the exception that certain provisions are not applied to employees who work for an employer for less than 24 hours a month, BCEA is applied equally to workers in both standard and non-standard employment, and rights and protection for part-time workers were extended compared to the previous BCEA. In 1998, two further important items of labor legislation, the Employment Equity Act, which includes provisions about affirmative action for blacks, women and disabled people, and the Skills Development Act, which aim to improve the skill levels of workers, were enacted. Through these reforms and the introduction of new legislation, South African labor regulations as a whole have shifted toward the extension of protection for workers who had been previously excluded.

3.3.2 Expansion of the social safety net

The Bill of Rights of the new constitution established that everyone has the right to access to "social security, including, if they are unable to support themselves and their dependants, appropriate social assistance" (Section 27(1)). In a pattern similar to that adopted in the sphere of labor legislation, reform of the social security system has also progressed toward the extension of protection for people who were excluded from the social safety net under the apartheid regime.

Firstly, in 1998 there was a reform of social grants for children. Social grants for children at that time were discriminatory and African households were virtually excluded from access to them. The newly introduced Child Support Grant was equally accessible for households of all races, and the number of recipients increased rapidly. By 2006, the total number of recipients of social grants – including the Old Age Grant, Disability Grant and Child Support Grant – stood at more than 10 million (Manuel 2006).

Another important reform concerned Unemployment Insurance. Under the terms of the new Unemployment Insurance Act, enacted in 2001, employers are now obliged to register domestic workers and seasonal workers for the UIF. Seasonal workers are by definition in non-standard employment, and although not all domestic workers are in non-standard employment, Von Holdt and Webster (2005) regarded them as "non-core" workers due to their extreme employment vulnerability. Therefore the Unemployment Insurance reform meant an extension of social security for workers in unstable and vulnerable employment. However, this does not serve as income security for the long-term unemployed and those who have been never registered for the UIF, because unemployment benefits cover only those who have contributed to the UIF, and are paid only for a limited period. As an additional means to address the issue of income security for the unemployed, in 2004 the government introduced a new public works program with a target of reaching one million people in five years. Access to the public works program is not a "right" of unemployed people, however, but the scale and locations of programs are determined according to budget constraints.

As Unemployment Insurance is under the jurisdiction of the Department of Labour, the contents of its reform were shaped through the NEDLAC process of consensus making. Meanwhile, social grants are under the jurisdiction of the Department of Social Development. Civil society organizations, including trade unions, churches, NGOs, and social movements, did engage in policy discussion about social grant reforms, yet it was mainly through lobbying the government and ANC as well as utilization of the mass media that they were carried through, and the role of NEDLAC was limited. The decision making in respect of social grant reforms has been made mainly by the government, and the opinions of labor, business, other civil society organizations and experts are only used as reference and do not bind government's decisions (Makino 2005). This is in contrast with the labor law reforms, where consensus of business and labor is required for any kind of change.

3.3.3 Limits of reforms, focusing on workers in non-standard employment

We have seen in previous sections that the labor and social security reforms after democratization were basically in the direction of strengthening and extending the protection and rights of workers in general. However, to have rights on paper and to enjoy the rights in reality are two different things. This is especially so for workers in non-standard employment.

Firstly, labor legislation is only applied to those who are "employed," and not to independent contractors who provide labor and services on contract. In fact, it is not always easy to distinguish between employment and service contracts, and firms often prefer, even for the same kind of work, to have service contracts with workers rather than employ them, so that labor legislation would not apply. As a response to this problem, LRA and BCEA were amended in 2002 so that any person who works for another person is presumed to be an employee, regardless of the form of contract, as long as the person is subject to the control or direction of the other person in terms of the manner in which the person works or hours of work, or the person is economically dependent on the other person for whom he or she works.

LRA establishes that it is regarded as dismissal if an employee reasonably expected the employer to renew a fixed-term contract of employment on the same or similar terms, but the employer offered to renew it on less favorable terms, or did not renew it (Section 186(1)(b)). However, it is not difficult for an employer to induce an employee to accept a contract which would not allow the employee to reasonably expect the employer to renew the contract on the same or similar terms. Temporary workers are vulnerable because of the complexity of employment relations and the difficulties involved in monitoring compliance. Theron et al. (2005: 29–31) points out that some labor brokers use contract forms with contents such as not allowing employees to have paid leave, or prohibit strikes. In addition, workers without written contracts and those who work informally and are not registered for Unemployment Insurance are more vulnerable and substantially outside of labor legislation regulations.

Secondly, in respect of social security reform, most workers in standard employment do have retirement provisions and also, to a lesser extent, medical schemes, as we have seen above. Income security for the non-labor force population and the unemployed also improved through social grant reforms and the extension of public works programs. However, there has been little progress in terms of social security for those who work in non-standard employment. In early 2007, the government proposed a social security reform plan that included a compulsory retirement provision and a wage subsidy for low-wage earners (Mbeki 2007; Manuel 2007). There will be consultation with various stakeholders including organized business and labor before any decisions are made, and it is unclear to what extent this proposed plan would cover workers in non-standard employment. The government initially aimed to introduce the new system by 2010, but a detailed set of proposals is yet to be finalized, and it is unlikely the new system will be introduced by that deadline (Joffe 2008). Compulsory social health insurance or national health insurance has been also on the agenda for years (Department of Health 2002; Taylor Committee 2002: ch. 8), yet it is still at the discussion stage and prospects remain uncertain.

Lund (2002) points out that the social security system in South Africa does not fit the needs of increasing numbers of workers in non-standard employment and the informal sector, as it was developed on the premise that most workers are in standard employment and that unemployment is usually only temporary. This is a historical problem, according to Lund, because the social security system in South Africa "was designed initially to protect the white population, especially the white working class" (p. 181). White workers were protected from competition with black workers and their risk of long-term unemployment or inability to find other than unstable non-standard or informal jobs was minimized by discriminatory policies in the fields of education and labor market regulations. Social grant reforms after democratization brought about a rapid increase in recipients of grants, which has played a big role in poverty alleviation (Van der Berg et al. 2006). However, those who are entitled to social grants are limited to non-labor force people (the elderly, disabled, or children), and social grant reform did not address changes in the risk structure, such as the increase in long-term unemployment and non-standard employment. Public works programs do function, to a certain extent, as income security for the unemployed, yet the employment provided through the programs is only temporary and is not accompanied by social security such as the Unemployment Insurance.

As seen above, Bezuidenhout et al. (2004) understands the increase in non-standard employment as a combination of casualization, externalization and informalization; in fact, all three of these processes do reduce the effectiveness of labor regulations. Taken as a whole, the labor law reform strengthened workers' rights and protection, yet at the same time an increase in non-standard employment has taken place, which means an increase in workers who do not substantially enjoy rights and protections under the new labor legislation and are excluded from social safety nets. In fact, it is the lack of regulations concerning non-standard employment itself that has enabled the increase in such unstable non-standard employment. Historically, the apartheid regime, which put African workers outside the protection offered by labor legislation and used them as a cheap, easily replaceable labor force, did not regulate the utilization of non-standard employment. After democratization, the protection of workers' rights was strengthened, and on paper this is equally applied to non-standard workers as well, yet the utilization of non-standard employment itself has been unregulated up to the present day. "Permanent temporary" workers are commonly observed, and there is no restriction on the type of business and period for which temporary workers can be used.

Returning to the dispute concerning whether the South African labor market should be considered to be either rigid or flexible, it can be said that it is rigid in terms of the wage level in the formal sector due to the system of centralized collective bargaining through BCs and sectoral determinations by the Labour Minister. However, in terms of the utilization of non-standard employment, the South African labor market has been quite flexible from the apartheid era to the present. If not, South African employers would not have been increasingly able to use flexible forms of labor to adapt to rapid economic liberalization. This is in contrast to many other countries where the flexibilization of employment relations were driven by deregulation of the labor market; in South Africa, labor law reform has been in the direction of the tightening of regulations, which paradoxically might have worked as an incentive for employers to use more non-standard employment so that the total labor cost would be suppressed (Department of Labour 2006: 16; COSATU Parliamentary Office 2000).

Now that several major labor law reforms have been implemented, the protection of workers in non-standard employment is one of the remaining issues for the Department of Labour. The Labour Minister stated in July 2006 that "I am of the view that the labour law should cushion and mitigate the adverse nature of atypical forms of employment and lack of protection for these workers" and "any proposed changes in the law in the next decade should ideally extend protection to vulnerable workers while balancing it with the needs of small employers" (Mdladlana 2006). The Department of Labour commissioned research about non-standard employment to Theron and other academics at the University of Cape Town in 2000 (Theron and Godfrey 2000). In addition, after the NEDLAC Growth and Development Summit in 2003, four additional research projects have been commissioned and implemented. Based upon these research results, a report particularly about the issue of non-standard employment was drafted by the Department of Labour in late 2006 (Department of Labour 2006).

According to various interviews conducted in October and November 2006 by the author with officials of the Department of Labour, employers' organizations, and trade unions, negotiations were taking place at that time on two points: the formulation of a Code of Good Practice stipulating who should be regarded as an "employee," and the introduction of some form of regulation on labor brokering. The Code of Good Practice was agreed upon and published in December 2006,[7] yet the future of the regulation of labor brokering remains uncertain. Organized business is against further labor law amendments to include such regulation, and hold to the opinion that what is needed to protect temporary workers is the improved effectiveness of, not amendments to, the current labor laws.[8] In contrast, COSATU demands tightening of regulations concerning labor brokers by labor law amendments, as well as the further regulation of fixed-term contracts (COSATU 2006). Atypical forms of employment were adopted as a NEDLAC key focus area for 2007/8, but the discussion was not concluded by the end of the year. As any amendment to the labor laws requires a consensus between organized business and labor, it seems that amendments in that direction are unlikely to take place in the near future, and if any further regulation is introduced, it is likely to be some form of self-regulation.

3.4 Conclusion

This chapter has tried to understand, from the nature of labor and social security reforms after democratization, the current status of the South African labor market, which is changing in contradictory directions, i.e. a strengthening of the rights and protection of workers at the same time as the flexibilization of employment. Although recent labor law reforms on the whole have strengthened the rights and protection of workers, it is workers in standard employment who have benefited most, and the merit has not been shared equally with workers in non-standard employment. Regulation concerning non-standard employment itself has not progressed much, except for the establishment of the Code of Good Practice about who is regarded as an "employee," and there is no regulation concerning the utilization of temporary workers in terms of the type of business, contract period, repeated renewal of contracts, and so on. In addition, as the basic structure of the social security system in South Africa has not changed since the apartheid era, in which it was designed to address the needs of white workers who were mostly in standard employment, social security for the unemployed and workers in non-standard employment remains insufficient.

Why has there been so little progress in terms of strengthening the rights and protection of non-standard workers? One answer would be that addressing unemployment, rather than non-standard employment, has been prioritized against the backdrop of an extremely high unemployment rate; yet this chapter has focused on another aspect, i.e. the limits of corporatist policy making. As we have seen above, post-apartheid labor law reforms have been the consequences of consensus and compromise between organized business and labor. The issue of insufficient protection for workers in non-standard employment is a part of the agenda of organized labor, yet in reality it has been the working conditions for workers in standard employment, the main constituency of trade unions, that have been the primary focus of negotiations. Trade unions have not been indifferent about organizing workers in non-standard employment; for instance, COSATU adopted the recommendation of the September Commission in 1997 that it should try to organize workers in flexible forms of employment in order to maintain its organizational base. However, there has been little progress since then in terms of the unionization rate of workers in non-standard employment in COSATU-affiliated trade unions (Webster 2006: 26). Although the issue of the protection of workers in non-standard employment has attracted more attention recently, it seems that the present labor legislation, which is acceptable for business because it is easy for employers to utilize non-standard employment and also for labor because the interests of workers in standard employment are protected, is the current equilibrium point reached as a result of a series of compromises between organized business and labor.

Notes

1. This chapter is a translated and updated version of my article, "Minami-Afurika ni okeru Hi-seiki-koyo no Zoka to Rodo-ho Shakai-hosho Seido Kaikaku (in Japanese)," in Koichi Usami ed. *Shinko Kogyo-koku ni okeru Koyo to Shakai-hosho* [Transformation of Employment and Social Security in the Newly Industrializing Countries], Kenkyu sosho (IDE Research Series) No. 565. Chiba: IDE-JETRO, 2007, pp. 147–81.
2. Not all consensuses were made through formal NEDLAC processes, some being reached through bilateral negotiations between organized business and labor, as well as other various informal consultations.
3. Speech of Labour Minister Tito Mboweni at the second reading debate of the National Economic Development and Labour Council Bill at the National Assembly, November 14, 1994.

4. Interview with Mr Thulani Lucas Mthiyane (National Engineering Sector Coordinator, National Union of Metalworkers of South Africa: NUMSA) on October 30, 2006.
5. Minute of a Meeting between Representatives of the Working Party and the Minister of Manpower Held at the Office of the Minister in Pretoria on September 13–14, 1990 (Laboria Minute), accessed at the COSATU Archive (Johannesburg) in October 2006.
6. There were some cases where negotiations outside of NEDLAC were important. For instance, amendments to LRA and BCEA in 2002 were based on bilateral negotiation between business and labor at the Millennium Labour Council, and not the tripartite negotiation at NEDLAC.
7. "Code of Good Practice: Who Is an Employee," General Notice 1774 of 2006, Government Gazette No. 29445, December 1, 2006. Retrieved February 17, 2007 from http://www.info.gov.za/gazette/notices/2006/29445.pdf.
8. Interview with Ms Corinna Gardner (Chief Officer Social Policy, Business Unity South Africa) on October 23, 2006; interview with Mr. John Botha (Confederation of Associations of Private Employment Sector) on November 8, 2006.

References

Adler, Glenn and Eddie Webster (eds). 2000. *Trade Unions and Democratization in South Africa, 1985–1997*. Johannesburg: Witwatersrand University Press.

Barchiesi, Franco. 2008. "Wage Labor, Precarious Employment, and Social Inclusion in the Making of South Africa's Postapartheid Transition." *African Studies Review* 51, no. 2: 119–42.

Baskin, Jeremy. 1991. *Striking Back*. Johannesburg: Ravan Press.

Baskin, Jeremy and Vishwas Satgar. 1996. "Assessing the New LRA: A Framework for Regulated Flexibility." In *Against the Current: Labour and Economic Policy in South Africa*, ed. J. Baskin. Johannesburg: Ravan Press.

Bendix, Sonia. 2004. *Industrial Relations in South Africa*, 5th impression (revised). Cape Town: Juta.

Bezuidenhout, Andries, Shane Godfrey, Jan Theron and Mmamagang Modisha. 2004. "Non-Standard Employment and Its Policy Implications." Report submitted to the Department of Labour, June 30.

Bhorat, Haroon. 2004. "Labour Market Challenges in the Post-Apartheid South Africa." *South African Journal of Economics* 72, no. 5: 940–77.

Bhorat, Haroon, Murray Leibbrandt, Muzi Maziya, Servaas Van der Berg and Ingrid Woolard. 2001. *Fighting Poverty: Labour Markets and Inequality in South Africa*. Cape Town: UCT Press.

Bhorat, Haroon and Morne Oosthuizen. 2006. "Evolution of the Labour Market, 1995–2002." In *Poverty and Policy in Post-Apartheid South Africa*, ed. H. Bhorat and R. Kanbur. Cape Town: HSRC Press.

Buhlungu, Sakhela. 2006. "Introduction: COSATU and the First Ten Years of Democratic Transition in South Africa." In *Trade Unions and Democracy: COSATU Workers' Political Attitudes in South Africa*, ed. S. Buhlungu. Cape Town: HSRC Press.

Casale, Daniela, Colette Muller and Dorrit Posel. 2004. "'Two Million Net New Jobs': A Reconsideration of the Rise in Employment in South Africa, 1995–2003." *South African Journal of Economics* 72, no. 5: 978–1002.
COSATU (Congress of South African Trade Unions). 2006. "Declaration and Resolutions, COSATU Ninth National Congress, Gallagher Estate, Midrand, September 18–21, 2006." http://www.cosatu.org.za/cong2006/congress06/finresolu.htm (accessed February 17, 2007).
COSATU, NACTU and FEDSAL. 1996. *Social Equity and Job Creation: The Key to a Stable Future*, Johannesburg: Labour Caucus at NEDLAC, incorporating COSATU, NACTU and FEDSAL.
COSATU Parliamentary Office. 2000. *Accelerating Transformation: COSATU's Engagement with Policy and Legislative Processes during South Africa's First Term of Democratic Governance*. Cape Town: COSATU Parliamentary Office.
Department of Finance. 1996. "Growth, Employment and Redistribution: A Macroeconomic Strategy." Pretoria: Department of Finance. http://www.treasury.gov.za/documents/gear/all.pdf (accessed February 17, 2007).
Department of Health. 2002. "Policy Options for the Future Covering: Inquiry into the Various Social Security Aspects of the South African Health System - Based on the Health Subcommittee Findings of the Committee of Inquiry into a Comprehensive System of Social Security." Pretoria: Committee of Enquiry – Health Chapter, Department of Health. http://www.doh.gov.za/docs/reports/2002/inquiry/ (accessed February 17, 2007).
Department of Labour. 1996. "Minimum Standard Directorate Policy Proposals for a New Employment Standards Statute Green Paper, 13 February 1996." Pretoria: Department of Labour. http://www.info.gov.za/greenpapers/1996/labour.htm (accessed February 17, 2007).
Department of Labour. 2006. "Changing Nature of Work and 'Atypical' Forms of Employment in South Africa: Synthesis Report." Unpublished document.
Friedman, Steven and Mark Shaw. 2000. "Power in Partnership? Trade Unions, Forums and the Transition." In *Trade Unions and Democratization in South Africa, 1985–1997*, ed. G. Adler and E. Webster. Johannesburg: Witwatersrand University Press.
Habib, Adam. 1997. "From Pluralism to Corporatism: South Africa's Labour Relations in Transition." *Politikon* 24, no. 1: 57–75.
Hirano, Katsumi. 1999. "Minami-Afurika ni okeru Tairyo Shitsugyo Mondai no Sangyo Kozo-ron-teki Bunseki" (in Japanese) [An Analysis on Mass Unemployment in South Africa: Perspective of the Industrial Structure Theory]. In *Shinsei Kokka Minami-Afurika no Shogeki* [Impacts of New South Africa], ed. Katsumi Hirano. IDE Research Series no. 495, Tokyo: IDE-JETRO.
Hirsch, Alan. 2005. *Season of Hope: Economic Reform under Mandela and Mbeki*. Pietermaritzburg: University of KwaZulu-Natal Press.
Houston, Gregory, Ian Liebenberg and William Dichaba. 2001. "Interest Group Participation in the National Economic Development and Labour Council." In *Public Participation in Democratic Governance in South Africa*. ed. Gregory Houston. Pretoria: HSRC.
Joffe, Hilary. 2008. "South Africa: Social Security Plan Faces Delay." *Business Day*, 15 September 2008. http://allafrica.com/stories/200809150510.html (accessed February 9, 2009).

Kenny, Bridget and Edward Webster. 1999. "Eroding the Core: Flexibility and the Re-segmentation of the South African Labour Market." *Critical Sociology* 24, no. 3: 216–43.

Kingdon, Geeta Ghandi and John Knight. 2004. "Unemployment in South Africa: The Nature of the Beast." *World Development* 32, no. 3: 391–408.

Lehmbruch, Gerhard. 1979 [1984]. "Riberaru Koporatizumu to Seito Seiji (in Japanese)" [Liberal Corporatism and Party Government]. In *Gendai Koporatizumu (I) Dantai Togo Shugi no Seiji to sono Riron* [Trends toward Corporatist Intermediation], ed. Philippe C. Schmitter and Gerhard Lehmbruch (translated by Yasushi Yamaguchi et al.). Tokyo: Mokutakusha.

Lund, Francie. 2002. "Social Security and the Changing Labour Market: Access for Non-Standard and Informal Workers in South Africa." *Social Dynamics* 28, no. 2: 177–206.

Makino, Kumiko. 2005. "Minshuka-go no Minami-Afurika ni okeru Shotoku Hosho Seido Kaikaku: Shakai Teate to Kokyo Jigyo Puroguramu" (in Japanese) [Income Security Policy Reform in Post-Apartheid South Africa: Social Grants and the Public Works Programme]. In *Shinko Kogyo-koku no Shakai Fukushi* [Social Protection Systems in Newly Industrializing Countries in the 21st Century], ed. Koichi Usami. IDE Research Series no. 548, Chiba: IDE-JETRO.

Manuel, Trevor A. 2006. "Budget Speech 2006 by Minister of Finance Trevor A Manuel." http://www.info.gov.za/speeches/2006/06021515501001.htm (accessed February 17, 2007).

Manuel, Trevor A. 2007. "Budget Speech 2007 by Minister of Finance Trevor A Manuel, MP." http://www.info.gov.za/speeches/2007/07022115261001.htm (accessed May 6, 2007).

Mbeki, Thabo. 2007. "State of the Nation Address of the President of South Africa, Thabo Mbeki: Joint Sitting of Parliament." http://www.info.gov.za/speeches/2007/07020911001001.htm (accessed May 6, 2007).

Maree, Johann. 1993. "Trade Unions and Corporatism in South Africa." *Transformation*, no. 21: 24–54.

Mdladlana, Membathisi. 2006. "Labour Law in the Next Decade: Time for a Change? – Speech by the Minister of Labour, M. Mdladlana, at the 19th Annual Labour Law Conference, Sandton Convention Centre, 6 July 2006." http://www.info.gov.za/speeches/2006/06070716451003.htm (accessed February 17, 2007).

Moll, Peter. 1996. "Compulsory Centralization of Collective Bargaining in South Africa." *American Economic Review* 86, no. 2: 326–9.

National Treasury. 2004. "Retirement Fund Reform: A Discussion Paper." December 2004. http://www.treasury.gov.za/documents/retirement/Retirement%20Fund%20Reform%20A%20Discussion%20Paper.pdf (accessed February 17, 2007).

National Treasury. 2007. "Social Security and Retirement Reform: Second Discussion Paper." February 2007. http://www.finance.gov.za/documents/national%20budget/2007/Social%20security%20and%20retirement%20reform%20paper.pdf (accessed February 9, 2009).

NEDLAC (National Economic Development and Labour Council). 2003. *Growth and Development Summit Agreement (GDS)*. Johannesburg: NEDLAC.

NEDLAC (National Economic Development and Labour Council). 2005. *10 Years of Social Dialogue: The Nedlac Experience*. Johannesburg: NEDLAC.

NEDLAC (National Economic Development and Labour Council). 2008. *Annual Report 2007/8*, Johannesburg: NEDLAC. http://www.nedlac.org.za/top.asp?inc=docs/reports/annual/2008/main.html (accessed February 2, 2009).

Rodrik, Dani. 2006. "Understanding South Africa's Economic Puzzles." NBER Working Paper no. 12565, Cambridge, MA: National Bureau of Economic Research. http://www.nber.org/papers/w12565.pdf (accessed December 1, 2006).

Schmitter, Philippe. 1979 [1984]. "Ima mo nao Koporatizumu no Seiki nanoka?" (in Japanese) [Still the Century of Corporatism?]. In *Gendai Koporatizumu (I) Dantai Togo Shugi no Seiji to sono Riron* [Trends toward Corporatist Intermediation], ed. Philippe C. Schmitter and Gerhard Lehmbruch (translated by Yasushi Yamaguchi et al.). Tokyo: Mokutakusha.

Seekings, Jeremy, and Nicoli Nattrass. 2005. *Race, Class and Inequality in South Africa*. New Haven, CT: Yale University Press.

South African Foundation. 1996. *Growth for All: An Economic Strategy for South Africa*. Johannesburg: South African Foundation.

Standing, Guy, John Sender and John Weeks. 1996. *Restructuring the Labour Market: The South African Challenge – An ILO Country Review*. Geneva: ILO.

Statistics South Africa. 2008. *Quarterly Labour Force Survey*, Quarter 3, 2008, Statistical Release P0211, Pretoria: Statistics South Africa.

Taylor Committee (Committee of Inquiry into a Comprehensive System of Social Security for South Africa). 2002. *Transforming the Present, Protecting the Future: Consolidated Report*, Pretoria: Department of Social Development.

Theron, Jan and Shane Godfrey. 2000. *Protecting Workers on the Periphery*. Cape Town: Institute of Development and Labour Law, University of Cape Town.

Theron, Jan, Shane Godfrey and Peter Lewis. 2005. *The Rise of Labour Broking and Its Policy Implications*, Monograph 1/2005. Cape Town: Institute of Development and Labour Law, University of Cape Town.

Valodia, Imraan. 2001. "Economic Policy and Women's Informal Work in South Africa." *Development and Change* 32, no. 5: 871–92.

Van der Berg, Servaas, Ronelle Burger, Rulof Burger, Megan Louw and Derek Yu. 2006. "Trends in Poverty and Inequality since the Political Transition." Working Paper no. 06/104. Cape Town: Development Policy Research Unit, University of Cape Town. http://www.commerce.uct.ac.za/Research_Units/DPRU/WorkingPapers/PDF_Files/WP06-104.pdf (accessed February 17, 2007).

Von Holdt, Karl. 1993. "The Danger of Corporatism." *SA Labour Bulletin* 17, no. 1: 46–51.

Von Holdt, Karl and Eddie Webster. 2005. "Wage Restructuring and the Crisis of Social Reproduction: A Southern Perspective." In *Beyond the Apartheid Workplace: Studies in Transition*, ed. E. Webster and K. Von Hold. Pietermaritzburg: University of KwaZulu-Natal Press.

Webster, Eddie. 2006. "Trade Unions and the Informalisation of Work." In *Trade Unions and Democracy: COSATU Workers Political Attitudes in South Africa*, ed. S. Buhlungu. Cape Town: HSRC Press, pp. 21–43.

Webster, Eddie and Karl Von Holdt (eds). 2005. *Beyond the Apartheid Workplace: Studies in Transition*. Pietermaritzburg: University of KwaZulu-Natal Press.

Webster, Edward and Glenn Adler. 1999. "Towards a Class Compromise in South Africa's 'Double Transition': Bargained Liberalization and the Consolidation of Democracy." *Politics & Society* 27, no. 3: 347–85.

4
The Impact of the Transformation of Labor Relations on Social Security System Reform in the People's Republic of China: The Growing Allure and Reality of Corporatism

Yukari Sawada

Introduction

The Chinese government is now groping for a new and effective system for attaining stability in its labor relations. What drives the government toward revision is the growing number of labor disputes and riots in recent years. Table 4.1, compiled from the government's official statistics, gives some details of labor disputes. The statistics show that the number of labor disputes was only a little more than 33,000 cases in 1995, but has increased almost tenfold within ten years – to 314,000 cases in 2005. During the same period, the number of workers participating in disputes also went up, from 123,000 to 740,000.

In response to the challenge, the government, under the leadership of General Secretary Hu Jintao and Premier Wen Jiabao, hammered out a new policy named *hexie shehui* (harmonious society) and started to put a greater emphasis than governments had done hitherto on the protection of workers' rights. In 2004, the minimum wage system was re-examined for the first time in ten years with the intention of guaranteeing workers a decent level of pay. In the same year, the Trade Union Law was revised, adding a new agenda for the protection of workers' rights. In 2005, the Standing Committee of the National People's Congress passed the new Labor Contract Law which tightens restrictions on employers seeking to terminate their employees' labor contracts.

Along with these changes in labor policy, the government started to lean toward the idea of applying corporatism to Chinese market-oriented

Table 4.1 Number of labor disputes accepted by arbitration committee (cases and workers involved), 1995–2005

	1995	1998	1999	2000	2001	2002	2003	2004	2005
Number of cases ('000)	33.0	94.0	120.0	135.0	155.0	184.0	226.0	260.0	314.0
year-on-year increase (%)	73.0	30.9	28.3	12.5	14.4	19.1	22.8	15.2	20.5
Workers involved ('000 persons)	122.5	359.0	474.0	423.0	467.0	610.0	800.0	760.0	740.0
year-on-year increase (%)	57.5	62.1	32.2	−10.8	10.5	30.2	31.1	−0.1	0.0
Number of collective disputes ('000 cases)	2.6	6.8	9.0	8.2	9.8	11.0	11.0	19.0	19.0
year-on-year increase (%)	NA	64.7	33.6	−8.8	19.4	12.0	0.0	72.7	0.0
Workers involved ('000 persons)	77.3	251.0	319.0	259.0	287.0	NA	NA	NA	410.0
year-on-year increase (%)	NA	89.4	27.0	−18.7	10.5	NA	NA	NA	NA

Source: MOLSS, *Annual Statistics Report on Development of Labour and Social Security Project*, 1995–2005 version. http://www.molss.gov.cn/gb/zwxx/node_5436.htm.

socialism as a means of stabilizing the new system of labor relations. On September 25, 2006, the 10th Tripartite Labor Relation Consultation, which consisted of representatives from the central government, employers, and employees, was held in Beijing. The consultation confirmed at the national level the decision to amend the upcoming draft of the Labor Contract Law and encouraged employers and workers to sign labor contracts. Moreover, the 2005 edition of the *Statistical Communiqué on Labor and Social Security Undertakings,* an official announcement released by the Ministry of Labor and Social Security, reported for the first time the progress of "tripartite consultation" as one of the major activities under way in terms of labor relations. This indicates the high expectation that the Chinese government held for this new labor coordinating procedure.

Despite governmental attempts to achieve stabilization, rapid economic growth in China is now undermining the basic assumptions underlying existing labor relations, namely, the presence of an abundant and inexpensive workforce. Following an influx of direct investment from overseas that has continued steadily for more than two decades, labor shortages among blue-collar workers became apparent in the Eastern coastal region where the labor-intensive export-processing industries had become concentrated. Yet contrary to what one might expect, the overall unemployment rate in China has been rising even during this period of unprecedentedly high rates of growth. Even college graduates have found it difficult to secure jobs, a trend that has become so widespread that it is now widely acknowledged as a social problem. The mismatch of supply and demand in the labor market created new risks for both employers and employees. Not only did it stimulate reforms in labor-related institutions, but it also affected the design of the social security system, since workers' choices are strongly influenced by the availability of social insurance schemes and social welfare services, especially when they are threatened with job dismissal or when they experience unfair labor practices. Social welfare reform is especially important for achieving stability among migrant workers and laid-off workers, since both groups lack representation in the official trade unions.

This chapter will analyze how far the new concept of the tripartite consultation mechanism, based upon corporatism, has to date met the Chinese government's hopes of securing cooperative relations between labor and management. I will also explore the extent to which the above consultation mechanism has compensated for the absence of a social safety net, which the social security system has so far failed to provide.

To better permit answers to these questions, the chapter has been divided into five sections. Section 4.1 evaluates the existing research, and section 4.2 identifies the factors that have led to labor disputes by outlining the current employment situation. Section 4.3 traces the labor reform's direction by examining the recent development of employment-related laws. Section 4.4 discusses the roles of two of the participants in the tripartite labor relation consultation – namely, trade unions and the employers' associations – and describes how each plays its role in the framework of corporatism. Section 4.5 evaluates the stabilizing effect of tripartite consultation by examining two groups that lie outside the scheme, namely the migrant workers who are registered as rural residents, and unemployed workers who have been laid off but who have urban registration. By looking into their survival strategies, this chapter explores the loopholes in the tripartite labor relations consultation scheme and draws attention to the defects of the present social security system.

4.1 Existing studies

The first studies to apply the concept of corporatism to the analysis of economic reform in the People's Republic of China were written by Chinese-speaking scholars based in western countries. In her 1992 work, Jean Oi used the term "Local State Corporatism" to describe the process by which local government authorities and managers of village-township enterprises collaborate during policy making. Gordon White's 1996 book observed civil society, whereas Anita Chan and Jonathan Unger (1995) considered the state and social organizations, and pointed out that the reform of political organization in China carried a strong possibility of transforming itself into "state corporatism". Under the influence of these earlier researches, the issue of corporatism drew scholars' attention as a component of political reform in China. The contributions of Zhang, Jing (1998) and Kang Xiaoguang (1999) are typical examples.

However, few academic works to date have employed the concept of corporatism to analyze labor relations reform and its impact on the welfare state. Zheng Bingwen was one of the earliest scholars to discuss corporatism in the People's Republic of China in the context of a labor relations system and a welfare state. Zheng's 2002 study reflected the social issue that stemmed from state-owned enterprise reform at that time. In the latter half of the 1990s, one of the major concerns in respect of enterprise reform was how to maintain stability among workers and their families while liberating the state-owned enterprises from their burden of social security contributions. To help facilitate this task, local governments and employees were also required to contribute to social security funds.[1] Zheng claimed that China can avoid problems that have beset many of today's welfare states by applying corporatism's tripartite cooperation mechanism (Zheng 2002: 77). Zheng perceived this way forward as a latecomer's advantage for China.

On the other hand, Yang Peng-fei argued that labor relations during the planned-economy era were themselves a variation of *state corporatism*, and pointed out that the rigid control of labor at that time had inflated personnel costs, causing a serious deficit in the central government budget. Furthermore, Yang criticized current labor relations for inclining too much toward neoliberalism. According to Yang, this new trend was generated by the very large numbers of Chinese students who had studied economic theories abroad, and especially by those who had returned from economics courses in the United States and the United Kingdom. The fact that the USA and the UK became China's major partners in international trade also lent strength to assertions that what China needed was a more flexible labor market. Labor reforms based upon this premise ruthlessly threw individual workers into the labor market without explicit institutional protection, forcing them to accept unfavorable treatment when they negotiated essential working conditions, such as wages and workplace safety, with employers. As a result, the era of reform enabled the employers to set their own terms in such matters (Yang 2006: 34).

Yang's prescription for redressing this power imbalance between employers and employees was to induce both parties to negotiate under "neocorporatism" (or social corporatism). Yang illustrated how in 2000 the Garden Hotel management collaborated successfully with its employees when Shanghai Municipality's new policy demanded that foreign joint-ventures must abolish employees' housing pensions.[2] Yang also noted that this hotel had formed a collective bargaining system regarding employees' pay rises since 1993. Based on his observation, Yang insisted that neocorporatism, in contrast to the preceding state corporatism, could effectively secure stability among employers and employees even in non-state-owned firms (Yang 2006: 37).[3] Chang Kai's survey of labor disputes in the Shenzhen Special Economic Zone confirmed Yang's analysis. According to Chang Kai, more than 90 percent of labor disruptions in the Special Economic Zone occurred in firms that lacked official labor unions. These unions are called *"gonghui"* in Chinese and had the exclusive right to represent workers. Chang's report made the authorities hopeful that neocorporatism, which assured the participation of labor in negotiations, would function as a stabilizer for labor relations in the era of reform (Ishii 2001: 24).

In contrast to the conclusions of Chinese scholars, Japanese researchers tend to hold negative attitudes toward both the feasibility and the efficacy of neocorporatism in China. In his 2006 paper, Ishii traced the history of the Chinese Communist Party (CCP) and pointed out that, in essence, corporatism in China is treated as the "institutional extension of the old United Front, such as the Political Consultative Conference, which was organized and directed by the CCP". According to him, trade unions fall into this category. Ishii believed that the true germination of social corporatism appeared in the period between the "separate government from the Communist Party" (*dangzheng fenkai*) in 1987 and the June Fourth Incident (also known as the "Tiananmen Square Massacre") in 1989. Evidence for this contention can be seen in the "fundamental plan" of the chairmen's conference of the All China Federation of Trade Unions in July 1988, and in the birth of the first independent trade union in China, the Beijing Workers' Independent Federation of Trade Unions which was established in June 1989 just before the Tiananmen Square Massacre. However, after the crackdown on the 1989 democracy movement by the People's Liberation Army, the All China Federation of Trade Unions (hereafter referred as ACFTU) adopted a highly restrictive attitude, referring to the independent labor union as "one who attempts an overthrow of the people's government". Thereafter, trade unions retreated to their earlier stance of forming a "United Front" under the supervision of the CCP. Ishii calls this adjustment a "withdrawal to state-corporatism." In Ishii's view, the numerous industrial associations and interest groups that emerged in the 1990s should be categorized as "organizations set up in a top-down style" meaning they were established on the *de facto* initiative of the CCP and that they maintain a low level of autonomy.

Kojima's 2006 research questioned the legitimacy of the ACFTU as an institution that is representative of the workers by analyzing its personnel affairs and finance. Kojima found that there were two contrasting trends inside the ACFTU in respect of the trade unions' *raison d'être*. One trend was motivated by the status quo, and insisted on maintaining current arrangements that kept the ACFTU close to the CCP and the government. The other trend was to give greater emphasis to the protection of workers' interests and rights by advocating the need for the ACFTU to achieve increased autonomy from the CCP. Kojima's paper illustrated how ACFTU leaders swayed between these two trends, and were unable to stick consistently to either of them. If we follow Kojima's logic, the ACFTU not qualified to be truly representative of the workers, and thus current efforts to promote industrial harmony through tripartite discussion, where only the ACFTU is allowed to represent labor, are invalid. This seems to suggest that the tripartite commissions are more or less ersatz wisdom that the Chinese authorities have acquired from the ILO. Uehara's survey on labor relations in state-owned enterprises resonates with Kojima's findings by claiming that the state-owned enterprise reforms weakened workers' relative capacity to negotiate and that the tripartite consultation system often favored the employer over the employee, because the CCP tended always to take the side of management.

These findings concerning the trade unions' degree of autonomy and their qualifications to represent the workers offer important insights into the problems of corporatism in China. However, one should not neglect those workers who lie outside the protection of the trade unions. More often than not most migrant workers from rural areas, whose number already exceeds 150 million, fail to join a union, and unemployed urban residents, who amount to at least 8.4 million, cannot voice their desires through the existing unions.[4] What is ironic is that these are the very groups that are most vulnerable to the infringement of rights. In reality, their needs are met by the social security system rather than by tripartite consultation. In order to clarify the role of corporatism in China, we need to analyze how the reformed social security system has compensated for the shortcomings of tripartite negotiation, especially in terms of providing a social safety net for those who are not members of unions.

Numerous studies have been carried out on this issue of the social safety net for workers in unstable occupations. Yang Yiyong and Xing Xiaobo (1999) conducted a field survey of laid-off workers and appealed for the creation of a new social safety net. Of the Japanese scholars who have worked on this issue, Ito (1998) and Tsukamoto (2006) carried out questionnaire surveys and interviews with laid-off workers in China, and described their actual circumstances together with the problems that they faced. Another important achievement was that of the Institute for Labor Studies, a research institution under the Ministry of Labor and Social Security. Every year the institute publishes a *Blue Book of Chinese Employment* which analyzes employment trends from various perspectives with regard to the issues that have come to public attention during the previous year. In the 2002 edition of this series, Mo Rong (2003) examined problems such as the oversupply of labor, fewer new employment opportunities, increased participation in the labor market of both women and the handicapped, and the working conditions of migrant workers from rural communities. Mo suggested the possibility of introducing vocational training and establishing a market for labor as a means of solving these problems. Furthermore, Mo regarded temporary employment and part-time labor in the small services sector as providing new job opportunities for those workers laid off by state-owned enterprises. At the same time, he pointed out the potentially illegal and undesirable aspects of such employment in the form of features such as unpaid wages and social insurance, wrongful dismissal, and unsafe working environments, all often characteristic of employment in small enterprises or among the self-employed, and drew attention to the loopholes in the existing social security system (Mo 2003: 157). Yan (2006) also mentioned the problem of irregular employment in the course of his survey of migrant workers in Shanghai and the surrounding region.

By contrast with the examples given above, there is a stronger tendency among Chinese scholars to focus on the positive effects of "irregular employment" because such employment creates more jobs. The work of Li Junfeng (2005) typifies this tendency. Li used data obtained from the second National Women's Social Status Sampling Survey, a joint survey carried out by the All China Women's Federation and the National Bureau of Statistics of China, and compared irregular employment in China with the levels observed in other countries. This comparative analysis led to the finding that the family-register system in China, which was originally designed to control the influx of peasants into the large cities, had accelerated the tendency of migrant workers to accept irregular employment. Li also found out that China differs from other countries in that there is almost no difference in the ratio of males and females engaged in irregular labor.

Another reason why researchers started to pay more attention to the inferior working conditions associated with irregular employment is the phenomenon of mismatching in the labor market. *Ming-gong huang* (migrant labor shortage) "started to emerge in Southern and Eastern coastal regions from 2002. Initially, this phenomenon was limited to the private factories and foreign firms where labor turnover rates were consistently high, but by 2005, it became prevalent even among the state-owned enterprises" (Inagaki 2005). Why should this be so? One possible explanation would be the "one-child" policy. The notoriously strict birth control regulations suppressed the increase rate of young unskilled workers, making peasants more reluctant to let their only child take the risk of leaving to look for a job far away from the home village, thus causing a shortage of labor supply among migrant workers. Although this may be true in the long run, at the moment, the number of entrants to the labor market is still expanding. Another likely cause may be the abolition of agricultural tax that has been initiated by Hu Jintao and Wen Jiabao. Their policies for reducing the fiscal burden on peasants and their support of agricultural production may have caused migrant workers to return to their home villages to resume their agricultural work.

However, Chinese scholars, and in particular researchers in Chinese government institutions, believe that the migrant labor shortage is caused by low pay scales and by the unstable employment structure. This can be seen from the report compiled by the Ministry of Labor and Social Security research group (2004). The report argued that the most appropriate countermeasure for tackling these issues would be for the government to refrain from direct intervention and promote more effective market mechanisms in the field of labor.

We may conclude from these studies that: (1) the analysis of corporatism in China has developed around the issue of the tripartite mechanism and the extent to which ACFTU can be regarded as fully qualified to represent labor; (2) studies of irregular employment have been done mainly as field surveys of groups of atypical workers, and assessments have tended to concentrate on whether or not irregular employment creates more jobs; and (3) the role of the government has been discussed in terms of the enhancement of the free market rather than of intervention, and workers' protection has been investigated in the context of advancing the development of the labor market. By contrast, this chapter examines the validity of the tripartite negotiation project as a means of actually maintaining stability among the workers. Special emphasis is given to workers who do not come within the purview of the scheme, and there is an examination of the impact of social security reform on these people is examined.

4.2 The present employment situation in China: the various factors that cause labor disputes

Let us explore why there has been an increase in the number of labor disputes in recent years. China has enjoyed rapid economic growth for the past thirty years. Its annual average GDP growth rate between 1979 and 2004 was 9.6 percent. Even though the rate declined slightly during the first few years of the twenty-first century, China still maintained an average growth rate of 8.8 percent between 2001 and 2005. The total number of employees in both urban and rural areas was 752 million in 2004, whereas in 1999 it was only 708.6 million. A simple calculation shows us that 46.14 million new jobs were created over a period of only five years, an increment that in size almost equals the total population of South Korea in 2005. Surprisingly, however, the unemployment rate also increased during those miraculous economic boom years. This is due to the sheer pressure of natural population growth. The statistics indicate that the unemployment rate on a registered base rose from 3.1 percent as of 1999 to 4.2 percent in 2004. Although GDP in 2004 showed 9.5 percent annual growth year-on-year, the fact that the unemployment rate continued to climb confirmed that the increase in the new population looking for jobs surpassed job creation.

What is noteworthy is the composition of the labor surplus. In the latter half of the 1990s, the majority of the labor surplus were laid-off workers as a result of the restructuring of the state-owned enterprises. However, in the 2000s, as the initial shock of state enterprise reform began to wear off, the annual increase in the number of laid-off workers started to fall, and unemployment among young people became the main concern in relation to conditions in the labor market (You Jun 2005: 5). If we take a look at the status of job seekers in the fourth quarter of the fiscal year 2004, the increase in the number of newly graduated young people who failed to find a job was 19.9 percent, whereas the increase in the number of laid-off workers was only 5.9 percent. This shows that at present the lack of job opportunities for new graduates is a more serious problem than the number of laid-off people.

Incidentally, the increase rate is also higher in the number of new graduates compared to the increase rate in the number of laid-off workers. In the fourth quarter of the fiscal year 2004, the increase rate of laid-off workers fell by 2.2 percent from the previous year. On the other hand, the increase rate for unemployed new graduates rose by 0.7 percent over the same period (You Jun 2005: 5).

However, further examination is needed before we can conclude that laid-off workers have ceased to be the main problem in the current labor market. If we focus on the total supply of urban labor, a somewhat different picture emerges. In 2004, the total amount of the labor supply in urban areas was 24 million. We can calculate the annual increase by young graduates to be 7.7 million by subtracting those who re-entered school after graduation (200,000) and those who enlisted in the army (500,000) from the total number of new graduates (8,400,000). This means that of the total supply of labor, about one-third was accounted for by new graduates. On the other hand, there are 2.6 million laid-off workers who used to work for state-owned and collective-owned firms, as well as eight million unemployed who were acknowledged as laid-off workers before they became jobless. If we add both groups together to show how much pressure the workers laid off in the state-owned sector exerted on the supply of labor, the number amounts to 10.6 million, easily surpassing the number of new graduates by 2.6 million. Other sources for the supply of labor are: (a) peasants whose residential registrations were transferred from rural to urban areas (such transfers can come about for various reasons, such as confiscation of farmland by the local government or a change in town classification); and (b) veteran soldiers demobilized from the army. But their numbers cannot be compared to those of the laid-off workers and the new graduates since they account for only (a) 1.4 million and (b) 0.5 million respectively (You Jun 2005: 17). Although at first it may appear that the employment problem of the laid-off workers has receded, the undercurrent of its pressure on the labor market is still strong and the problem has yet to be solved.[5]

At the same time, the existence of migrant workers from rural communities must be taken into account if we are to understand the instability in the labor market. Numerous instances of labor disputes among them have been covered by local newspapers and magazines. One example was a demonstration in Beijing held by 60 or so migrant workers from Hebei, Jiangsu, Henan, and Sichuan, who hung up a banner in front of a labor shark's office on February 5, 2007. They all claimed to have been deprived of several months of wages, and demanded the settlement of the debt before the Lunar New Year (*Channel NewsAsia*, February 5). This particular case also occurred on a construction site, but similar incidents have occurred throughout manufacturing industry.

To understand the background of recent disputes among migrant laborers, we will first ascertain the kind of employment in which the migrants have been engaged. It is apparent that migration in search of work has been directed disproportionately toward the large cities of the coastal provinces. *China Labor Statistical Yearbook 2005* shows that Guangdong Province had the largest number of urban new recruits in 2004, accounting for 12.3 percent of the annual national increase in labor supply in that year. As Table 4.2 shows, Beijing (9.1 percent) came second, followed by Fujian (7.0 percent), Shanghai (7.0 percent), and Jiangsu (7.0 percent). These high-ranking provinces have one common trait — more than 30 percent of their new recruits are migrant workers from rural areas. In other words, peasants flock specifically to the three economic regions that are most open to the global economy, namely: (1) the Bohai Gulf

Table 4.2 Increase of employment in urban units by region (2004)

	Region	Total	Recruited from countryside	Recruited from cities and towns	Recruited from demobilized troops & transferred from army	Recruited as graduates	Transferred into the region	(persons) Others
	national total	11,175,565	3,595,015	1,851,155	245,549	1,802,738	1,662,358	2,018,750
	%	100%	32.2%	16.6%	2.2%	16.1%	14.9%	18.1%
Top five provinces	Guangdong	12.3%	18.1%	15.2%	8.9%	13.9%	5.0%	4.5%
	Beijing	9.1%	7.6%	9.4%	3.6%	7.3%	10.1%	13.0%
	Shanghai	7.0%	2.7%	7.1%	1.7%	3.3%	8.8%	17.2%
	Fujian	7.0%	13.1%	5.9%	4.2%	4.3%	2.3%	3.8%
	Jiangsu	7.0%	5.4%	9.0%	4.9%	9.7%	5.6%	6.9%

Source: *China Labour Statistical Yearbook 2005*, p. 305.

area, which includes prominent cities such as Beijing, Tianjin, Qingdao, and Dalian; (2) the Changjiang Delta area, where Shanghai functions as the headquarters for many Chinese and foreign companies; and (3) the Pearl River Delta, where the business network connects Hong Kong, Shenzhen, Macau, Zhuhai, and Guangzhou. According to the abovementioned labor statistics, in 2004 these three economic spheres accounted for 57 percent of annual new recruits into the labor market.

We must note that these three regions are well-known destinations for FDI in China, and new recruits are more likely to find jobs among foreign enterprises. In addition, since private enterprises and self-employed businesses tend to be more labor-intensive than FDI establishments, they absorb more labor, as is shown in Table 4.3. Private companies and the self-employed accounted for one-third of the total number of job vacancies available during the third quarter of 2006. FDI, private firms and self-employed businesses have already replaced the state-owned and collectively-owned enterprises as the main sources of job creation.

Table 4.3 Job vacancies by ownership (3rd quarter, 2006)

	No.	(persons) %
1. Enterprise	3,893,439	96.4
Mainland China capital	3,012,131	74.6
State-owned	146,434	3.6
Collectively owned	132,656	3.3
Firm with share holding stock ownership	185,313	4.6
Firm under joint ownership	95,919	2.4
Limited	795,539	19.7
Corporate	480,487	11.9
Private-enterprise	1,010,208	25.0
Others	165,575	4.1
Hong Kong, Macau, Taiwan capital	214,333	5.3
Foreign capital	305,871	7.6
Individual (self-employed)	361,104	8.9
2. Operation unit	23,606	0.6
3. Institution	8,071	0.2
4. Others	114,988	2.8
Total	4,040,104	100.0

Source: China Labour Market Info Monitor Center, 2006.

The problem with these generators of new jobs is that they tend to cause an expansion of atypical forms of employment, such as part-time, temporary, and casual employment. Migrant workers have often encountered unstable working arrangements in these types of employment, and have frequently taken jobs without written contracts. Even urban citizens with local residential registrations have not been able to escape the impact of instability in these new types of employment. If they are unskilled or have had an inferior education, they are likely to end up in casual employment and must compete with migrant workers for the jobs that are available. The excess supply of labor, combined with more flexible forms of employment, has weakened the bargaining power of individual workers vis-à-vis their employers, as can be seen from the declining labor distribution rate. On December 10, 2005, *Jiefang Ribao*, a Shanghai-based newspaper, reported that the average level of migrant workers' wages in the Pearl River Delta had increased by only 68 RMB over the previous 12 years. There can be no doubt that if inflation is taken into account, wage levels did indeed decline during those years in spite of remarkable levels of economic growth. By contrast, the capital formation of private companies increased rapidly. Thus some 49 private firms with more than 1 million RMB of assets enlarged their total assets by 19.4 times within a five-year period, allowing their annual average increase rate in asset values to reach 55.6 percent (Yang 2006: 35). It seems very likely that the widening disparity in employers' and employees' income distribution is contributing to the rising number of labor disputes.

4.3 The transformation of labor-related laws and restrictions

Although the Chinese government authorities have shown much concern over the growing number of labor disputes, if we examine the planning and revision of labor-related laws and regulations, little priority seems to be given to worker protection. Rather, legal reforms have been designed to promote the market economy and to introduce legislation to encourage flexibility in the rigid labor relations that were the legacy of the planned economy. Let us now consider the transformation of China's labor laws and regulations.

The labor laws took a major turn after a market economy was introduced into the People's Republic of China in 1979. During the planned economy era, urban workers' jobs were essentially guaranteed for their lifetime by the permanent employment system that was followed by the state-owned and collective enterprises. However, with the introduction of the market economy, foreign investors and village-and-township firms that lay outside the state's planned economy were able to hire migrant workers on a contract basis, the contracts usually expiring after a period of one or two years. The employers of these firms were free if they wished to adjust the amount of their labor to fluctuations in market demand. As a result, these firms compressed their labor costs sharply. Since migrant workers are almost exclusively peasants whose wages were very low compared to those of urban residents, state-owned enterprises soon found their own rigid permanent employment system to be a huge obstacle preventing them from competing with these newly emerging firms. As the market economy spread throughout the nation, many state-owned companies started to complain that they were bearing the extra burden of maintaining jobs for redundant workers, and this accumulation eventually led to the generation of large deficits.

In response to this problem, in 1986 the State Council announced that from that time new recruits should all become contract-based workers and only those who were hired prior to the announcement were permitted to enjoy the benefits of the lifetime employment system. As the economic reforms of the 1980s allowed state-owned industries greater freedom of management from the state, by the same token they also opened up the possibility for their going bankrupt. This meant that workers at state-owned enterprises needed a new form of employment security, so an unemployment insurance scheme was set up and 1 percent of the worker's basic salary was collected as the premium. According to Yamamoto (2000: 331), these labor system reforms were arranged into four sets of regulations, namely "Provisional Regulation to Exercise the Labor-Contract System Among State-owned Enterprises", "The Unemployment Insurance System for Workers Discharged for Various Reasons", "Open Recruitment for Hiring Workers", and "Disposal of Workers by the Disciplinary Infraction". They are sometimes referred as the four major new labor regulations.

Initially, the above regulations were designed to protect the vested rights and interests of those who already held permanent employment status, and they were introduced at the expense of new recruitment. The double standard for the smooth transition was apparent from the slogan "New regulations for new recruits, old ways for old workers" (*Xinren Xinbanfa, Jiuren Jiubanfa*). However, Deng Xiaoping's determination to promote market-oriented reforms and the Chinese government's decision to join the World Trade Organization made it necessary to make drastic changes to the arrangements. Even though the shocking

June Fourth Incident (Tiananmen Square Massacre) forced the process to slow down, more flexibility was introduced into the labor market after 1992. The *Labor Law of the People's Republic of China* (hereinafter referred to as the *Labor Law*), which symbolizes these changes, was passed on July 5, 1994 and put into force in the January of the following year. This marked the end of the old permanent employment system. The act changed the status of all employees, including even the older generation hired before 1986, to contract-based workers, and thus paved the way for the loss-making state-owned enterprises to start massive employee layoffs.

New laws and regulations relevant to this act have continued to appear since this time. Because the new labor act promoted the mobilization of the workforce through the labor market, the *Provisional Regulation on Job Placement Service* (1998) was enforced. Furthermore, the responsibility for providing workers' welfare programs including benefits such as old-age pensions and medical care was taken away from the management of the state-owned enterprises and handed over to relevant public institutions such as the social security funds and the public hospitals.[6] In some cases, enterprise-based service activities such as catering services and clinics were transferred to the private sector. Prior to the reform, the workers' welfare programs provided by enterprises had often hindered the smooth transition to a more open labor market. Employees were reluctant to leave their "unit" for fear of losing the accumulated benefits that were based upon the number of consecutive years that they had been in service. The separation of welfare programs from corporate management encouraged workers to seek job opportunities outside the original "unit". The new social-security system was also designed to encourage the increasing mobility of labor. The *Provisions on Collection of Social Insurance Premium* (1999), *Unemployment Insurance Provisions* (1999), and *Work-related Injury Insurance Provisions* (2003) were implemented to ensure that the new policy took effect.

On the other hand, although the Ministry of Labor proclaimed the *Minimum Wage Provision regarding Companies* in 1993, the minimum wage was in fact left unchanged for a decade despite the high rates of inflation that had accompanied rapid economic growth. When the new *Minimum Wage Provision* (Ministry of Labor and Social Security Order No. 21) was finally proclaimed, on January 20, 2004 (enforced on March 1 of the same year), again, its main purpose was to encourage greater flexibility in the labor market and to acknowledge the existence of atypical employment. This provision related to many aspects of social welfare reform. For example, the new provision allowed for the hourly publication of the minimum wage standard, whereas the previous provision had defined minimum wages only on a monthly basis. As a result, this 2004 provision succeeded in securing minimum payment for part-time workers with hourly pay contracts. Furthermore, the provision stated that when the hourly minimum wage was the result of a conversion from the monthly minimum wage, the stated amount did not include basic pension contributions and basic medical insurance payments. These two mandatory insurance payments were to be added *after* the hourly minimum wage was determined (Ministry of Labor and Social Security 2004b).

In addition, there was also a tightening of the restrictions on working hours. It was specified that overtime hours, together with special extra allowances for hazardous employment such as work carried out in high temperatures or in tunnels, must be excluded from the minimum wage. Article 6 specifies that "when determining or adjusting the hourly minimum wage, the gap between full-time and non-full-time workers concerning the safety, intensity, and fringe-benefits of their work must be taken into consideration". On the other hand, a 1993 provision defined the premise of the minimum wage as one that must be for work "within statutory working hours", whereas the 2004 provision stated it be to for work "within statutory working hours, or working hours set by a labor contract", giving much greater importance than hitherto to the labor contract (Ministry of Labor and Social Security 2004b; Zhou 2004).

Another significant change is that the 2004 provision imposed a biannual evaluation of the minimum wage standard. According to article 7, local governments at the provincial level are responsible for conducting examinations of the standard and must report the results to the central government. This procedure generates a disparity between localities. Let us, for example, consider the three metropolises of Beijing, Shanghai, and Shenzhen, where minimum wages for full-time workers are around the same level. When we compare the minimum wage standard for non-full-time workers, Beijing's and Shanghai's standards are substantially higher than those found in Shenzhen. In fact, Beijing's non-full-time worker's minimum wage standard is more than double the level in Shenzhen. One of the reasons for Beijing's higher standard could be the inclusion of social insurance premiums. But social insurance alone does not explain why the gap is so wide, and Shanghai's standard, which excludes social insurance contribution, is still 1.5 times higher than Shenzhen's. (Li Shu-guo 2005).

The above example shows that while endorsing to a certain extent the right of former state-owned firms' workers to maintain their privileges, the government authorities are indeed refining new labor legislation, resulting in the encouragement of atypical employment. It was therefore necessary for the new legislation to include a demarche designed to protect workers from unpaid wages, a problem that has occurred widely in the world of atypical employment in China, and especially on construction sites. On November 4, 2004, the Ministry of Labor and Social Security announced the *Transitional Provision on Pay Management of the Seasonal-workers in the Construction Industry* and notified employers that unpaid wages and intermediary exploitation by wage sharks is forbidden under law.

The protection of workers' rights was, in fact, already contained in the 1994 Labor Law. Under this law, all labor departments above county level were to establish Labor and Social Security Inspection Agencies to supervise and inspect employers' compliance with labor legislation. However, violations of workers' rights, including the avoidance of social insurance contributions, the imposition of excessive working hours, and the non-payment of wages got worse every year, driving the government to put in place a legal basis to deal with this specific issue. The *Regulations on Labor Protection Inspection* (hereafter referred to as the *Labor Inspection Regulations*) has been in force since December 1, 2004.

The Labor Inspection Regulations authorized local labor administrations to rectify any unlawful labor contracts (article 24) and empowered them to conduct on-site inspection for labor security. Local administrations were also given the right to collect evidence across a wide range of issues (article 15). The Regulation also granted both employers and employees the right to notify their local administration of any violation of the law or regulation (article 9), and clarified which issues should be subjects of inspection. These issues included the establishment of a corporate by-law on labor security, labor contracts (both their contents and their execution), working hours, levels of payment including abidance by the minimum wage standard, and social insurance contributions (article 11), to give just a few examples. The inspector must complete his investigation within 60 days after a case is placed on file, although the labor administration in charge may permit a 30-day extension if the case is complicated (article 17).

At the same time, the regulation clarifies the amount of compensation and fines payable in the event of unlawful conduct. Article 23 lists issues that are considered to violate the rights of women and minor workers, and imposes fines of 1,000–5,000 RMB on employers. As regards unpaid and underpaid wages, as well as wages below the minimum wage standards, article 26 empowers the local labor administration to order an employer to pay the worker the full amount owed up until a set date, and if the employer fails to pay by the deadline, additional payment must be made as compensation, within a range of 50 percent or more up to double the amount of the wage owed. The local labor administration also has the power to warn and order an employer to stop illegal overtime working hours, and can impose a fine of more than 100 and less than 500 RMB per worker in cases of infringement (article 25). Regarding avoidance of social insurance contributions, if an employer makes a false claim concerning the amount of the total wage bill, or the size of the workforce, the labor administration may impose a fine that is more than double and less than triple the amount of the wages concealed. The same rule applies to the reception of social security benefits and social security fund expenditure (article 27). Finally, article 29 guarantees the workers' right to organize a trade union. It forbids an employer to relocate workers or to cancel their labor contract based upon their union activities (Department of Population and Social, Science and Technology Statistics, National Bureau of Statistics, PRC: Department of Planning and Finance, Ministry of Labor and Social Security, PRC 2004: 524).

As can be seen from the contents of the above regulation, the protection of workers' rights has focused on the completion and strict observance of labor contracts. This direction can be seen in the strengthening of collective labor contracts. Collective labor contracts were defined by the Labor Law and the Trade Union Law of the People's Republic of China (hereafter referred as the Trade Union Law). Based on these two laws, an employer and employees may sign a collective labor contract that determines important labor conditions such as wages, working hours, recess and rest hours, workplace safety, social insurance, and benefit programs. The details were set out in the Regulation on Collective Labor Contracts, which was promulgated on December 5, 1994 by the Ministry of Labor. However, it was not until ten years after that the regulation was revised into *The Provision on Collective Labor Contracts*, which was promulgated by the Ministry of Labor and Social Security on January 20, 2004, becoming effective on May 1, 2004. The 2004 *Provision* includes protection for women and minor workers. This is another indication of why the year 2004 marked a turning point for the protection of workers' rights in terms of law making.

Nevertheless, we should keep in mind that the change was brought in as a necessary procedure for coping with the diversification of employment patterns without deterring ongoing rapid economic growth. Needless to say the law-making was important, but for the laws and regulations to have any actual impact on the improvement of labor conditions, workers must have the opportunity to voice their desires. Otherwise, these articles might turn into empty promises. In this regard, recent statistics on labor disputes, as mentioned in the introduction of this chapter, seem to cast serious doubts on the efficacy of these legal efforts.

One way to improve the legal effectiveness of legislation is to arrange for the relevant parties to participate actively in its implementation and to take part in monitoring its outcomes. In China's case, the tripartite scheme of corporatism that allows representatives from labor, management and the government to negotiate labor-related issues was considered to be a sound way forward. According to the official definition of corporatism, only one organization is permitted to represent each party. Thus the ACFTU, the central trade union, and the China Enterprise Confederation/China Enterprise Directors Association (hereafter referred as CEC/CEDA), a business association, act respectively as the sole representatives of the employees and employers at national level. Yet one cannot help but find their qualifications to represent their constituents somewhat debatable. The following section examines the reality that surrounds these national organizations that are crucial components of the tripartite consultation scheme.

4.4 Trade unions and employers' associations in the context of tripartite consultation

4.4.1 ACFTU: a national center of trade unions

The first trade union law following the socialist revolution of 1949 was enacted in 1950. As the result of the socialist revolution, trade unions became affiliate organizations of the CCP and all trade unions were put under the control of the ACFTU. However, with the outbreak of the Great Cultural Revolution, the CCP froze the ACFTU's assets and forced it to halt supervision of its subsidiary organizations in January 1967. It was not until April, 1978 that the ACFTU resumed its official activities (Ito 1998: 160–1).

The economic reforms gave trade unions a new mission. According to the Trade Union Law, governments at various levels are to establish a tripartite consultation mechanism with the trade unions and the representatives of enterprises at the corresponding level to analyze and solve important issues regarding labor relations (article 34).

This tripartite consultation mechanism was adopted from the ILO convention, and was established in August, 2001 by three parties, namely the Ministry of Labor and Social Security (representing central government), the ACFTU (in its capacity as the labor unions' national center), and the CEC/CEDA (the sole representative of employers at the national level). Zhang, Yanning and Chen Lantong (2005: 130–48) state that as a general rule, tripartite consultations at national level are called once every four months. The three parties take turns to provide a venue for the meetings, or arrange a "neutral" venue unconnected with any one of the parties concerned. Although local-level tripartite consultations are supposed to follow those at the national level, there are some differences due to the diverse circumstances of the various localities.

What makes Chinese trade unions unique is the fact that managers and employers are also eligible for union membership. Because of this, some scholars have questioned whether or not the trade unions are properly qualified to represent workers' interests. We should also bear in mind the extent to which the Chinese trade unions are independent from the state. If we focus only on the financial and personnel aspects of ACFTU's work, the union seems sufficiently self-governing, and is equipped with its own fund and separate account, and enjoys independent control over its human resources. Yet the new Trade Union Law promulgated in 1992 reflected the impact of the June Fourth Incident and acknowledged the ACFTU as the one and only legal trade union in the People's Republic of China. In comparison to the 1950 Trade Union Law, the 1992 version made it clear that the trade union's duty toward the CCP and the State takes precedence over the union's responsibility to the workers (Ishii 2006).

Moreover, the *Decision on Amending the Trade Union Law (Guanyu Xiugai Zhonghua Renmin Gongheguo Gonghui-fa)* made at the 24th Meeting of the Standing Committee of the Ninth National People's Congress on October 27, 2001, while stating that the trade unions represent workers, at the same time emphasized that the unions should follow government supervision and should support economic growth. Chapter 1 ("General Provision") of the 2001 Trade Union Law declares that

> Trade unions shall... take economic development as the central task, uphold the socialist road, the people's democratic dictatorship, leadership by the CCP and Marxist-Leninism, Mao Zedong Thoughts and Deng Xiaoping Theory, preserve in reform and the open policy, and conduct their work independently in accordance with the Constitution of trade unions.

The above declaration shows the trade unions' independent activities are conditional on the willingness of the unions to follow the CCP's guidance.

What is more important for the tripartite consultation system is that the amendment confirmed the trade unions' right to coordinate labor relations on an equal footing and to arrange collective labor contracts (article 6). It also acknowledged the trade unions' responsibility for guaranteeing the rights of unions at higher levels "to dispatch their members to assist and supervise the workers of enterprises to set up their trade unions", and that "no units or individuals may obstruct the effort" (article 11). This means that local trade unions have the authority to operate inside not only state-owned enterprises, but also in foreign and private-enterprise firms.

The Trade Union Law also assigns unions to represent workers and approves their right to demand employers to rectify violations of labor laws or infringements of workers' rights as listed in article 22. These violations are: (a) the embezzlement of workers' wages; (b) failure to provide adequate occupational safety and health conditions; (c) the arbitrary extension of working hours; (d) infringement of the special rights of women and minor workers; and (e) serious infringement of other labor rights detrimental to the interests of workers. When the unions make demands under the Trade Union Law, employers are obliged to review the issue and must make a formal reply to the unions. If an employer refuses to take remedial action, the trade union may appeal to local government to take legal action. Regarding the trade unions' role in social welfare, article 38 states that the trade union in the enterprise/institution shall have its representative or representatives in attendance at any meetings held by the employers to discuss matters relating to wages, welfare, occupational safety and health, social insurance and other issues that affect the immediate interest of the workers.

However, the 2001 Trade Union Law Amendment has left ambiguity regarding one of the fundamental conditions for the definition of corporatism, that is, the trade union's monopoly on workers' representation. While the 1950 Trade Union Law explicitly prohibited the creation of any trade union outside the ACFTU and made its existence illegal (article 3), the 2001 version states only that "Trade Unions are mass organizations of the working class formed by the workers on a voluntary basis. The ACFTU and all the trade unions under it represent the interest of the workers and safeguard the legitimate rights and interests of the workers according to the law" (article 2). In reality, there are numerous voluntary organizations inside enterprises to which many workers belong. These include *tongxiang-hui* (fellow countrymen associations), *xiongdi-hui* (brotherhood associations), *lianyi-hui* (friendship associations), *yuangong julebu* (workers' clubs), and *gongren fuli-hui* (workers' welfare associations). Although some of their activities overlap with those of the trade unions, they are allowed to sustain activities as long as they pay for the expenses of union activity and provide union membership fees to the trade unions. As is indicated by a case study in the final section of this chapter, from time to time these associations have functioned as shock absorbers for the changing labor market. Therefore, it can be said that the lack of explicit prohibition of workers' organizations other than ACFTU implies that the law tolerates their existence of these organizations because of the stabilizing effect they bring to the workplace (Peng 2002: 98).

Moreover, the *Trade Union Law* grants neither trade unions nor workers the right to call a strike. Since they are not legally entitled to go on strike, it is impossible for the unions to use the withdrawal of labor as a means of accomplishing their goals during collective bargaining (Peng 2002: 103). Trade unions must seek other means to obtain bargaining power in the tripartite consultation system. Trade unions in China cannot exert strong influence as constituent bodies like the unions in Latin American countries, because there is almost no popular direct election at the national level. Ultimately, the trade unions' power lies in their ability to collect information and opinions from the workers and transmit them to the government. They are valuable intermediaries that form a connection between the government with the workers, and they function more as a governmental consultation institution on labor issues than an institution representing the workers.

One factor that makes it difficult for trade unions to claim their legitimacy to represent the workers is the decrease in the level of union membership in recent years. The ratio of organized labor rose during the 1980s as the result of a rebound from the circumstances of the Great Cultural Revolution, an era during which all trade unions were forced to halt their activities. The number of unions doubled from 329,000 units in 1979 to 617,000 in 1992. The union membership increased 2.5 times during the same period – from 51.47 million persons to 132.2 million. But this trend was reversed during the 1990s and by 1999, the number of unions had declined to 510,000 units while membership had plunged to 86 million. The major causes of the downturn were: (a) the massive reductions in the workforce which took place in state-owned enterprises that were the main pillar of the Chinese trade union movement; (b) more new jobs were offered by foreign enterprises and private sector businesses in which trade unions were either inactive or nonexistent; and (c) the there was a decline in the rate of unionization among young workers.

In response to this new predicament, ACFTU has mobilized local trade unions and has also reinforced efforts to organize trade unions inside the private sector (Japan Institute for Labor Policy and Training (JIL) 2003). One of the major obstacles to unionization was large number of migrant workers in the private sector. They are often used as a means to adjust the level of employment within the firm, and their turnover rate is quite high. It is difficult for a typical in-company trade union to represent a highly fluid workforce. Despite this obstacle, a recent statement by Sun Chunlan, the ACFTU Vice Chairperson and First Secretary, addressing the Sixth Session of 14th ACFTU Executive Committee, indicated that the unionization rate among foreign enterprises nationwide has reached 73.1 percent (Sun). Considering that the rate was only 33 percent in 2005, ACFTU's exertions have not been fruitless in terms of raising the unionization rate (Kamata 2006: 180).

On the other hand, we must note that the unionization rate reported by the ACFTU is not the share of union members among total employees, but rather the proportion of companies which have trade unions. Furusawa's 2005 survey suggests that the rising unionization rate did not directly lead to stronger trade union influence. Furusawa's questionnaire survey was based on 102 valid responses from Japanese enterprises and 100 responses from American firms located in China, and revealed that the Japanese companies have a notably higher rate of unionization (69.3 percent) than found in American firms (31.3 percent).[7] What is interesting is that there was a higher proportion of companies that experienced labor disputes among the Japanese firms than among the American ones, the percentages being 15.3 percent for the former and 5.2 percent for the latter. The survey also showed that among the Japanese enterprises, those with in-company trade unions were more likely to encounter labor disputes than those without in-house unions. Thus 20.6 percent of the Japanese firms with in-house unions had experienced labor disputes while the equivalent percentage for those with no in-house unions was only 4.0 percent. The same tendency held true for the American companies, where four out of five companies that experienced labor disputes had established trade unions inside (Furusawa 2006: 21).

Furthermore, Furusawa's data revealed that most of the Japanese firms drew up their labor contracts under the initiative of the local ACFTU branch and the local government. Of the 40 that firms responded, 22 replied that labor contracts were initiated by the local ACFTU branch, 14 answered that they followed the demands of local government, while 12 stated that they had responded to a demand from their in-company trade union.[8] If we make a closer examination of the Japanese companies that experienced labor disputes, we can see that whether or not these companies have signed labor contracts with the workers appears to be irrelevant to the labor disputes. Some 23.7 percent of those with labor contracts encountered labor disputes, compared with 19.2 percent of those without labor contracts (Furusawa 2006: 15, 20).

In respect of the issue of managers holding union memberships, the survey shows that among non-full-time trade union chairmen in Japanese firms, 92.3 percent held a position equal to or higher than division chief, and 53.8 percent had a status equivalent to a department director or higher. What is noteworthy is that the vast majority of union chairmen are not full-time union officials, contrary to the guidelines in the *Trade Union Law*. In this survey, non-full-time chairmen accounted for 86.8 percent in Japanese firms and 82.8 percent in US firms (Furusawa 2006: 16).

These findings seem to suggest that a rising unionization rate does not necessary imply an improvement in unions' effectiveness to negotiate and to represent employees on equal terms with the government and employers at the tripartite consultations. In his paper, Furusawa concludes that the trade unions play a limited role in preventing or solving labor disputes (Furusawa 2006: 24).

4.4.2 CEC/CEDA: a national center of employers' associations

CEC/CEDA is the organization that represents employers in the National Tripartite Consultation System, where the Ministry of Labor and Social Security represents the government and the ACFTU represents employees. This is stated clearly in Article 2 of CEC/CEDA's Constitution. Furthermore, the Constitution stipulates that CEC/CEDA must guide Employers' Confederations and Enterprise Directors' Associations in each locality and in each industry to establish a "sound tripartite consultation mechanism" and to participate in the labor relations coordination process (CEC/CEDA 2003: Article 7). The Constitution also declares that CEC/CEDA is to be the sole organization to represent China in international employers' institutions (CEC/CEDA 2003: Article 8). Furthermore, when the *Labor Law* was enacted in 1994, CEC/CEDA joined the procedure, along with the Central Government and the ACFTU.

However, CEC/CEDA is not unlike ACFTU in the effectiveness of its representation. From the time of its foundation, CEC/CEDA has come under the strong influence of the government[9] and even today, CEC/CEDA's chairman is a high-ranking cadre of the Central Government and the CCP. For example, Wang Zhongyu, the current chairman of CEC/CEDA, successively held prominent positions in the Central

Government, including the vice-chairman of the Chinese People's Political Consultative Conference (2003 to 2008), the secretary general of the State Council (1998–2003), and the minister of the State Economic and Trade Commission (1993–1998). He was also a member of the 14th and 15th Central Committees of the CCP (CPPCC 2007). Chen Jinhua, the former chairman, was also a famous politician who used to be the vice-chairman of the Chinese People's Political Consultative Conference, and the minister of the State Economic Planning Commission. Moreover, in the early days of its history, CEC/CEDA's memberships were held by the directors of the state-owned enterprises and these remain the core groups even today. These facts suggest that CEC/CEDA's nature is closer to that of a government-affiliated institution rather than that of an independent organization established by self-supporting entrepreneurs. Moreover, since CEC/CEDA was launched after the introduction of economic reform, the association is less well known than the ACFTU at prefectural, village-township, and *jietao* (neighborhood) levels, whose history dates back to foundation of the People's Republic of China.

In fact, the All China Federation of Industry and Commerce (ACFIC) could be seen as a more prevalent association, and one that is more closely related to the actual entrepreneurs of China.

According to its official website, ACFIC has a far longer history than CEC/CEDA since it was established in 1953 and has a large membership that spreads down to village-township and *jietao* level. According to Chairman Huang Mengfu of ACFIC, in September 2007 ACFIC's membership amounted to 2.139 million, with enterprises accounting for 782,000. There are 3,296 locality-based FICs (Federations of Industry and Commerce, that are subordinate organizations of ACFIC), and 8,611 industry-based FICs. At the grassroots level (township-village, *jiedao*, or below), there were 23,000 FICs.

At the same time, we must note that ACFIC, too, is closely tied to the government. ACFIC proclaims itself to be "a non-governmental chamber of commerce composed of Chinese industrialists and business people under the leadership of the CCP, and an organization assisting the government to manage China's non-public economy, and also a bridge linking the Party and Government and non-public economic personages" (ACFIC 1999). However, what separates ACFIC from CEC/CEDA is the emphasis on the private sector. Of the 412 members of ACFIC's 9th Executive Committee, 233 (56 percent) were chosen from the "non-public" or private sector. This is the first time in the history of ACFIC that the majority of top leaders were representatives of "non-public" firms, and in fact Chairman Huang at that time said, "non-public representatives are the main body of ACFIC" (Renmin Wang 2002).

ACFIC also plays an active role in presenting the employers' views to the law-makers. When laws such as the *Realty Law,* the *Corporate Income Tax Law,* and the *Anti-Monopoly Law* were drafted or revised, ACFIC submitted its opinion publicly, demanding equal protection for private ownership rights and equality in the burden of taxation on various companies. More importantly, ACFIC has collaborated with the Ministry of Labor and Social Welfare and ACFTU to solve unemployment problems in both rural and urban areas. ACFIC has claimed that in the large cities, such collaboration created jobs for 2.025 million people over a three-year period (Huang 2007).

Considering these facts, it is little wonder that in some localities, FICs have become a part of the tripartite consultation system on labor relations. Reports from the Changjiang Delta region, where the local economy contains a high ratio of private enterprises, show that FICs act as employers' representatives. According to the Anhui Provincial FIC, when the Wuhu Municipality established the Wuhu Municipal Tripartite Consultation Institution on Labor Relations in July 2006, there were actually four members, namely the Municipal Labor and Social Security Bureau to embody government views, the ACFTU to stand for the workers, and the CEC and the ACFIC to represent the employers. We can see that, contrary to the definition of corporatism, the employers' representatives are not limited to a single organization. The main agenda set by the four organizations in the Wuhu Municipal Tripartite Consultation Institution were: to establish a healthy labor contract system, to compensate for unpaid and underpaid wages, and to settle accounts on social security contributions (Anhui 2006).

In October 2006, Yuhang District government in Hangzhou Municipality (Zhejiang Province) formulated a three-year program to improve the labor contract system through a tripartite labor relations consultation institution in response to the demands of central government. The district announced that the program was expected to promote subscriptions to the industry injury insurance scheme and that the administration would select a model enterprise regarding labor–management relationships while aggregating their experience. Again, it was the Yuhang District FIC, rather than the ACFTU subsidiary, that attended the District Labor Relations Tripartite Consultation Institution as a representative of the employers. On December 9, 2008, the Seventh Meeting of the District's Tripartite Labor Consultation was called and hosted by the Yuhang District FIC (Cao Chen 2008).

According to Zhang and Chen, other various employers' associations were allowed to participate in the tripartite labor relations consultation institutions in Fujian and Shanghai on the condition that they followed CEC/CEDA's guidance (Zhang Yanning and Chen Lantong 2005: 144–5). At the grassroots level, even organizations such as the State-owned Assets Supervision and Administration Commission, the Economic and Trade Commission, the Individual Laborers Association, and the Private Enterprise Associations had become the employers' representatives in the tripartite consultation institutions.

The above evidence suggests that, overall, tripartite labor relations consultation institutions are less likely to function as an adjustment program for employers' and employees' representatives to negotiate on an equal footing with government, and instead tend to lean toward being a convenient machine for the government to collect data and receive advice on labor policy from relevant actors. Furthermore, even in terms of supplying data, employers have multiple channels to reach government as can be seen in the case of the adoption of the *Labor Contract Law*.

When the first draft of the *Labor Contract Law* was submitted to the Standing Committee of the 10th National People's Congress' 19th Meeting in December 2005, the central government called for a public hearing through the People's Congress at various locality levels on March 20, 2006. Since in comparison with the *Labor Law*, the draft was designed in favor of workers' protection, it contained many new restrictions closely related to the immediate interests of both employers and employees. For example, if an employer and an employee do not swiftly sign a labor contract in spite of the fact that they are already in an employment relationship, workers will be deemed to have unlimited contracts that cannot be terminated without a justifiable cause until the retirement of the employee. The employee's probationary period of six months based upon the *Labor Law* was reduced to less than a month per one year contract in the case of non-technical workers, and to two months for technical staff.

The disclosure of the draft provoked a strong reaction from the general public. Within a period of just one month, some 191,849 letters were sent to the government, expressing a variety of views. This was the largest public response in the history of the PRC since the 1954 public hearings about the formation of the first Constitution. Although the *Labor Contract Law*'s draft had already passed a Tripartite Labor Relations Consultation which included ACFTU, the government, taken aback by this massive response to the draft, decided to postpone the promulgation at the end of 2006 (Zhu Zhe 2006). Heated debates among researchers and experts also seemed to affect the government decision to revise the original draft. On January 2007, ACFIC called on the conference entitled the *Round-Table Discussion on Revision of the Labor Contract Law (second draft)* to gather comments and proposals from the private sector (*Chinese Industry & Commerce Times*, January 22, 2007). The whole process implies that the tripartite labor consultation institution plays only a superficial role in determining important labor relations issues, therefore, strictly speaking, the institution is not to be treated as a variation of corporatism.

4.5 Social safety net for migrant workers and the unemployed

If the official labor consultation mechanism is not effective, who should the workers turn to in order to protect their rights and protect their employment? If the workers' wishes were simply to keep their jobs and if the government's principal target was to prevent labor-related social disturbances, various types of social welfare program would have been sufficient. Unemployment insurance, industrial injury insurance and medical insurance are expected to function as a social safety net. However, migrant workers and the laid-off workers of former state-owned enterprises would most likely be left out, without some form of subscription to social security.

Between November and December 2005, the author conducted a joint research project with Dr Zhang Qixin, an Associate Professor of the Economic Research Institute in the Shanghai Academy of Social Science. We collected questionnaires from 200 women who are migrant workers and 200 women urban residents who were formerly employees of state-owned enterprises.[10] The questionnaires asked whether the respondents had subscribed to various types of social insurance. The results are set out in Table 4.4.

Before being laid off, 85 percent of the 200 urban women were covered by health insurance and old-age pensions. Yet once they were laid off, even among those who found "stable employment" (we defined the term as "an employment continued for three months or more) at their first job after the lay-off, there only around 20 percent of them were still covered by social insurance arrangements and by permitted sick leave. As for those in "unstable employment" (i.e. less than three months), social insurance and various benefits had almost all disappeared.

Table 4.4 Did your employer provide these social security payments and allowances?

	1. Laid-off workers/before dismissal				2. Laid-off workers/first stable job after dismissal			
	Yes	No	Don't know	Valid responses	Yes	No	Don't know	Valid responses
Heath insurance	168	23	5	196	12	43	1	56
Old-age pension	165	26	5	196	11	43	2	56
Unemployment insurance	156	27	12	195	10	44	2	56
Industrial injury insurance	74	81	40	195	3	47	6	56
Sick leave	150	39	6	195	8	45	3	56
Maternity leave	147	41	7	195	7	45	4	56
Housing allowance	122	57	16	195	3	50	3	56
Paid holidays	130	58	7	195	5	49	2	56

	3. Laid-off workers/unstable job after dismissal				4. Migrant workers (comprehensive insurance)			
	Yes	No	Don't know	Valid responses	Yes	No	Don't know	Valid responses
Health insurance	1	73	0	74	137	68	0	205
Old-age pension	2	71	1	74	137	68	0	205
Unemployment insurance	1	73	0	74	137	68	0	205
Industrial injury insurance	0	74	0	74	137	68	0	205
Sick leave	0	74	0	74				
Maternity leave	0	74	0	74				
Housing allowance	0	74	0	74				
Paid holidays	1	72	1	74				

*1–3 respondents were laid-off women workers with Shanghai residential registration. 4 was put to migrant women workers.

Some 67 percent of migrant women workers are covered by a social insurance package, a figure that suggests that migrants are better protected in terms of a social safety net than those urban workers that have been laid off (Table 4.4). However, we need to realize that the migrant workers' social insurance package is completely different from that of urban residents. Initially, migrant workers are not covered by any social insurance unless they return to their home village. In 2002, the Shanghai Municipal Government launched a new social security program called "Wailai Renshi Zonghe Baoxian" (A Comprehensive Security for Non-local Persons) which was designed exclusively for workers who did not have Shanghai residential registration. This program covers industrial injury, hospital admission, and old age. In addition, medical expenses are reimbursed up to a ceiling of 20 RMB per month. Two notable aspects of this new social insurance package are: (a) the contribution is made solely by the employers; and (b) the amount of the contribution is fixed, regardless of the differences in wage levels among the migrant workers. The contribution is calculated using the average wages of Shanghai employees during the previous year.[11] For example, in 2005, when we carried out the survey, the amount of contribution was 152.5 RMB for every migrant worker. This is quite a small amount compared to the local social insurance program for urban residents, and the program spread quickly among the migrant workers. At the end of 2004, the number of workers covered by this new insurance package had already reached 2.06 million. At the same time, the level of insurance reimbursement is so low that the prospect of using the insurance to support oneself during one's old age is an unrealistic one.

Taking these facts into account, the migrant workers' social safety net is by no means superior to that of the laid-off locals. The new program is in effect an insurance scheme with a low level of contribution and reimbursement, and as such is more of a minimum social support than a sufficient safeguard. Moreover, the provision of a separate social security scheme for migrants may institutionally consolidate disparities between locals and migrants. This means that both the migrants and the laid-off workers must somehow find a way to survive with little support from social welfare.

This prompted us to ask in our survey who migrant women turn to for help when they encounter a problem that is difficult to handle on their own. The results are shown in Table 4.5. We can see from the table that to find a job, the overwhelming majority answered that they would first turn to relatives for help. Their next choice was friends and fellow countryfolk. Few said that they would ask the local community

Table 4.5 Migrant women workers' replies to the question "Who do you to approach for help when you face the following problems?"

Issues	Relatives*	Fellow countryfolk	Neighborhood people	Friends	Your employer	Trade union	Judicial court	Local government	Government back home	Migrants' NGOs	Mass media	Others	Take no action	Total
1. Seeking new job														
1st choice	113	30	1	21	18	4	4	2	0	4	3	0	4	204
2nd choice	8	30	3	62	10	1	1	7	0	20	6	5	2	155
2. Unexpected amount of financial needs occurred														
1st choice	142	21	0	23	12	0	0	1	0	4	0	1	0	204
2nd choice	4	38	2	75	13	4	0	3	0	8	0	2	2	151
3. Serious injury/ illness														
1st choice	123	22	0	19	27	1	1	3	0	6	1	0	1	204
2nd choice	6	34	3	48	24	12	1	7	2	10	0	2	4	153
4. Wage payment delayed/cut without just reason														
1st choice	36	16	q1	6	49	2	12	54	0	22	1	1	4	204
2nd choice	4	9	2	11	11	6	2	17	0	76	5	0	5	148
5. Lack or safety in workplace														
1st choice	44	18	2	7	62	3	22	20	0	23	0	1	1	203
2nd choice	1	12	0	11	15	2	20	21	0	54	5	4	5	150
6. Unjust dismissal														
1st choice	27	15	1	4	39	1	25	60	0	20	0	3	8	203
2nd choice	1	9	0	8	7	2	5	15	0	89	5	2	7	150

*Relatives that are not parents, brothers or sisters.

(neighborhood) for help. From these answers, we can assume that migrant workers feel that their personal connections that remain rooted in their home village are more effective than their connections with the host community. One of the interesting reactions was that when migrant women workers fall ill or face financial difficulties, more of them consider talking directly to their employers rather than approaching their trade union. This may be due to the size of their workplace. Many migrant workers are hired by small and medium-sized companies, so it is likely that the distance between employer and employee is close enough for the employer to show some kind of paternalism and compensate for the lack of social security.

In respect of labor disputes, many migrants apparently do not depend on help from relatives or from friends back in their home villages. Their first choice of someone to assist them is their employer or the local government authorities. Between the two, over questions relating to delays in wage payment and unjust dismissals, those approaching local government authorities for help significantly outnumbered those who turned to employers for assistance. More significantly, perhaps, almost none of the workers would turn to trade unions for help over labor-related trouble, even though trade unions are supposed to represent workers in the tripartite consultation system. Even the second-best choice in such issues is not the unions but the beneficial associations for migrant workers (the NGOs).

According to Yang's study, in Shanghai a noteworthy effort has been made to establish trade unions not inside companies, but based in communities, thus increasing the opportunities for migrant workers in private enterprises to join trade unions. The campaign started in 1999 and by March 2003, 101 community-based unions were organized at *jiedao* (neighborhood) level. As a result, the unionization rate in private enterprises reached 96.94 percent, and trade union membership rate rose to 98.49 percent (Yang 2006: 36).

If Yang's survey reflects the reality of unionization as it affects migrant workers, it appears from Table 4.4 that migrant workers have low expectations for the ability of trade unions to solve their actual labor issues regardless of the unions' ready accessibility. The results in Table 4.5 also suggest that the local judicial courts, which hardly featured in the answers concerning livelihood issues, are thought to be more reliable than friends and home countryfolk in labor-related issues, especially for troubles related to workplace safety and unjust dismissal.

In essence, when labor-related grievances are felt, migrant workers consider negotiating with employers individually, or appeal directly to the local government or the local judicial court rather than seeking trade union support. On September 22, 2006, I myself witnessed sit-in protestors at the main gate of the Guangdong Provincial Government in Guangzhou. About 20 elderly women were holding up a banner demanding fair treatment for former state-owned enterprise retirees. When I asked one of the protestors why they were demonstrating, she answered that she had been laid off by a state-owned enterprise and was receiving an old age pension from their former employer at that time but found the amount unbearably low. A slogan on the banner also insisted that the amount of their pension was insufficient even for survival per se. This could be seen as an example of a direct appeal by the workers to the local government over a grievance toward employers on an issue of social security.

Furthermore, our questionnaire survey in Shanghai confirmed that the unemployed women registered in Shanghai follow a similar trend (Table 4.6). For personal financial needs, local unemployed women are most likely to call on their relatives for assistance. The only preference that differed between migrants and local unemployed women was the importance that was given to neighborhood organizations. In all categories of difficulties other than the financial, unemployed women picked the neighborhood organization as their choice. Local social welfare institutions are a secondary choice following neighborhood organizations and former colleagues. In respect of unjust dismissals, the most frequent replies were "not to take any action", but we cannot decide whether to attribute this to their sense of helplessness or to the age range of the respondents. The majority of the unemployed women in our survey were middle aged or older, so there is a possibility that their passive attitude stems from the expectation of receiving an old age pension in the foreseeable future. At any rate, so far as the respondents were concerned, turning in the first place to the trade unions for assistance was out of the question. Unemployed urban women perceive judicial courts to be more effective than trade unions.

The above findings suggest that despite recent attempts by the Chinese government to institutionalize tripartite labor relations consultation, and despite the efforts of the trade unions to expand membership among private sector employees, trade unions figure hardly at all among workers who have employment grievances or who have work-related problems to solve. We can safely say, therefore, that the tripartite labor relation consultation to date has not measured up to the expectation of exerting a stabilizing influence on fragile labor relations at a time of rapid transformation.

Table 4.6 Replies of unemployed women with Shanghai residential registration to the question in Table 4.5

	Relatives*	Former colleague	Neighborhood organization	Social security agency	Trade union	Judicial court	Re-recruitment service center	NGO	Mass media	Others	Take no action	Total
1. unexpected amount of financial needs occurred												
1st	123	12	52	6	0	0	1	0	0	0	4	198
2nd	9	8	68	40	6	4	17	0	1	4	7	164
2. wage payment delayed/cut without justful reason												
1st	36	50	74	13	1	5	0	0	0	1	7	187
2nd	6	7	24	49	17	32	12	1	0	1	6	155
3. unjust dismissal												
1st	34	36	52	19	2	14	3	1	1	0	27	189
2nd	15	0	10	23	9	38	45	3	1	3	7	154

Note: *Relatives that are not parents, brothers, or sisters.

4.6 Conclusions

The Hu Jintao administration, well aware of widening inequalities in Chinese society, has been opening multiple channels to respond to public opinion. According to Aoyama, in the absence of direct popular elections in the PRC, the masses have five options for making their opinions known. These are: (1) to send their opinions to the mass media; (2) to express their views via scholars and experts; (3) to appeal to local representatives; (4) to send petitions or to visit the government directly; and (5) to post messages on Internet bulletin boards. Of these, options (4) and (5) are the ones most frequently used by the general public (Aoyama 2005: 16).

However, both of these methods have their flaws as main channels of communication. The central government has been alarmed by the recent increase in the number of visitors appealing directly to the administration, a phenomenon that has been led to the creation of their own settlement, known as "petitioners' village", in Beijing. The village encountered enforced clearances and in May 2005, the central national government enforced "Regulations on Letters and Visits" which sets a limit to the number of petitioners per visit[12] (Aoyama 2005: 18).

In respect of the postings on Internet bulletin boards, it is true that the Internet, which is becoming increasingly popular in China, has become an important means for the government to monitor public opinion. On January 23, 2007 the China Internet Network Information Center reported that the online population has reached 137 million, which is equivalent to 10.5 percent of the total population. In the case of Beijing, the rate now exceeds 30 percent (CNNIC 2007). But this channel of communication tends not to be available to the poor. As can be seen from the gap between the national average of Internet usage and that in Beijing, Internet access tends to be greater in wealthy coastal areas, and especially in the large cities. This means that there is likely to be a digital divide between urban residents and the peasants.

In search of a more reliable channel for settling labor disputes, the Hu Jintao administration introduced the tripartite labor relations consultation scheme. Its original design could be seen as a variation of state corporatism, but as the reports and surveys in this chapter have shown, of the three Commission representatives, two do not strictly fit the definition of corporatism, being not solely representative of the constituents whose opinions they are supposed to listen to. CEC/CEMA often shares its representative seats with local FICs at the grassroots level, and multiple workers' organizations are active inside enterprises. Furthermore, the tripartite consultation institution has yet to live up to the government's expectation that it will bring stability, as can be seen from prolonged opposition during the drafting procedure of the new *Labor Contract Law*, the last-minute dismissal of workers before the law's enforcement, and labor disturbances in its aftermath.

However, my belief is that tripartite labor relation consultation is meaningful, not as a stabilizer, but as a process for the government to institutionalize workers' rights and as a forum in which the direction of labor policy can be announced. As we have seen, a tripartite consultation institution functions as a labor advisory group under the government's initiative. By establishing tripartite consultation institutions throughout the nation, the government announced to the public that the present administration attaches importance to the rising number of grievances among the workers and that the government has at its disposal a channel to deliver the workers' voices to employers that is supposedly more fair and transparent than individual negotiations or wildcat strikes. In other words, tripartite consultation was a signal given by the Hu Jintao administration that it was anxious to reach local government and to show workers at the grassroots level that their concerns are not being neglected. So far, the local governments are responding to the signal. For example, the Guangdong Provincial Government listed the formation of tripartite labor relations consultation institutions among 11 important policy targets for the year 2007, and has set up such institutions at the prefectural level (Guangdong Provincial Government 2007). The same is true of Shanghai and Quanzhou, to name only two examples (Shanghai Municipal Government 2007; Quanzhou Municipal Government 2006).

This also means that if the government is seeking to resolve workers' actual hardships, it needs to look beyond tripartite labor relations consultation. Our questionnaire survey results show that although the workers mostly depend on families and friends in times of trouble, migrant workers prefer to turn to local governments and NGOs as sources of assistance on labor-related issues rather than to trade unions. In respect of local laid-off workers, they have higher expectations of help from neighborhood organizations and social welfare agencies than from trade unions. The replies suggest that labor relations policy needs to take the social safety net into consideration and to coordinate the social security system with support from community organizations and NGOs. In reality, social security policies for employees have focused on social insurance reforms, which in fact hold are of little significance for migrants and workers who have been laid off. Therefore, my conclusions are that tripartite labor consultation fulfills neither the criteria of corporatism nor the expectation of the government for more secure and stable labor relations through corporatism. Social security reform for maintaining a decent living standard has a greater potential for stabilizing labor relations than existing social insurance reform based on workers' self-responsibility.

Notes

1. Prior to the reform, only employers had been held responsible for the social security premium payment.
2. The hotel abolished the housing pension but compensated for this by adding an extra housing fee to the workers' wages.
3. "Non-state-owned firms" refers to those companies that are neither state-owned nor collectively owned.
4. The number is limited to officially registered unemployment.
5. The issue of unemployed young people has become a focus of public attention as more and more Chinese university graduates encounter difficulties finding jobs. The number of students enrolling for tertiary education has increased dramatically, with the annual number almost tripling in four years from 1.17 million persons in 2001 to 3.4 million in 2005. Meanwhile, however, the placement rate for new graduates dropped from 70 percent in 2004 to 64.7 percent in 2005. The number of students who have failed to a secure job has increased year after year, from 750,000 in 2003 to 990,000 in 2004, reaching 1.2 million in 2005 (You Jun 2005: 198–9). However, if we compare these numbers to that of laid-off workers, both current and previous, the latter is far greater. Nonetheless, the media and the academics in China have shifted their focus of interest from laid-off workers to unemployed new graduates. This probably reflects the shared memory that only a decade ago, university graduates were considered to be an elite and that they were in great demand. It has been quite shocking for the public to witness a rise in unemployment amongst people who have acquired tertiary education degrees and diplomas.
6. More details in Kizaki (1995) and Suehiro (2006).
7. If we include those enterprises that plan to organize trade unions in the near future, the unionization rate for Japanese firms is 74.3 percent and 49.6 percent for American firms (Furusawa 2006: 14).
8. Multiple answers were allowed in this survey (Furusawa 2006: 15). Many media reports confirm that unionization was carried out under the initiative of local governments and local ACFTU branches. In Guangdong Province, where a large number of private and foreign enterprises are concentrated, the Communist Party's Provincial Committee announced on January 26, 2007 that it would set up trade unions inside these companies within five years. In response, the provincial trade unions set themselves the target of raising the unionization rate in foreign-run companies to 80 percent and in private companies to 60 percent (Ri Jing).

9. CEC was founded in 1979 under the name of China Enterprise Management Association (CEMA) and CEDA was established in 1983 under the leadership of the State Economic and Trade Commission (SETC), a central government organ. They were merged into one institution in 1988. CEMA was renamed CEC in April 20, 1999 (Taylor, Kai Chang, Qi Li: 72).
10. This questionnaire survey was funded by JSPS (Japan Society for the Promotion of Science) as a 2005 Grant-in-Aid for Scientific Research Project Number 16402028, entitled *Globalization of Economy and Changes of Gender Regimes in Asia*, led by Professor Nobuko Yokota (Faculty of Economics, Yamaguchi University) as a Principal Researcher. The first draft of the questionnaire was prepared by the present author, and was revised by Dr Zhang Qixin. Dr Zhang was in charge of the distribution and collection of the questionnaires.
11. Amount of contribution = 12 percent × 60 percent × previous year's average wage.
12. Article 18 of the Regulations limited the number of representatives to no more than five. At the same time, the central government demands that local governments respond to petitioners whether the petition is accepted or not, and to solve the issue within sixty days if the petition is accepted (Aoyama 2005: 18).

References

Japanese

Aoyama, Romi. 2005. "Chūgoku ni okeru seron keisei no mekanizumu" [Mechanisms for forming public opinion in China]. *Tōa*, no. 458: 12–21.

Furusawa, Masayuki. 2006. "Chūgoku no kōkai: genzai chūgoku nikkei kigyō ni okeru rōshi kankei no genjō to kadai: 'Gonghui' o meguru jōkyō no kōsatsu" [Trade unions in China: the current situation and the problem of labor relations in China based on Japanese enterprises: observations on issues regarding the "trade union"]. *Kokusai Keizai Rōdō Kenkyū* 64, no. 9: 7–25.

Ishii, Tomoaki. 2006. "Chūgoku ni okeru kōporatizumu no genzai" [Present situation of corporatism in China]. Shinpoziumu hōkokusho "jiritsuka" shakai no gabanansu: gurasu rūto chūgoku no henyō to seiji-teki resuponsu [A symposium paper, "Governance of an 'autonomous' society: changes at grass-roots level in China and the political response"]. Hosei University, Research Institute of Chinese Grass-root Politics, December 10. http://www.i.hosei.ac.jp/~hhishida/001.htm (accessed February 17, 2007).

Ishii, Tomoaki. 2001. "Chūgoku ni okeru rōshi-kankei no tenkai: chūka zenkoku sōkōkai o chūshin ni shite" [Development of labor relations in China: focusing on FACTU]. The Ohara Institute for Social Research, Hosei University, *Ohara shakai mondai kenkyūjo zasshi*, no. 514: 22–49.

Inagaki, Hiroshi. 2005. "Kanan o chūsin to suru chūgoku no rōdōryoku fusoku mondai: jittai wa issō fukakka suru ka" [Labor shortage in China with particular reference to South China: will the situation get worse?] *Mizuho sōken ronshū*, no. 3: 1–57. http://www.mizuho-ri.co.jp/research/economics/pdf/argument/mron0503-2.pdf (accessed January 16, 2006).

Ito, Shoichi. 1998. *Gendai chūgoku no rōdō-shijō* [The labor market in modern China]. Tokyo: Yuhikaku.

Japan Institute for Labor Policy and Training (JIL). 2004. "Chūgoku "rōdōhō" kōfu kara 10 nenkan no seika to kadai" [Achievements and problems ten years after the enactment of the "Trade Union Law"]. 2004–10. http://www.jil.go.jp/foreign/jihou/2004_10/china_01.htm (accessed January 30, 2006).

Japan Institute for Labor Policy and Training (JIL). 2003. "Zenkoku sōkōkai soshikiritsu ga ōhaba kaifuku" [Great recovery in ACFTU's unionization rate]. 2003-03. http://www.jil.go.jp/kaigaitopic/ 2003_03/chinaP01.html (accessed January 30, 2006).

Kamata, Fumihiko. 2006. "Rōdō keiyakuhō (sōan) no kōhyō to iken kōbo" [Disclosure of the labor contract law (draft) and public comments]. *Gaikoku no rippō*, no. 229: 180–3.

Kizaki, Midori. 1995. *Gendai chūgoku no kokuyū kigyō kaikaku: naibu kōzō kara no shiren* [State-owned enterprise reform in modern China: a test of the internal structure]. Tokyo: Japan Association for Asian Studies.

Kojima, Kazuko. 2006. "Chūgoku no shijō keizaika to 'kōkai' o meguru giron" [Marketization and arguments on "gonghui" (trade unions) in China]. *Ajia Kenkyū* 52, no. 1: 1–18.

Ma, Chengsan. 2000. *Chūgoku shinshutsu kigyō no rōdō mondai: nichibeiō kigyō no hikaku ni yoru kenshō* [Labor issues in FDIs in China: a comparative study of Japanese, American and European enterprises]. Tokyo: Japan External Trade Organization.

Peng, Guanghua. 2002. "Chūgoku kaisei kōkai (rōdō kumiai) hō no seiritsu to kadai" [Enactment and problems of trade union law revision]. *Hōsei Kenkyū* (Kyushu University) 69, no. 1: 93–116.

Peoples Daily. 2002. "Zenkoku kōshōren shikkōi de hi-kōyūsei no daihyō ga hansū ijō ni" [The representatives from non-publicly-owned-enterprises reach a majority on the ACFIC's executive committee]. Peoples Daily Online. 2002-11-28. http://j.peopledaily.com.cn/2002/11/28/jp20021128_23749.htm (accessed January 31, 2007).

Suehiro, Akira, ed. 2006. *Higashi Ajia no fukushi shisutemu no yukue: kigyō nai fukushi to kokka no shakai hoshō seido (ronten no seiri to deeta shu)* [The nature of social security systems in East Asia: enterprise-based welfare and social welfare of the various countries (summary of moot points and data)]. Institute of Social Science, University of Tokyo.

Tsukamoto, Takatoshi. 2006. *Chūgoku no kokuyū kigyō to rōdō irō hoshō* [State owned enterprises and labor and health security in China]. Tokyo: Otsuki Shoten.

Uehara, Kazuyoshi. 2000. "Kokuyū kigyō kaikaku to rōdōsha" [State owned enterprise reform and workers]. In *Gendai chūgoku no kōzō hendō: keizai kōzōhenkō to shijōka* [Economic fluctuations in modern China: economy, structural fluctuations, and marketization], ed. Nakagane Katsuji. Tokyo: University of Tokyo Press.

Yamamoto, Tsuneto. 2000. *Gendai chūgoku no rōdō keizai (1949–2000): "gōriteki teichingin seido" kara gendai rōdō shijō e* [Labor economics of modern China (1949–2000): from the "rational low wage system" to the modern labor market]. Tokyo: Sōdosha.

Yan, Shanping.2005. *Chūgoku no jinkō idō to minkō: makuro-mikuro deeta ni motozuku keisan bunseki* [Migration and migrant workers in China: Econometric analysis based on macro and micro data]. Tokyo: Keiso-Shobo.

Chinese

All China Federation of Industry and Commerce (ACFIC). 2006. "Zhonghua quanguo gongshanglian jienjie" [ACFIC: a brief introduction]. ACFIC. http://www.acfic.org.cn/cenweb/portal/user/anon/page/introducePage.page (accessed February 2, 2006).

All-China Federation of Trade Unions (ACFTU). 2002. *Zhongguo guonghui tongji nianjian 2001* [China trade unions statistical yearbook 2001]. Beijing: China Statistics Press.

Anhui Federation of Industry and Commerce. 2006. "Anhui-sheng Wuhu-shi jianli xietiao laodong guanxi sanfang huiyi zhidu" [Wuhu Municipality in Anhui Province establishes tripartite labor relations consultation institution]. http://www.acfic.org.cn/cenweb/portal/user/anon/page/acfic_CMSItemInfoPage.page?appId=00000000000000000122&category=030010020130&metainfoId=BBC00000000000014966 (accessed February 17, 2007).

Cao, Chen. 2008. "Yuhang District Tripartite Labor Relation Consultation's Meeting Called by the District Federation of Industry and Commerce", Yuhang District FIC. December 24, http://www.hzgcc.org/xqcz.asp?id=3050 (accessed January 3, 2009)

Channel NewsAsia. 2007. "Mingong Shiwei Kangyi Gongtou Tuoqian Gongzi" [Migrant workers hold demonstration to protest about arrears of wages from a laborshark]. 2007-02-05. http://www.asianews.it/view4print.php?=zh&art=840, (accessed February 15, 2007).

Chang, Kai. 1995. *Laodong guanxi, laodong-zhe, laoquan* [Labor relations, workers, and workers' rights]. Beijing: Zhongguo Laodong Chubanshe.

China Business Times. 2007. "Sun Xiaohua chuxi 'laodong hetongfa' zhengshou xiugai yijian zuotanhui" [Sun Xiaohua attends public hearing round-table discussion on revision of "Labor Contract Law"]. 01-22.

China Enterprise Confederation/China Enterprise Directors Association (CEC/CEDA). 2003. "Zhongguo qiye lianhe hui, zhongguo qiyejia xiehui zhangcheng (xiuzheng'an) [Constitution of CEC & CEDA (revised draft)]. CEC/CEDA. 09-15, http://www.cec-ceda.org.cn/china/zc.php (accessed January 2, 2009).

China Internet Network Information Center (CNNIC). 2007. "di 19 ci zhongguo hulian wangluo fazhan zhuangkuang tongji diaocha" [19th statistical survey on the development of the Internet in China]. CNNIC. 01-23. http://www.cnnic.cn/uploadfiles/pdf/2007/1/23/113114.pdf (accessed January 31, 2007).

China Labor Market Info Monitor Center. 2006. "2006 di san jidu bufen chengshi laodongli shichang gongqiu zhuangkuang fenxi" [Supply and demand analysis of the labor market in selected cities in the third quarter of 2006]. http://www.lm.gov.cn/gn/data/2006-10/27/content_141073.htm (accessed November 6, 2006).

Chinese People's Political Consultative Conference (CPPCC). 2007. "Wang Zhongyu". 02-14, http://www.cppcc.gov.cn/English/cv/vcm/200702150145.htm (accessed January 2, 2009).

Department of Population and Social, Science and Technology Statistics, National Bureau of Statistics, Department of Planning and Finance, Ministry of Labor and Social Security, 2005. *Zhongguo tongji nianjian 2005* [China labor statistical yearbook, 2005]. Beijing: China Statistics Press.

Guangdong Provincial Government. 2007. "Guangdong zhengfu 2007 nian gongzuo baogao" [Guangdong provincial government annual activity report, 2007]. http://www.e-gov.org.cn/ziliaoku/news002/200703/54337.html (accessed April 28, 2007).
Huang, Mengfu. 2007. "Walk Firmly and Unshakably Down the Path of Socialism with Chinese Characteristics, Make Great Effort to Create a New Phase for ACFIC: Report to the ACFIC 10th Congress (Report on Top Ten Issues)", ACFIC. November 22, http://www.acfic.org.cn/cenweb/portal/user/anon/page/acfic_CMSItemInfoPage.page?metainfoId=ABC00000000000021103 (accessed January 1, 2009).
Kang Xiaoguang. 1999. "Jingji zengzhang, shehui gongzheng, minzhu fazhi yu hefaxing jichu" [Economic growth, social justice, democratic governance and the foundation of legitimacy], *Zhanlue yu Guanli*, no. 4.
Li, Jungfeng. 2005. *Zhongguo fei-zhenggui jiuye yanjiu* [Research on atypical employment in China]. Zhengzhou: Henan People Publishing House.
Li, Sugu. 2005. "Beijing Shanghai Shenzhen Xi'an Fujian dengdi fenbie tiaogao zuidi gongzi biaozhun" [Minimum wage standards adjusted to higher level in Beijing, Shanghai, Shenzhen Xi'an Fujian and other regions] Chinanews.com. 2005-07-01. http://www.chinanews.com.cn/news/2005/2005-07-01/26/593723.shtml# (accessed February 5, 2006).
Ministry of Labor and Social Security (MOLSS). 2006. "Guojia xietiao laodong guanxi sanfang huiyi dishici huiyi jiyao" [Bulletin of the tenth national tripartite labor relations consultation conference]. http://www.molss.gov.cn/gb/ywzn/2006-12/11/content_152776.htm (accessed February 15, 2007).
Ministry of Labor and Social Security (MOLSS). 2005. "2004 nian laodong he shehui baozhang shiye fazhan gongbao" [2004 annual statistical report on development of the labor and social-security project]. http://www.molss.gov.cn/column/index_p5.htm (accessed January 27, 2006).
Ministry of Labor and Social Security (MOLSS). 2004a. "Jiti hetong guiding" [Collective contract regulation]. MOLSS order no. 22, promulgated 2004-01-20. http://www.molss.gov.cn/news/2004/0205b.htm, (accessed January 31, 2006).
Ministry of Labor and Social Security (MOLSS). 2004b. "Zuidi gongzi guiding" [Minimum wage regulation]. MOLSS order no. 21, promulgated 2004-1-20. http://www.molss.gov.cn/news/2004/0205b.htm, (accessed January 31, 2006).
body-politic labor sum social-security part subject group – [2004 MOLSS Project Team. 2004. "Guanyu mingong duanque de diaocha baogao" A survey report on the migrant labor shortage]. http://www.molss.gov.cn/news/2004/0908a.htm (accessed January 31, 2006).
Mo, Rong. 2004. *Jiye Lanpi shu 2003–2004 nian: Zhongguo jiuyebaogao: Zhongguo jiji jiuyezhengce de shijian* [Blue book of Chinese employment 2003–2004: China's active employment policy in practice]. Beijing: Zhongguo Laodong Chubanshe.
Mo, Rong. 2003 *Jiye Lanpi shu 2002 nian: jingji tizhi gaige he jiegou tiaozheng zhong de jiuye wenti* [Blue book of Chinese employment 2002: Employment issues under economic system reform and structural adjustment, and China's active employment policy in practice]. Beijing: Zhongguo Laodong Chubanshe.
Quanzhou Municipal Government. 2006. "Quanzhou-shi zhengfu gongzuo baogao (zhaiyao)" [Quanzhou municipal government's annual activity report (summary)]. http://www.e-gov.org.cn/ziliaoku/news002/200612/45044.html (accessed April 28, 2007).

Ri, Jing. 2007. "Shijie 500 qiang zaiyue qiye jinnian quan yao jian gonghui" [All the top 500 enterprises in Guangdong must establish unions this year]. Jinyang Net. 2007-01-26. http://www.ycwb.com.2007-01/26/content_1364710.htm, (accessed January 30, 2007).

Shanghai Municipal Government. 2007. "Shanghai-shi 2007 nian zhengfu gongzuo baogao" [Shanghai municipal government annual activity report, 2007]. http://www.e-gov.org.cn/ziliaoku/news002/200701/48142.html (accessed April 28, 2007).

Sun Chunlan. 2008. "Sun Chunlan zai quanzong 14 jie 6 ci zhiwei huiyi shang de gongsuo baogao (zhaiyao)" [The Work Report Delivered at the Sixth Session of 14th ACFTU Executive Committee (Abstract)]. ACFTU. 2008-09-25, http://www.acftu.org/template/10004/file.jsp?cid=318&aid=80816 (accessed February 31, 2008).

Yang, Pengfei. 2006. "Xin-hezuo zhuyi nengfou zheghe zhongguo de laozi guanxi: yi Shanghai shi de shijian wei li" [Can neo-cooperation coordinate relations between labor and capital in China? A case study of practices in Shanghai]. Shanghai: Shanghai Academy of Social Science. *Journal of Social Sciences*. no. 8: 32–40.

Yang, Yiyong. 1999. *Shiye Chongji bo* [Unemployment shock wave]. Beijing: Jinri Zhongguo Chubanshe.

Yang, Yiyong and Xing Xiaobo. 1999. "Xiagang zhigong jiben shenghuo baozhang he zaijiuye de diaocha" [Survey on laid-off workers' basic livelihood protection and re-employment]. In 1999 *Zhongguo shehui xingshi fenxi yu yuce* [1999 Analysis and forecast of the Chinese social situation (blue book of Chinese society)]. In ed. Ru Xin, Lu Xueyi, and Li Peilin. Beijing: Social Sciences Academic Press.

You, Jun. 2005. *Jiye Lanpi shu 2005 nian: tongchou chengxiang jiuye* [Blue book of Chinese employment, 2005: Unifying plan for urban–rural employment]. Beijing: China Labor and Social Security Publishing House.

Zhang, Jing. 1998. *Fatuan zhuyi* [Corporatism]. Beijing: Social Sciences Academic Press.

Zhang, Yanning and Chen Lantong, ed. 2005. *Zhongguo Qiye laodong guanxi Zhuangkuang Baogao 2005* [Report on labor relations situation in Chinese enterprises, 2005]. Beijing: Enterprise Management Publishing House.

Zheng, Bingwen. 2002. "Hezuo zhuyi: Zhongguo fuli zhidu kuangjia de chonggou" [Corporatism: Restructuring the framework of the social security system in China]. *Economic Research Journal*. no. 2: 71–9.

Zhong, Lan. 2002. "Fenxi 3: Shehui baozhang jianquan, laozhe yannian yishou" [Analysis 3: Social security improves, elderly longevity extends yearly]. National Bureau of Statistics, 2002-03-31. http://www.stats.gov.cn/tjfx/ztfx/zgsnrjzs/t20020628_23975.htm (accessed February 3, 2006).

Zhou, Fang. 2004. "'zuidi gongzi guiding' zhongdian shiyi" [Solving questions on important points of the "minimum wage regulation"]. Jinyang net. 2004-03-03. http://www.ycwb.com/gb/content/2004-03/03/content_650756.htm (accessed February 5, 2006).

English

Chan, Anita, and Jonathan Unger. 1995. "China, Corporatism and the East Asian Model." *Australian Journal of Chinese Affairs*, no. 33: 29–53.

Oi, Jean. 1992. "Fiscal Reform and the Economic Foundation of Local State Corporatism in China." *World Politics*, no. 45: 99–126.
Taylor, Bill, Kai Chang and Qi Li. 2003. *Industrial Relations in China*. Cheltenham: Edward Elgar Publishing.
White, Gordon, Jude A. Howell and Shang Xiaoyuan. 1996. *In Search of Civil Society: Market Reform and Social Change in Contemporary China* (IDS Development Studies Series). Oxford: Clarendon Press.
Zhu Zhe. 2006. "Vote on Labor Contract Law Put Off." *China Daily*, December 27.

5
The Tripartite Relationship and Social Policy in Taiwan: Searching for a New Corporatism?

Yasuhiro Kamimura

Introduction

The purpose of this chapter is to shed light on how tripartite relations in Taiwan have changed since the 1980s, and also to highlight the influence of these changes on social policy related to labor market flexibility. It should be noted that 1980 was the year when leaders of the Democratic Progressive Party fought against the previous authoritarian system as defendants or lawyers in the "Kaohsiung Incident." Ten years later, in 1990, President Lee Teng-hui of the Nationalist Party pushed for democratic reform; if we again advance ten years further, in 2000, the Democratic Progressive Party administration gained power for the first time. It is impossible to give a full elaboration of this turbulent period in Taiwan's history in just a few pages.

To make clear the changes in tripartite relations, rather than simply following a chronological table, it will probably be more effective to describe the following three elements as ideal types. The first element is the legacy of state corporatism, which still remains after the lifting of martial law in 1987. The second element is the trend of pluralism, which goes back to 1984. The third element is the emergence of social corporatism since 2001. These three elements, rather than each representing a discrete period of history, continue to coexist while struggling against each other in present-day Taiwan.

As a result, this chapter is structured as follows. Section 5.1 relies on Schmitter's theory of corporatism to explain how to compose and apply the above-mentioned ideal types. In section 5.2 there is a description of the elements of state corporatism in Taiwan's tripartite relations, considering them at both the national level and the enterprise level. Section 5.3 deals with elements of pluralism which were formed through the different stages of democratization. In section 5.4, there is an analysis of two advisory council meetings held under the Democratic Progressive Party administration, in order to reveal the emergence of social corporatism, the legacy of state corporatism and the elements of pluralism, and to measure the effect that these three conflicting elements have on social policy. Finally, in section 5.5 there is an analysis concerning the nature of the flexible labor market in Taiwan, which works independently of the political process, and how it is related to social policy.

5.1 Corporatism as a cognitive tool

In this chapter I would like to invoke Schmitter's famous concept of corporatism as an auxiliary tool in order to identify the locations of tripartite relations and social policy in Taiwan. However, this concept is quoted, not because it literally represents Taiwan's political structure, nor because Schmitter himself has listed Taiwan as an example of a corporatist regime (Schmitter 1979: 11). The purpose is rather to describe the actual issues that Taiwan is facing, by measuring the deviation of Taiwan's current political structure from Schmitter's concept of corporatism. Ideal types are to be used in this way. Here I would like to summarize very briefly the differences between corporatism and pluralism, and the two subcategories of corporatism.

According to Schmitter, in corporatism the number of interest groups in each category is limited, and the inner structure of each group is ordered hierarchically like a pyramid. These groups are granted a representational monopoly within each category by the state, in exchange for accepting certain controls and assistance from the state (ibid.: 13). Although Schmitter devised this ideal type when he was observing the Brazilian and Portuguese political systems, he found that it is also applicable to many countries in Europe and Latin America.

The concept of corporatism was proposed as an alternative to the pluralist theory that occupied the mainstream of American political science at that time. According to the pluralist theory, various interest groups are organized, in unrestricted competition, and having horizontal relationships with each other. Each group is organized voluntarily, and they are neither subject to controls or assistance from the state, nor granted a representational monopoly by the state (ibid.: 15). It can be said that the pluralist model was an ideal type drawing on the reality of American society of those days.

According to Schmitter, the way corporatism appears, and the character it assumes as a result, varies greatly between advanced countries and latecomer countries. In advanced countries, in order to maintain the stability of the highly developed capitalist system over the long term, interest groups voluntarily and slowly develop corporatism from below (social corporatism). The number of interest groups becomes gradually restricted as the result of deliberations among existing groups, and in response to requests from these groups, they are recognized and assisted by the state (ibid.: 20, 23, 38). This is a feature of the "neocorporatism" found in postwar western countries.

On the other hand, in latecomer countries, in order to overcome immediate critical situations such as internal strife or external subordination, the state builds up corporatism compulsorily and suddenly from above (state corporatism). The numbers of interest groups are restricted by force and they are compelled to accept controls and assistance from the state (ibid.). These are features of regimes that were seen in countries such as those of the postwar Iberian Peninsula and Latin America. Schmitter puts this type of corporatism together with former corporatism systems such as those of Fascist Italy and Nazi Germany (ibid.: 22), and he distinguishes it from neocorporatism (Schmitter 1982: 268).

Drawing on all of these theoretical models, I will now outline the hypothesis of this chapter which deals with the history of tripartite relations in Taiwan after the 1980s. With democratization in the latter half of the 1980s, the model of government–labor–management relations changed from *state corporatism* into *pluralism*. However, since the latter half of the 1990s, when Taiwan was facing an adverse economic situation, a search for a policy-making style of *social corporatism* started.[1] This was also because of the rapid change in the industrial structure posed by the shifting of the production base to mainland China which, accompanied by the economic crisis, demanded some kind of policy agreement and cooperation between the Taiwan government, labor organizations and management. For the following reasons, however, the path toward a new corporatism has to be a bumpy road.

First, the legacy of state corporatism interferes with the formation of social corporatism. As Schmitter states, in a country where state corporatism has once taken root, the transition toward social corporatism becomes extremely difficult. This is because the formal organizations built up by state corporatism neither function voluntarily nor can have the support of the general members. Schmitter predicted that in such a country, there is no other choice than to "degenerate" into fractious pluralism (Schmitter 1979: 41).

Secondly, since the 1980s, adverse conditions for social corporatism have started to appear even in advanced western countries. According to Schmitter, adverse conditions for social corporatism may occur in the following six places: (1) Rebellion of the general members: The general members of unions stop following the undemocratic union leaders who are entangled in symbiotic relationships with tripartite counterparts. (2) Class mobilization: The working classes, who think that corporatism is a disadvantageous transaction for them, are mobilized into a left-wing party and aim at a socialist revolution. (3) Newly licensed organizations: The affiliation of ethnic groups and feminist groups, which were not previously members of corporatism, makes corporatist decision-making difficult. (4) Single-issue movements: People who focus on new issues such as ethnicity, gender and environment, attack corporatism from the outside. (5) Civil servants and professional politicians rebel against corporatist practices. (6) The capitalist class, which thinks that corporatism is a disadvantageous transaction for itself, returns to neo-liberalism. Schmitter gave special importance to the possibility of 4 and 6 (Schmitter 1982: 267). Probably some of these adverse conditions will strike mercilessly at Taiwan's infant social corporatism.

Researchers in Taiwan object to the immediate application of the abovementioned tools proposed by Schmitter to Taiwan's system of tripartite relations. They maintain that tripartite relations in Taiwan before democratization cannot be termed state corporatism. I think that such objections stem from a misunderstanding in the method of using an ideal type. I would like to briefly introduce these objections and refute them.

First, according to Hong Shi-cheng, labor unions in Taiwan were simply instruments used to legitimize the party-state regime, and their role in interest representation was very limited. Hong argues that identifying this with state corporatism by merely considering the formal aspect leads to overlooking the importance of interest representation in the theory of corporatism (Hong 2006: 67). However, in corporatism there are two aspects – representation and control – and the degree of effectiveness of each aspect varies depending on the country. The weak function of Taiwan's unions in representation is not sufficient reason to reject the state corporatism hypothesis.

Next, according to Huang Chang-ling, the CFL (the Chinese Federation of Labor) did not have the ability to express the interests of the working class nor the instruments to control lower-level unions. In Taiwan neither wages nor employment were regulated by corporatism. Therefore, it is not possible to assert the existence of state corporatism simply by judging from appearances (Huang 2002: 312). Certainly it is likely that in Taiwan at the time, the type of tripartite relations might not be considered as typical state corporatism. But its features will be clearly highlighted when compared with the ideal type of state corporatism.

Finally, according to Shen Tzong-ruey, Taiwan's interest groups were controlled by the KMT (Nationalist Party) government and their role in decision-making was not significant. Shen argues that although it would be more appropriate to consider Taiwan's regime to be a hybrid of state corporatism and monism (totalitarianism), the features of state corporatism finally became more prominent in the 1980s (Shen 2001: 109). However, it is what Shen calls a "hybrid" type that closely resembles the ideal type of state corporatism. After the 1980s, on the other hand, one can gain greater insight by comparing Taiwan's regime with the ideal type of pluralism.

In any case, there is no use in confusing the ideal type with reality or worrying about the difference between them. Obviously, an ideal type, being a model, does not correspond exactly to reality. It is important to handle the concept of corporatism as a cognitive tool. Firstly, a researcher should examine the characteristics of the model itself and the way it operates. The next step is to interpret the historical facts by comparing them with the model. In the following sections, I would like to interpret the situation of Taiwan by referring to the models which were examined in this section.

5.2 Legacy of state corporatism

How close to the ideal type of state corporatism were tripartite relations in Taiwan before democratization? In addition, how does this continue to affect Taiwan after democratization? Here, I would like to consider industrial relations at both the national level and the enterprise level.

5.2.1 Industrial relations at the national level

Features close to Schmitter's ideal type of "state corporatism" could be seen in the tripartite relations of Taiwan before democratization. This can be observed in both the ideological and the organizational aspects.

The ideological characteristics have been expressed in the following text of the Nationalist Party called the "Basic Principles of the Labor Policy of *Sanmin-zhuyi* (the Three Principles of the People)" (1951) (Fan 2004: 263).

1. The interests of the people exceed the interests of the classes. The essence of labor policy in liberalist states is individual interest; the essence of nationalist labor policy is to strengthen the national power for preparing war of aggression; the essence of labor policy in the Soviet Union is class interests. On the one hand, the labor policy of Sanmin-zhuyi considers the people's interest as the core. However, it pursues the freedom and equality of the people, differing from aggressive nationalism. It pursues the happiness of the whole nation, differing from nationalism which, in the name of industrial harmony, in effect submits the workers to the command of capitalists.

2. Industrial harmony. So far no opposition can be observed between capital and labor in China. It is because opposition is annulled by applying the principle of restricting private capital,[2] and by promoting harmony and cooperation in order to attain the purpose of welfare for the whole nation, and by preventing various evils seen in capitalist societies such as the UK and the USA.

3. Social democratization. The principle of so-called social democratization points out that the organization and activities of workers should be returned to the free will of the workers; and that the government should put neither pressure nor force on them.

In essence, it declares that the people's interests should be pursued through industrial harmony, and that the government should prepare the conditions for this harmony, though retaining its position in the western bloc. In response, the labor organization, having as its first goal the winning of the war against the Communist Party, was willing to avoid labor disputes in a spirit of industrial cooperation (Fan 2004: 301).[3]

Though it could be said that such industrial harmony is no more than an ideology, it legitimized the following type of organizational structure. The structure of the organizations stipulated here clearly shows the features of state corporatism. The following text was extracted from the "Civil Associations Act During the Extraordinary Period", promulgated in mainland China in 1942 and which continued in force until 1989 (Shen 2001: 110).

> Those who engage in occupations must, according to law, organize an occupational organization and join the corresponding organization ... Lower level organizations shall join the upper level organization. (Article 4)

The existence of more than one organization of the same type and the same category within the same region is not allowed, unless it is stipulated separately by law. (Article 8)

Here we can see fulfillment of Schmitter's requirements of corporatism through the use of terms such as "singular", "compulsory", "noncompetitive", "hierarchically ordered", and "functionally differentiated" (Schmitter 1979: 13). Taiwan's economic organizations as well as labor organizations came to be organized under these principles.

There are three economic organizations at the national level. The first is the Chinese National Federation of Industries, representing the manufacturing sector. This federation has its precedent in the Chinese National Association of Industries (established in 1942), and was established in 1948 in Nanking under the Industrial Association Act (Lee 2000: 340; Shen 2001: 115). Later, under the Industrial Group Act enacted in 1974, the federation was reorganized as shown in Figure 5.1, and it was located as part of the "perfect state corporatist model" (Shen 2001: 116).

The second organization is the General Chamber of Commerce of the Republic of China, which represents the service sector, and has a

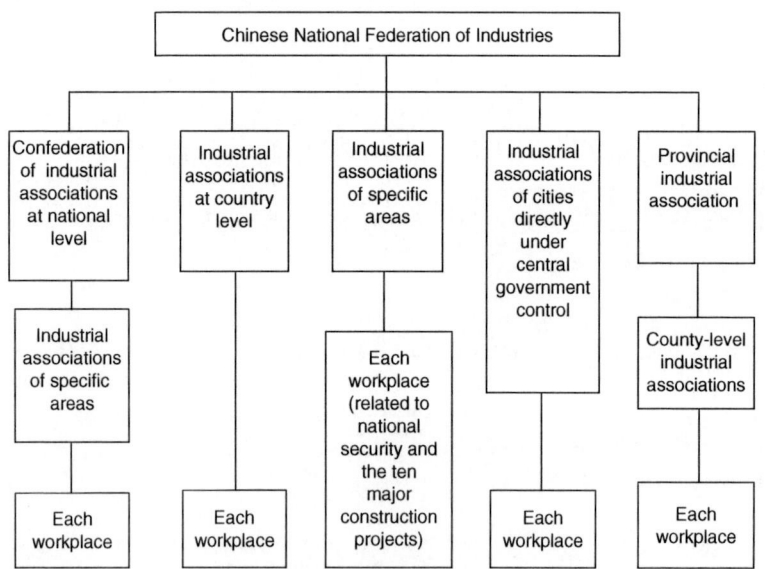

Figure 5.1 Organization chart of the Federation of Industries
Source: Adapted from chart 6.1 of Shen (2001: 117).

similar structure to the first organization. Its predecessor was the National Federation of Chambers of Commerce established in 1946 in Nanking, which was renamed under the Commercial Group Act enacted in 1973.[4] The third is the Chinese National Association of Industry and Commerce, established in 1952; this organization has key major companies as members. Koo Chen-fu, the well-known leader of the Koo's Group and chairman of the Straits Exchange Foundation, held the post of chairman of this association for 33 years from 1961 to 1994. This organization has as a predecessor the Chinese Association of Industry and Trade established upon the proposal by the business leaders of Taiwan before the above two organizations moved to Taiwan;[5] thus, it cannot be affirmed that it presented the features of state corporatism at the time of its establishment. However, of these three organizations, the voice of this one has had the most influence on the government since the pre-democratization period. However, before democratization, these three groups had a close relationship with the KMT (Nationalist Party), as the representatives of these organizations were chosen by the President (Shen 2001: 119).

Before democratization, there was only one labor organization, the Chinese Federation of Labor (CFL), established in 1948. This federation was the only labor organization officially recognized under the Labor Union Law (enacted in 1929). More than two-thirds of its expenses are covered by government subsidies. The KMT sought to use the CFL to mobilize workers, and for this reason it was usual for the chief director of the CFL to be appointed as a member of the legislature (Chen et al. 2003: 322). The CFL was structured as shown in Figure 5.2 (Shen 2001: 118). The structure was similar to that of the Chinese National Federation of Industries shown in Figure 5.1, so one can see that a corporatist regime was established at least in the formal sense.

Above I used the expression "formal" because there are doubts as to whether, in reality, the pyramidal organization placing the CFL at the top functioned actively. On this point I am in agreement with the Taiwanese researchers introduced in section 5.1. Labor unions in Taiwan were usually only nominal and kept unions such as "vase unions" (mere ornamentations) and "bean curd unions" (too fragile) (Hong 2006: 6). Moreover, the CFL was also a kind of "Perennial National Assembly" where the directors who were elected in mainland China remained in office. The retirement of all directors elected in mainland China finally occurred in 1991 (Economic Daily News, March 28). Nevertheless, it is certain that this organization had the function of connecting workers of large public and private enterprises to the party state. Although it was a mere façade, features close to the ideal type of state corporatism were apparently present.

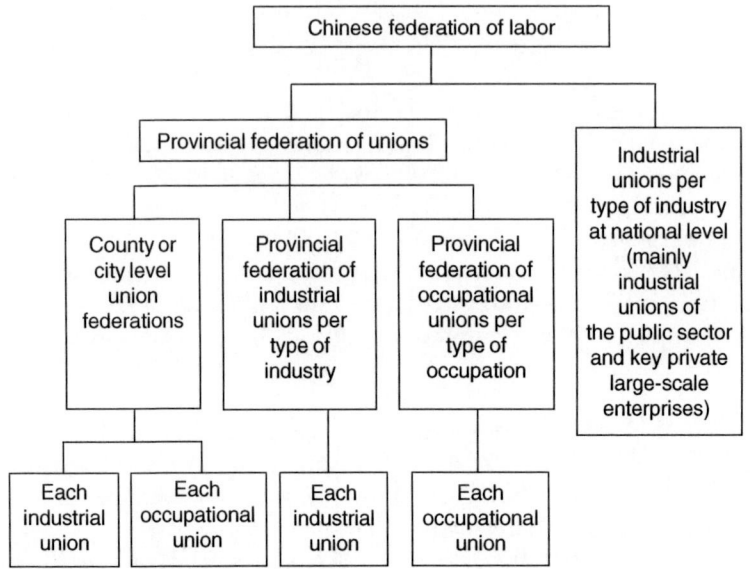

Figure 5.2 Organization chart of the Labor Unions Federation
Source: Adapted from chart 6.2 of Shen (2001: 118).

5.2 Industrial relations at the enterprise level

In order to identify the features of industrial relations in Taiwan, it is necessary to examine them not only at the national level but also at the enterprise level. In order to judge the extent that state corporatism was effective in the past, and the extent that it has changed, it is necessary to understand the corporatism at the enterprise level.

Labor unions in Taiwan are divided into two types under the Labor Union Law, namely "industrial unions" and "occupational unions". Industrial unions are trade unions organized on a company basis. Occupational unions are organized by region, and represent workers who do not work for a specific employer. The latter, rather than calling them unions, should be regarded as mutual aid organizations, where most of the members are self-employed and became affiliated in order to join the labor insurance scheme (it is impossible to join the labor insurance program without being a member of an occupational union) (Chen et al. 2003: 320).[6]

As of 2004, establishments having organized industrial unions numbered 1,109, which represented 3.5 percent of the total number of business establishments with 30 or more employees covered under the

Labor Union Law. The unionization rate of employees is 19.6 percent.[7] As can be seen from these numbers, the arena for union activities is mainly limited to large enterprises.[8]

Industrial relations at the enterprise level in Taiwan are regulated by law. According to the Labor Standards Act (enacted in 1984), "An establishment shall hold meetings to coordinate worker–employer relationships, promote worker–employer cooperation and increase work efficiency" (Article 83). The worker–employer meetings are not an innovation of this law enacted in 1984, as the Factories Act enacted in 1929 already provided for "factory meetings" (Wei 2001: 120). As there are no penal provisions in the abovementioned article 83 of the Labor Standards Act, it cannot be affirmed that such meetings have been held in all establishments. However, as of 2004, worker–employer meetings were set up in 4,386 establishments (947 in the public sector and 3,439 in the private sector),[9] a figure that exceeds the number of the above-mentioned industrial unions. In other words, even in the enterprises where unions have not been set up, room for labor–management consultation is provided. When looking at the activities of the industrial unions, 60 percent of them provide for worker–employer meetings; 15 percent answered that they hold the meetings every month and 16 percent answered that they do so on a quarterly basis. If we look at the average of those enterprises with unions, the meetings are held five times per year.[10] The topics dealt with at these meetings are: company benefits (62 percent), participation in human resource management (56 percent), year-end bonuses (53 percent), and wages (50 percent) (ibid.). Though enterprises holding meetings are limited mainly to large companies, this feature has great importance when considering industrial relations at the enterprise level.

Along with worker–employer meetings, the employees' welfare committees also provide a channel for industrial relations within a company. These committees were set up under the Employees' Welfare Funds Act (enacted in 1943), which made their establishment compulsory. According to the act, at the time of an enterprise's founding, it must set aside 1–5 percent of its total capital as a welfare fund for the employees. In addition, a monthly amount corresponding to 0.05–0.15 percent of the company's business income and 0.5 percent of the salary of each employee must also be contributed. The purpose of the employees' welfare fund is decided by the employees' welfare councils (comprising ten employee representatives and five management representatives), and the decisions of these councils are not directly influenced by the management's human-resource strategy. As of 2004 there were 13,162 establishments with employees' welfare councils,[11] a number that greatly exceeds the number of the abovementioned industrial unions and worker–employer meetings. Table 5.1 gives a breakdown of the benefits offered by the enterprises and those offered by the employees' welfare councils in enterprises where the councils have been established. From this table we can see the important role of the employees' welfare councils in such matters as leisure activities support, emergency assistance funds and scholarships for the children.

Industrial unions in Taiwan are expected to support corporatism at the enterprise level, but as the foregoing discussion shows, these unions have become established in only a portion of the large companies. At the enterprises where unions have not been established, organizations such as the worker–employer meetings and the employees' welfare councils, both stipulated by law, have been in charge of "industrial cooperation", which provides indirect, passive support of state corporatism.

5.3 Democratization and the shift to pluralism

To what extent did the tripartite relations in Taiwan shift toward the pluralist model with the coming of democratization? At the time, how did the legacy of state corporatism operate? In this section I will examine the movements of independent unions in the late 1980s and the 1990s, and the increase in the interest groups after the shift of power in 2000.

5.3.1 Independent labor movement

The year 1984 was the starting point for the independent labor movement in Taiwan. On May 1, while the martial law imposed by the KMT government was still in force, legislators of the "outside-the-party" movement (a force opposing the KMT which would develop into the Democratic Progressive Party in 1986) came together to establish the Taiwan Labor Legal Assistance Association (later the Taiwan Labor Front; hereinafter referred to as the Labor Front). At the beginning this association intended to give logistical support through legal assistance to the labor movement (Taiwan Labor Front 2004: 2). Thereafter, it played a key role in the formation of an independent labor movement not submitting to state corporatism. Moreover, in 1979, following the breaking off of Taiwan–United States relations that year, the Labor Standards Act was enacted under pressure from the United States (ibid.), which helped drive the labor movement.

When martial law was lifted in July 1987, the labor movement rose up in unison. Between the end of 1987 and the spring of 1988,

Table 5.1 Company benefits and employees' welfare council benefits

Size of business entity	Supplied by the company				Total	Supplied by the Employees' Welfare Council				Total
	1–29 workers	30–99 workers	100–299 workers	300 workers or over		1–29 workers	30–99 workers	100–299 workers	300 workers or over	
Company cafeteria	29.8	39.1	52.5	63.0	43.4	2.7	5.1	14.5	29.1	11.2
Company housing	27.1	42.1	44.8	62.1	41.7	1.9	3.5	8.5	13.2	6.0
Group life insurance	23.6	26.2	28.4	47.2	30.3	2.1	4.5	10.2	14.0	6.8
Leisure activities	27.8	29.3	25.3	22.6	26.6	5.7	22.0	38.5	44.4	24.1
Recreation facilities	15.0	12.8	22.6	32.3	19.6	2.9	9.7	25.8	28.8	14.6
Emergency Assistance Fund	17.3	16.2	14.5	23.1	17.8	3.0	12.4	20.4	31.0	14.7
Transportation	10.3	11.3	19.7	31.6	17.0	1.5	1.5	4.6	6.9	3.2
Library facilities	7.3	6.8	19.5	40.3	16.6	1.6	5.1	12.3	21.0	8.6
Scholarship, school expenses	4.5	9.4	16.6	30.2	13.5	2.5	9.2	26.2	36.2	15.8
Daily necessities	5.3	4.9	5.1	14.2	7.2	1.7	3.0	10.6	32.7	10.5
Housing loans	3.3	3.3	5.8	7.7	4.7	1.9	1.7	7.8	11.2	4.9
Nursery facilities	1.9	2.0	1.1	2.4	1.8	0.6	1.0	1.2	2.4	1.2

Source: Government of the Province of Taiwan, Labor Department, Workers' Living Conditions Survey Report, 1997.

there were frequent labor disputes throughout Taiwan over demands such as year-end bonuses, unpaid wages and overtime allowances. In 1988 a large-scale strike was launched by drivers of the Taoyuan Bus Corporation, the Miaoli Bus Corporation and the National Railway. This led to the outbreak of 32 serious disputes nationwide (Hong 2006: 8). Behind these disputes was the powerful organizing strategy by the Taiwan Labor Front, which was then still known as the Taiwan Labor Movement Support Association (Taiwan Labor Front 2004: 2). However, following the 1989 strike at the Far Eastern Chemical Fiber Plant, which was suppressed by over 2,000 policemen, the labor movement and its outburst of activity suffered setbacks (Hong 2006: 8). Next the Taiwan Labor Front (renamed in 1992), while continuing to organize independent unions and building strength, expanded its activity as a social movement organization involved in the promotion of the National Health Insurance and the National Pension Scheme and opposition to the privatization of state-run enterprises (Taiwan Labor Front 2004: 2).

Although the independent labor movement became active in line with the democratization of society, this did not mean an immediate shift to pluralism of tripartite relations. This is because the legacy of state corporatism obstructed the process. As seen in the organizational chart of the Chinese Federation of Labor in Figure 5.2, county- or city-level union federations (local branches of the Chinese Federation of Labor) are formed by occupational unions and industrial unions. Occupational unions consist mainly of unions of self-employed workers who, in exchange for receiving benefits such as subsidies and labor insurance from the government, functioned as a vote-gathering machine for the KMT. As can be seen in Table 5.2,[12] the membership of industrial unions as of 2005 numbered approximately 600,000 workers, which was only a quarter of that of occupational unions. County- or city-level union federations were controlled by the representatives of occupational unions supported by the KMT (Shen 2001: 173). In these circumstances, along with the county- or city-level union federations, a movement to establish county- or city-level federations of industrial unions started to emerge from the mid-1990s. First the Confederation of Trade Unions was established in Taipei County (1994), then in Kaohsiung County (1996), Taipei City and Kaohsiung City (1997) and by 1998 they were already established in several places such as Tainan County, Hsinchu County, Yilan County and Miaoli County (Taiwan Labor Front 2004; Lee 1999: 161). These county- or city-level federations of industrial unions became a part of the Taiwan Confederation of Trade Unions, which will be dealt with in the next section.

Table 5.2 Unionization rate, 1987–2005

	Industrial unions			Occupational unions		
	No. of unions	No. of members	Unionization rate	No. of unions	No. of members	Unionization rate
1987	1,160	703,526	30.7	1,286	1,396,287	36.3
1988	1,285	696,515	29.5	1,680	1,564,070	42.8
1989	1,345	698,118	30.6	1,883	1,721,546	42.8
1990	1,354	699,372	31.3	2,083	2,057,248	50.7
1991	1,350	692,579	29.3	2,217	2,249,187	59.7
1992	1,300	669,083	28.3	2,271	2,389,331	59.7
1993	1,271	651,086	28.5	2,333	2,521,030	61.2
1994	1,237	637,095	27.4	2,382	2,640,738	60.3
1995	1,204	598,479	25.4	2,413	2,537,396	58.1
1996	1,190	587,559	23.6	2,422	2,460,711	56.7
1997	1,196	588,997	23.0	2,427	2,363,886	53.3
1998	1,176	575,606	22.1	2,464	2,345,794	52.1
1999	1,175	613,963	22.5	2,534	2,313,398	50.3
2000	1,128	588,832	20.9	2,613	2,279,498	49.2
2001	1,091	584,337	20.9	2,726	2,295,290	50.9
2002	1,104	561,140	20.3	2,848	2,299,158	49.2
2003	1,103	558,195	19.4	2,902	2,343,777	49.8
2004	1,109	593,907	19.6	3,024	2,370,704	49.0
2005	1,027	618,006	19.6	3,119	2,368,798	48.0

Source: The Council of Labor Affairs, *Yearbook of Labor Statistics 2006*.

While the independent labor movement increased in strength through the 1990s, the unionization rate of industrial unions, on which the movement was based, decreased by some 10 points, from a little over 31 percent in 1990 to less than 21 percent by 2000 (Table 5.2). Although union organizing in Taiwan has been obstructed by an excess of small and medium-sized enterprises, the fall in the unionization rate still seems surprising, considering that there was a considerable increase in the number of large-scale enterprises during the 1990s. As shown in Figure 5.3, in the manufacturing industry, people working in establishments of 500 or more workers increased from 10 percent to 30 percent during the 1990s, while people working in establishments with fewer than 30 workers decreased from 51 percent to 31 percent. Moreover, the situation in family-style traditional companies, where union organizing has been difficult, has begun to change. As shown in Figure 5.4, the rate of persons employed through the introduction of a friend or a teacher has decreased gradually while that of those applying through

156 *Non-Standard Employment under Globalization*

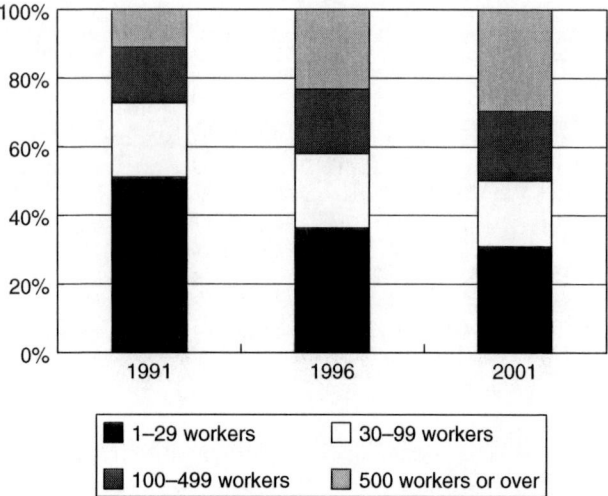

Figure 5.3 The ratio of employment by size of establishment in the manufacturing industries
Source: The Directorate-General of Budget, Accounting and Statistics, *1991 Industry, Commerce and Service Census* (1993), and *2001 Industry, Commerce and Service Census* (2003).

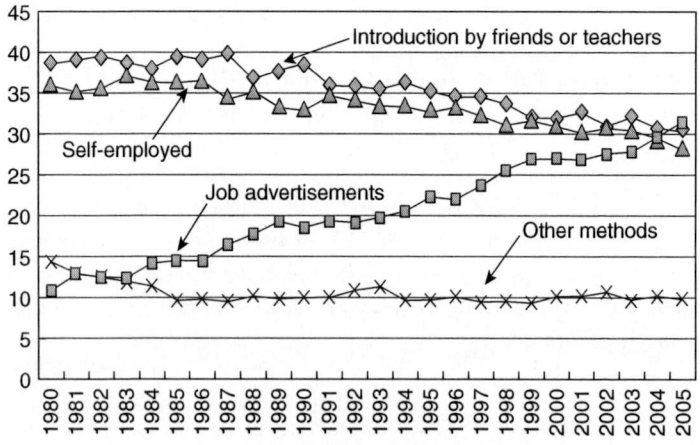

Figure 5.4 Method of applying for current employment (%)
Source: The Council of Labor Affairs, *Manpower Utilization Survey 2005*.

job advertisements has increased. The decreasing importance of personal contacts in obtaining a job will bring changes in human relations in workplaces. It will surely produce a change from a family-like relational culture to a businesslike market-type labor relationship. These changes will be advantageous for union activity. However, despite these changes, there was a fall in the unionization rate. There were two reasons for this: the increase in high-tech companies employing mainly white-collar workers where no unions are usually organized, and the privatization of public enterprises with highly active unions. Thus, the growth potential of the independent labor movement was limited by these conditions.

5.3.2 The shift of power and the explosion of union organization

In 1998, in defiance of the Chinese Federation of Labor (a legacy of state corporatism), independent unions established the "Preparatory Committee for the Taiwan Confederation of Trade Unions". This organization was made up of county- or city-level union federations (mentioned in the previous section) and the unions of public enterprises (Lee 1999: 161). Having come to power inn 2000, the Democratic Progressive Party government, on May 1 of the same year it promulgated a presidential decree recognizing the establishment of independent unions, and the Taiwan Confederation of Trade Unions (TCTU), a legitimate national center parallel to the Chinese Federation of Labor, was established (Chen et al. 2003: 326). Huang Ching-hsien, from the Taiwan Petroleum Worker's Union and a former head of the Taiwan Labor Front, became its first chairman. Most leaders of the TCTU and its union affiliates have been from the Taiwan Labor Front (Taiwan Labor Front 2004: 59).

At the same time, the Chinese Federation of Labor began to fracture. In April of that year, Lin Hui-kuan, a reformer from the Railway Union, was elected chairman, defeating Ho Tsai-feng who had been the safe candidate supported by the KMT. This triggered strife within the board which caused the federation to split into six groups: the National Trade Union Congress (NTUC), established in August 2000 and led by Wu Hai-rui; the Chinese General Labour League (CGL), established in September 2000 and led by Ho Tsai-feng; the Chinese National Federation of Labor (CNFL), established in February 2001; the Chinese Federation of Occupational Labour (CFOL), established in March 2001; the National Labor Congress (NLC), established in March 2001; and the Taiwan Province Confederation of Labor, established in 1948 and renamed the Taiwan Confederation of Labor (TCL) in 2002 (Hong 2006: 361; United Daily News, 2000, April 3, April 8, July 11). The opposition among the union leaders was the direct cause of the CFL's breakup, fueled by the collapse of the old political structure following the resignation of the KMT, and the formation of the TCTU with the support of the DPP, which meant that the pluralism of national centers was officially recognized.

Such change is closely related to the opposition among the political parties. At present, the chairman of the Chinese Federation of Labor, Lin Hui-kuan, is a legislator (elected by nationwide constituency) from the People First Party (a party that separated from the KMT); the chairman of the Chinese General Labour League, Ho Tsai-Feng, is a legislator (elected by nationwide constituency) from the KMT. The chairman of the Taiwan Confederation of Labor, Chen Chieh, is also a legislator (elected by Changhua County) from the KMT; while Lu Tien-lin, a legislator from the DPP (elected by nationwide constituency), is a former chairman of the TCTU. Moreover, there are a great number of politicians from the Taiwan Labor Front who became legislators for the DPP.[13] Thus in tandem with the increasing competition between the political parties after the shift of government, labor organizations also started to accept pluralism.

The organizational structure of the TCTU, the leading actor in the era of pluralism, is shown in Table 5.3. The table lists the unions affiliated with the TCTU, gives a breakdown of the number of members. As can be seen, of the 270,000 members,[14] nearly 120,000 belong to county- or city-level union federations, and nearly 150,000 members are workers from public enterprises in the process of privatization. Among the enterprises in Table 5.3, only Tatung, a consumer electronics maker, was originally a large-scale private enterprise. This imbalanced structure explains the reason why the labor movement made anti-privatization the main issue of its protest activities during the 1990s (Taiwan Labor Front 1999).

This imbalanced organizational structure can be explained by the industrial structure of Taiwan, which is dominated by small and medium-sized enterprises. There are no labor unions in most of the small and medium-sized enterprises. Table 5.4[15] compares the affiliation rates of the industrial unions in Taiwan (i.e., the unionization rates) by type of industry with those of Japan. Though the percentage of workers in the manufacturing industry in Taiwan is 13 points higher than in Japan, the unionization rate is 13 percent which is 13 points lower than that found in Japan. It should also be noted in the case of Taiwan that the unionization rate in sectors other than water, electricity, gas, transportation, finance, and manufacturing, is extremely low. Thus, the union movement in Taiwan is based on a shaky foundation.

Table 5.3 Unions affiliated with the Taiwan Confederation of Trade Unions, 2006

Organization	Established	No. of members
Kaohsiung County Federation of Trade Unions		10000
Kaohsiung City Confederation of Trade Unions		31000
Tainan County Federation of Trade Unions		10000
Yilan County Confederation of Trade Unions		3000
Miaoli County Confederation of Trade Unions		8794
Hsinchu County Confederation of Trade Unions	**1998	3285
Taipei City Confederation of Trade Unions	1997	34400
Taipei County Confederation of Trade Unions		5379
Taichung City Confederation of Trade Unions		11578
Tatung Corporation Industrial Union	1959	5631
Taiwan Power Labor Union	1958	24780
Taiwan Tobacco & Liquor Corporation Federation Union	*1956	6625
First Commercial Bank Industrial Union of Taipei City	1995	4500
Taiwan Bank Industrial Union of Taipei City		4628
Taiwan Business Bank Industrial Union	1996	4741
Hua Nan Financial Holdings Industrial Union of Taipei City		5000
Taiwan Cooperative Bank Industrial Union of Taipei City	1996	5315
Land Bank of Taiwan Industrial Union	2001	4822
Taiwan Petroleum Workers' Union	1959	14849
Chunghwa Telecom Workers' Union	*1957	28700
China Airlines Employees Union		8962
Taiwan Water Corporation Industrial Union	*2001	5187
Taiwan Sugar Federation of Trade Unions	*1955	4687
Chunghwa Postal Workers' Union	*1932	24926
Total		270789

Source: Taiwan Confederation of Trade Unions, *2006 May Day Passport*.
*website of each union; **website of the Council of Labor Affairs.

Table 5.4 Unionization rate by industry, 2005

	Taiwan			Japan	
	Unionization rate	% among employees		Unionization rate	% among employees
Total	8.4	100.0	Total	18.7	100.0
Agriculture, Forestry, Fishing, Pasturage	3.1	1.0	Agriculture, Forestry, Fishery	3.5	0.9
Mining, Quarrying	14.1	0.1	Mining	21.6	0.1
Manufacturing	12.6	33.3	Manufacturing	25.7	19.8
Water, Electricity, Gas	175.7	0.5	Electricity, Gas, Heat supply, Water	58.6	0.6
Construction	1.4	9.0	Construction	20.3	8.6
Wholesale, Retail trade	0.2	12.7	Wholesale, Retail trade	10.1	17.7
Hotels, Restaurants	0.3	4.3	Restaurants, Hotels	3.2	4.8
Transport, Storage, Communications	42.4	5.0	Transport	29.4	5.5
Finance, Insurance	13.6	5.5	Finance, Insurance	48.6	2.8
Real estate, Renting	0.0	1.0	Real estate	3.0	1.1
Education	0.1	7.1	Education, Learning assistance	24.4	4.7
Health, Social welfare services	0.5	3.9	Health, Welfare	8.4	9.8
Culture, Sports, Recreational services	7.0	2.2	Service industry	6.0	13.9
Public administration	2.9	4.8	Public administration	50.7	4.2
Professionals, Science, Technology services	0.0	3.4	Information and communications	22.3	3.2
Other services	0.3	6.6	Compound services	44.3	1.3

Source: Council of Labor Affairs, *Yearbook of Labor Statistics 2005*; Ministry of Health, Labor and Welfare, *Labor Unions Basic Survey 2005*.
Note: The unionization rate exceeding 100% for the "Water, Electricity, Gas" industries in Taiwan is due to an error in the original data.

5.4 Searching for a new corporatism?

Although Taiwan's interest-group politics is exhibiting a growing pluralism, at the same time, as mentioned in the section above, a movement searching for a new corporatism can also be seen. In this section, I will focus on the two advisory council meetings held under the Chen Shui-bian administration in order to examine the extent that elements of "social corporatism" can be found. I would also like to know what the primary factor obstructing the formation of a new corporatism is.

5.4.1 Two advisory council meetings

Two important advisory council meetings were held under the Chen Shui-bian administration which was inaugurated in 2000: the "Economic Development Advisory Council (EDAC)" held in August 2001, and the "Conference on Sustaining Taiwan's Economic Development (COSTED)" held in July 2006. In his famous book *Modern Capitalism*, Shonfield described corporatism as follows: "The major interest groups are brought together and encouraged to conclude a series of bargains about their future behaviour" (cited in Schmitter 1979: 29). The outward appearance of both advisory council meetings fits this description exactly. But to what extent can this be called the beginning of "social corporatism"? This will be examined in the next section after a brief description of the contents of these meetings. Here I would like to look at the following aspects of both advisory council meetings: (1) background and nature of the meetings; (2) structure of the meetings and selection of members; (3) issues agreed upon; and (4) evaluation from the parties concerned and public opinion.[16]

The Economic Development Advisory Council (EDAC)

The Economic Development Advisory Council meeting (2001) took place against the backdrop of difficulties facing the minority ruling party in the government administration, and the economic crisis that was about to lead Taiwan to record its first negative growth figures and mass unemployment. In order to deal with these pressing issues, this council meeting was non-partisan and called by the presidential office.

There were five topics on the meeting agenda: rising unemployment, the deteriorating investment environment, cross-strait economic and trade relations, loss of industrial competitiveness, and fiscal and monetary policy. The topics were discussed in a series of workshops: Employment Workshop, Investment Workshop, Cross-strait Workshop, Industrial Workshop and Fiscal–monetary Workshop. Of a total of 121 council members, only four were representatives of labor organizations: Huang Ching-hsien (chairman of the Taiwan Confederation of Trade Unions), Bair Jeng-sharn (chairman of Tatung Corporation Industrial Union), Huang Shui-chuan (chairman of the National Federation of Bank Employees Union), and Lin Hui-kuan (chairman of the Chinese Federation of Labor). With the exception of Lin Hui-kuan of the Nationalist Party (who later shifted to the People First Party), the remaining three members were labor movement leaders from the Taiwan Labor Front and belonged to the TCTU and the Democratic Progressive Party. Though the labor organization leaders were a minority, all four labor leaders attended the Employment Workshop (which had only 13 members), where they were balanced by three representatives of economic organizations (United Daily News, July 23, August 5).

The overall tone of the council meeting was encapsulated in the following slogan: "active opening and effective management" (changing policies toward an actively open economic relationship with mainland China). Consensus regarding social policy issues was reached and the main points were: (1) the minimum wage should not be abolished; moreover, foreign workers should not be exempted from the application of the minimum wage; (2) the flexibility of working hours should be increased; female workers should be permitted to work the night shift; (3) the labor pension (legal retirement benefit) scheme should be made "portable" among companies and be deposited in individual accounts; (4) the Protective Act for Mass Redundancy of Employees should be enacted; and (5) the total number of foreign workers should be controlled.

Looking at the evaluation from the parties concerned and public opinion concerning the above issues, economic organizations were demanding either the abolition of the minimum wage or the exemption of foreign workers from the application of the minimum wage. However, these demands were not accepted. This caused discontent in the business community (Economic Daily News, August 15).

On the other hand, Huang Ching-hsien, the Chairman of the TCTU and a member of the Employment Workshop, held a joint press conference with labor organizations, social welfare organizations and environmental organizations, where he criticized the shift to the right of the Democratic Progressive Party administration by "being on good terms with capitalists and exercising pressure on labor" (Economic Daily News, August 22), and summoned all labor organizations to a protest demonstration (United Daily News, August 22). However, to counter the arguments of the labor movement organizations, such as the Alliance for Actions on Labor Legislation and the Coalition for 84 Working

Hours, which called for withdrawal in protest from the Council, he replied, "Our defense is doing well. Why should we withdraw?" By this he meant that were labor to withdraw, it would lose the right to speak and there would be nobody to prevent the passage of adverse legislation against workers (Economic Daily News, August 26). Since decisions in the council were taken not by majority vote but by consensus-building procedure,[17] the presence of labor organization representatives was important, even though their number was small. They were able to prevent the abolition of the minimum wage or the exemption of foreign workers from its application. This indicates that the demands of labor organizations were recognized.

The Conference on Sustaining Taiwan's Economic Development (COSTED)

The Conference on Sustaining Taiwan's Economic Development (COSTED) (2006) took place against the backdrop of a decline in support for the Democratic Progressive Party, the minority ruling party, due to various scandals from the previous year involving its members. On the other hand, Taiwan's economy registered positive growth in 2002, and the unemployment rate stabilized after 2004. In this mixed context, the Executive Yuan sponsored a non-partisan meeting in order to debate measures for dealing with long-term economic issues, such as population ageing and globalization.

The conference focused on five main subjects: completion of the social security system; the improvement of industrial competitiveness; fiscal and monetary reforms; global structure and cross-strait trade; and the improvement of government efficiency. Discussions on each subject were conducted separately in the following workshops: the Social Security Workshop, the Industrial Workshop, the Fiscal–monetary Workshop, the Global and Cross-strait Workshop, and the Government Efficiency Workshop. Though the conference members totaled 159, no more than six labor representatives could be identified among these members. On the other hand, the presence of representatives from social movements, such as social welfare organizations and environmental protection organizations, was a feature that had not been seen in the previous meeting. When focusing on the make-up of the Industrial Workshop handling labor policies (57 members), it can be shown that there were 6 government representatives, 8 legislative members, 11 researchers, 18 members from the business sector, 5 members from social movements, 4 from labor organizations, and 5 from other bodies. The relatively large number of business representatives can be explained by the fact that this workshop discussed industrial policies. As this workshop also dealt with energy and environment-related policies, social movement representatives were also present. In comparison with the former Employment Workshop, there were fewer representatives of labor organizations. These were: Shih Chao-hsien (chairman of the Taiwan Confederation of Trade Unions), Wu Ching-pin (chairman of the Kaohsiung City Confederation of Trade Unions), Chuang Chueh-an (chairman of the Taiwan Petroleum Workers' Union), and Hsieh Chuang-chih (secretary-general of the Taiwan Confederation of Trade Unions). All four of these members belong to the TCTU. Lin Hui-kuan (the chairman of the Chinese Federation of Labor) also participated in this workshop as a legislative member.

In place of the slogan of the previous Economic Development Advisory Council meeting, the overall tone of this council meeting was expressed as "active management and effective opening" (to be understood as the government actively taking the management and responsibility for reducing the risk involved in the opening of economic relations with mainland China). The following important issues regarding social policies, particularly labor policies, were agreed upon:[18] (1) the easing of legal restrictions on atypical employment should be considered; (2) the Dispatched Worker Protection Law should be enacted; (3) the rate of female and senior citizen participation in the workforce should be increased; (4) the total number of foreign workers should be controlled.

Considering the evaluation of the parties concerned and public attitudes about the above issues, compared with the previous Economic Development Advisory Council, the level of public interest in labor policies was low. This was because in addition to dealing with labor policies, the Industrial Workshop also discussed industrial and environmental policies. As a result, attention was focused on the sharp exchange between the economic and environmental protection organizations. Unable to withstand the criticism of the environmental protection groups, the economic organizations hinted at leaving the meeting (Economic Daily News, July 8, and July 12). Moreover, they voiced disappointment with the fact that there was no prospect of a solution to the labor shortage problem (which referred to the increased acceptance of foreign workers and their exemption from the application of the minimum wage) (Economic Daily News, July 12).

Meanwhile, labor movement organizations, including the Labor Rights Association and the National Federation of Independent Trade Unions, staged a massive street demonstration against measures designed to increase labor flexibility, such as the enactment of the Dispatched

Worker Law. In respect of this point, Lee Ying-yuan, chairman of the Council of Labor Affairs, argued that the Dispatched Worker Protection Law was to be enacted in order to protect dispatched workers who were in a vulnerable position (United Evening News, July 27).

5.4.2 Adverse factors for social corporatism

In this section, I would like to consider the significance of the two advisory council meetings. Did these meetings have any substantial significance? Did they lead to the development of a more flexible labor market? Can they be regarded as the beginning of social corporatism? What adverse factors have been hindering the formation of a new corporatism in Taiwan?

Examining first the significance of the two meetings, what kind of legislation has actually been enacted based on their proposals? After the Economic Development Advisory Council meeting in 2001, the Labor Standard Law was amended in December 2002 in order to increase the flexibility of working hours. Specifically, it included such changes as: the "two-week irregular working hour system", the "eight-week flexible working hour system",[19] the deregulation of overtime working conditions (though limited to a maximum of four hours per day, 46 hours per month), and the deregulation of night-shift work for female workers (Council of Labor Affairs 2005). In addition, the Protective Act for Mass Redundancy of Employees took effect in May 2005, which states that in the case of large-scale restructuring, there must be prior notice and negotiation. Furthermore, the new Labor Pension Act (legal retirement benefits) was introduced in June 2004 (implemented in July 2005). The old system, enacted in 1984, stipulated that a worker who switched jobs was not entitled to receive retirement benefits. Thus, many employers of small and medium-sized enterprises, anticipating the possibility of a job switch by their employees, did not set aside the required amounts for the retirement reserve funds. The new system stipulated that even when switching jobs, workers could receive retirement benefits through the implementation of an individual account system. In this way, most issues agreed upon at the Economic Development Advisory Council were legislated, and for the most part in accordance with the proposals. In this sense, it can be said that the consensus reached during the meeting had a substantial significance. As of January 2007 (the termination date of this study), the proposals of the Conference on Sustaining Taiwan's Economic Development in 2006 had yet to be implemented as of January 2007: however, it is said that the formulation of the Dispatched Worker Protection bill is in progress at the Council of Labor Affairs.

Did the meetings lead to more flexibility in the labor market? Certainly, measures such as the irregular working-hour system and the deregulation of overtime working conditions are a form of flexibility, but these changes are not as radical. On the other hand, the pension reform is tightening regulations on small and medium-sized enterprises that have not established retirement reserve funds. It is also important to consider the reforms not implemented. Measures demanded by economic organizations, such as an increase in the acceptance of foreign workers and the exemption of foreign workers from basic wages, neither reached consensus in the meetings nor were they implemented.[20] To a certain extent, the labor organizations were able to defend their position during the meetings, and as a result, flexibility was inhibited. However, as Huang Mei-ling, a member of the policy council of the Democratic Progressive Party, argued, there may not have been a rigid labor market in Taiwan to be made flexible (United Daily News, July 29, 2001). As will be argued in the following section, job shifting has been frequent phenomenon in Taiwan, and arguably the labor market has been flexible from the very beginning.

Can these two meetings be regarded as the beginning of social corporatism in Taiwan? First, it should be noted that the Taiwan Confederation of Trade Unions (TCTU), which grew out of the independent labor movement, gained the position as labor representative, displacing the Chinese Federation of Labor, which was the actor of state corporatism. Though this can be seen as evidence of a decline in state corporatism and the formation of social corporatism, it is also a sign of the fragility of social corporatism. To a great extent, personal connections with the Democratic Progressive Party explain the success of the TCTU in becoming the labor representative at both meetings. Thus, if the KMT regains power in the next presidential elections,[21] the TCTU could easily be deprived of its position. Moreover, as stated in section 5.3.2, the total number of members in the TCTU is only 270,000. This number represents less than half of the 600,000 members in industrial unions. Furthermore, it represents only 2.7 percent of the 10,000,000 workers in Taiwan. Thus the TCTU's position as the representative of labor appears to be increasingly insecure. Likewise, the mode in which discussions were carried out during the meetings, and the unions' street demonstrations, were not typical features of corporatism. Rather than a "concertation mode" akin to the typical social corporatism, there was a strong pluralist "pressure mode" component (Schmitter 1982: 263). Furthermore, only in the Labor Affairs Workshop of the Economic Development Advisory Council was it possible to see a number of participants somewhat similar to a tripartite structure; if we consider the meeting as a whole, the labor representatives were a mere minority. As for the Conference on Sustaining Taiwan's Economic Development, during the debate of non-labor issues such as environment and welfare, the presence of environmental protection groups, social welfare groups, and women's organizations acquired great importance, thus becoming more distant from the typical tripartite structure. In other words, what we are seeing is a nascent social corporatism that is extremely weak.

What factors hinder the formation of a new corporatism in Taiwan? I will try to examine factors following Schmitter's hypotheses, which were introduced in section 5.1. First, the legacy of state corporatism interferes with the formation of social corporatism. Even today the Labor Union Law restricts the existence of labor unions to only one organization within a region or within a company. Therefore, unions affiliated with the TCTU are also paying the membership fee to the Chinese Federation of Labor, which means that there is an overlap of membership.[22] In such circumstances, it is difficult for the TCTU to exercise nationwide control of all unions. Tangled up in political party competition, "pluralist" competition between national centers will probably continue for some time. Second, the same headwind facing social corporatism in advanced western countries has also started to hit Taiwan, although less severely. As described above, the existence of the labor organizations has become overshadowed in the Conference on Sustaining Taiwan's Economic Development by the rise of "newly entitled organizations" such as environmental protection groups, social welfare groups and women's organizations. During both meetings, the labor activists connected to the TCTU always attacked corporatism "from the outside" with street demonstrations. Probably the TCTU itself, which should play a role "within" corporatism, still maintains the character of a social movement. But the most important point is that the economic sector, whose support the Democratic Progressive Party administration has tried to keep, will probably demand neo-liberal policies and will strengthen their determination to exit the tripartite meetings. Thus it looks like the nascent social corporatism in Taiwan is soon to be stricken by a strong, countervailing wind.

5.5 Was flexibilization obstructed?

Above, I pointed out how Taiwan's nascent social corporatism is somehow hindering the demands of economic organizations for market flexibility. However, as also suggested above, the labor market in

Taiwan originally had a flexible structure. In other words, it is necessary to examine the nature of the labor market itself, detached from the political process. I would like to conclude this chapter, therefore, by looking at the flexibility issue from a slightly different angle. I would like to shed more light on the degree of labor market flexibility in Taiwan by analyzing the macro labor statistics, and also examining how the reforms in the labor law and social security carried out in the 2000s are related to this flexibility.

Table 5.5 shows indicators pertaining to Taiwan's labor market between 1980 and 2006. The unemployment rate remained constant at low levels into the 1990s, but for the first time in 2000 it exceeded 3 percent, and rose to 5.2 percent in 2002. As was mentioned above, this unprecedentedly high unemployment rate was the backdrop to the meeting of the Economic Development Advisory Council. Meanwhile, there was an increase in the number of employed persons and white-collar workers, even though Taiwan is an industrial society with a strong aspiration for self-employment.

If we consider the situation for women, elderly people and foreign workers, who are often expected to be the most flexible portion of the labor market, the most remarkable change over the course of the last quarter-century is the increase in the number of economically active women, especially women with children. Because this change has occurred without implementing adequate child-care services, the total fertility rate declined sharply to 1.12 in 2005.[23] The enactment of the Gender Equality in Employment Act in 2002 was a belated response to this change. Meanwhile, the participation rate of elderly men in the labor force has decreased. Behind this change have been the economic stagnation and business restructuring since the latter half of the 1990s as well as the expansion of welfare allowances for elderly people (Kamimura 2005: 51). Regarding foreign workers, although during the 1990s there was an increase in the acceptance of foreign workers, the ratio of these workers (the ratio to the economically active population) has remained constant since 2000, contrary to the demands of economic organizations.

Considering the high rate of labor mobility and how it supported the flexibility of Taiwan's labor market, average job tenure showed a slight rise, reflecting the ageing of the population, and the annual staff turnover rate[24] decreased from 39.5 percent in 1980 to 27.5 percent in 2006. However, when set against the annual turnover rate in Japan, the level of mobility in Taiwan is still comparatively high. The annual turnover rate of Japan in 2005 was 13.8 percent for general workers and 30.3 percent

Table 5.5 Labor indicators for Taiwan, 1980–2006

	Unemployment rate	Employees ratio	White-collar workers ratio	Participation rate of 30–34 year old females	Employment rate of mothers with children under 6 years old	Participation rate of 60–64 year old males	Foreign workers ratio	Average job tenure (in years)	Annual job turnover rate
1980	1.2	64.4	21.6	39.7	26.4	62.4	–	7.7	39.5
1990	1.7	67.6	29.5	53.3	43.3	56.4	0.2	7.7	38.0
2000	3.0	71.1	38.4	64.2	51.2	53.9	3.3	8.3	31.2
2006	3.9	74.6	43.0	73.7	57.9	46.9	3.2	8.6	27.5

Source: Data for unemployment rate, employees ratio, white-collar workers ratio, workforce rate by age from: DGBAS, *Monthly Report on Manpower Survey Statistics, December 2006*. Data for average job tenure and workforce rate of mothers from: DGBAS, *Manpower Utilization Survey 2006*. Data for the ratio of foreign workers from: The Council of Labor Affairs, *Monthly Report on Labor Statistics, January 2007*. Data for annual job turnover rate (data in 2006 cell corresponds to 2005) from: DGBAS, *Earnings and Productivity Statistics*.

for part-time workers.²⁵ In other words, Taiwan's turnover rate is broadly similar to that of Japanese part-time workers.

In what sense can it be ascertained that Taiwan's labor market is "flexible?" Here, I would like to apply Regini's definition of flexibility. According to Regini, labor flexibility includes the following four elements: (1) numerical flexibility; (2) functional flexibility; (3) wage flexibility; and (4) temporal flexibility (Regini 2000: 16).

Numerical flexibility refers to the employer's ability to adjust the number of employees, according to fluctuations in demand or technological innovation. It also includes the ability to replace the workforce by atypical employment (ibid.). In Taiwan, atypical employment, such as part-time work or dispatched work, is not yet widespread. The percentage of part-time workers in 2006 was only 3.4 percent.²⁶ This rate is extremely low when compared with 25.8 percent in Japan and 9.0 percent in South Korea (in 2005).²⁷ The rate of enterprises employing dispatched workers is only 7.9 percent; and even at enterprises with 500 or more workers, the rate comes to only 35.0 percent.²⁸ However, Taiwan's extremely high level of labor mobility, as described above, is enough to guarantee numerical flexibility. Legislation such as the Protective Act for Mass Redundancy of Employees enacted in 2003, and the Dispatched Worker Protection Law, which is currently being drafted, seem intended to regulate this high level of mobility so that it has no adverse effects on the workers.

Functional flexibility refers to the employer's ability to introduce measures such as job rotation and modifications in job description. This type of flexibility can substitute for numerical flexibility, since it is a way to try to guarantee flexibility by retraining or multi-skilling instead of firing employees (ibid.). In Taiwan there are neither the strict seniority rules nor the rigid job descriptions which are found in Anglo-Saxon countries. Therefore raising the level of functional flexibility would not seem to be a difficult task, but a deeper examination of the actual situation in Taiwan's enterprises is beyond the scope of this chapter.

Wage flexibility means that the employer can alter wage levels and wage systems relatively independently of collective agreements or statutory regulations (ibid.). In Taiwan, the employer is free to set the level of wages if they do not fall below the minimum wage. In that sense, wage flexibility seems to be fully guaranteed, but we do not have the space for a complete analysis. The minimum wage currently, though it is to be revised by the tripartite representatives in the Basic Wage Commission, is a monthly salary of 15,840 NT$, a daily wage of 528 NT$ and an hourly wage of 66 NT$, and these minimums have not been increased since 1997.²⁹

Temporal flexibility refers to the employer's ability to adjust the working hour in a day, week or year in accordance with cyclical or seasonal shifts in demand (ibid.: 17). This type of flexibility was to some extent put into practice in Taiwan by the revision of the Labor Standards Act in 2002, which was agreed upon at the Economic Development Advisory Council, namely, the "two-week irregular working hour system" and "eight-week flexible working hour system" mentioned above.

As clearly indicated above, the flexibility of Taiwan's labor market is based principally on the long-standing high levels of mobility within the workforce, rather than on its accelerated promotion by the recent policy changes. Moreover, the flexibility guaranteed by the subcontract networks between enterprises, and the division of labor with the factories opened abroad in countries such as mainland China, Vietnam and Myanmar, cannot be overlooked either. It can be mentioned too that in the past ten years, the numbers of stallholders, who symbolize the strong inclination for independent business of the Taiwanese people, have increased rather than decreased. Their number, which stood at 234,335 in 1988, had increased to 291,064 in 2003, illustrating another aspect of the labor market's flexibility.[30]

Finally, in respect of social security, the reforms suitable for a highly fluid labor market have been implemented. The National Health Insurance program enacted in 1995 covers all citizens regardless of their workplace. After the earlier-mentioned portable Labor Pension scheme was introduced in 2005, 37.8 percent of workers joined this new scheme, mainly younger workers who are more likely to switch jobs.[31] On the other hand, the number of persons who registered with the Employment Insurance scheme, began in 2003, has remained at 51.8 percent of the labor force. The number of unemployed persons was 428,000 in 2005, but there were 250,600 cases of people receiving unemployment benefits.[32] The limits of the current scheme can be seen in the fact that the unemployed people who answered that unemployment benefits are an important income for living remained at 1.0 percent in 2006.[33]

5.6 Conclusion

This chapter has described how current Taiwan tripartite relations have advanced with uncertainty toward social corporatism, encumbered by the legacy of state corporatism and carrying elements of pluralism. Although the nascent social corporatism is resisting the increased flexibility of the labor market, this social corporatism itself is in a sense standing on the unstable base of an original flexibility in Taiwan's industrial structure.

Of course, this description can also be refuted. It may be that Taiwan's state corporatism was only an appearance; and considering the current situation an embryonic social corporatism may be ridiculed. Other ideal type can be proposed, but for me the real issues that Taiwan's tripartite relations and social policies are facing have become clearer through the use of the ideal type described in this study.

Notes

1. In recent years in Europe, the decline of the type of social corporatism based on Keynesian policy and the emergence of competitive corporatism which aims at balancing flexibility and security has been pointed out (Rhodes 2001). However, Schmitter's concept of social corporatism, used in this chapter, is not necessarily related to a specific kind of policy. Rather, competitive corporatism should be considered as a subcategory of the social corporatism discussed here. As will be seen below, the "contents" of the policy which seeks agreement in contemporary Taiwan are nothing more than those of competitive corporatism.
2. This refers to the regulation and control of capital by the state. Along with the "equalization of land ownership", it is a measure to implement the "principle of people's livelihood", one of the Three Principles of the People advocated by Sun Yat-sen.
3. "The platform for the wartime operations of the Taiwan Provincial Confederation of Labor" (1958).
4. According to the website of ROCCOC.
5. According to the website of the CNAIC.
6. Since 1995 the unionization rate of the occupational unions has declined. This may be explained by the fact that in the same year, the National Health Insurance program was implemented. This scheme applies to people who have not joined an occupational union, and consequently the importance of the Labor Insurance system decreased.
7. Council of Labor Affairs, *Yearbook of Labor Statistics 2005*.
8. Ibid.
9. Ibid.
10. Council of Labor Affairs, *Industrial Unions General Situation Survey Report 2002*.
11. Council of Labor Affairs, *Yearbook of Labor Statistics 2005*.
12. There is a difference in the unionization rate in Tables 5.2 and 5.4. In Table 5.2 the unionization rate for industrial unions in 2005 is 19.6 percent, while in Table 5.4 the rate is 8.4 percent. Table 5.4 was prepared by the author, and its figures are suitable for international comparison. On the other hand, Table 5.2 reproduces the figures of the government statistics. According to the Labor Union Law (Article 6), the formation of labor unions in establishments with less than 30 employees is prohibited. Consequently, according to the official statistics, the unionization rate for industrial unions is calculated by dividing the number of industrial union members by the "total number of employees of the establishments with 30 or more employees."

13. According to the website of the Legislative Yuan.
14. It should be noted that the Chinese Federation of Labor is still the organization with the largest membership. According to the CFL website, the official number of members is 1,100,000.
15. See footnote 13.
16. Data about the structure and content of debate of the meetings derived mainly from the following websites: the Executive Yuan Council for Economic Planning and Development (Economic Development Consulting Council: http://find.cepd.gov.tw/president/home.htm; the Conference on Sustaining Taiwan's Economic Development: http://find.cepd.gov.tw/tesg/). Other information has come from the following newspapers: *United Daily News*, *Economic Daily News*, and *Liberty Times*.
17. The Conference on Sustaining Taiwan's Economic Development, which will be discussed below, also adopted the consensus-building procedure.
18. I do not include references to welfare policies discussed in the Social Security Workshop.
19. The "two-week irregular working hour system" allows for the transfer of fixed working hours corresponding to two days within two weeks, to other days, with the consent of the labor unions or the labor–capital conference. However, only two hours per day are allowed to be transferred. Regarding the "eight-week flexible working hour system", it allows the transfer the fixed working hours within eight weeks, to other days with the consent of the labor unions or the labor-capital conference. However, the fixed working hours of one day cannot exceed eight hours, and the fixed working hours of one week cannot exceed 48 hours (Council of Labor Affairs 2005).
20. According to the website of the Council of Labor Affairs, the number of foreign workers remained constant from 2001 to 2006 at about 300,000 persons.
21. The KMT returned to power in May 2008.
22. According to the interview with Ms Huang Chi-ling, Deputy Secretary of the TCTU (August 31, 2006).
23. DGBAS, *Statistical Yearbook of the Republic of China 2005*.
24. However, the "annual turnover rate" in Table 5.5 includes: "job leavers", "dismissed workers", "retired workers" and "others". "Others" includes categories such as "temporary leave without pay", "death", and "rotation within the same enterprise". In the strict sense, those who do not correspond to "job leavers" are also included. As the survey form itself considers "others" as one item, it is not possible to calculate the exact number of "job leavers". Nevertheless, the overall trend is apparent.
25. Ministry of Health, *Labor and Welfare, Survey on Employment Trends 2005*.
26. DGBAS, *Report on the Manpower Utilization Survey 2006*; the percentage of workers with less than 35 working hours per week: males 3.1 percent, females 3.8 percent.
27. The percentages for Japan and Korea are from the Labor Force Statistics of the OECD website.
28. Council of Labor Affairs, *Bulletin of Occupation Wage Survey 2005*.
29. From the website of the Council of Labor Affairs.
30. DGBAS, *Statistics on the General Situation of Stallholders 1998*, *Statistics on the General Situation of Stallholders 2003*.

31. Data for 2005. Council of Labor Affairs, *Monthly Bulletin of Labor Statistics*, January 2007.
32. Council of Labor Affairs, *Monthly Bulletin of Labor Statistics*, January 2007.
33. DGBAS, *Report on the Manpower Utilization Survey 2006*.

References

Chinese

Chan, Hou-sheng, ed. 2001. *Labor Policy in the New Economic Century: Socio-Labor Part of Welfare White Paper*. Taipei: Welfare Foundation.

Chu, Jou-juo. 2005. "An Evaluation of Labor Problems and Policy in Taiwan." In *Social Problems in Taiwan 2005*, ed. Chiu Hei-yuan and Chang Ly-yun. Taipei: Chuliu Publishers, pp. 248–75.

Council of Labor Affairs. 2005. *The Handbook of the New Working Hour System*. Taipei: Council of Labor Affairs.

Fan, Ya-jiun (ed.) 2004. *Documentary Collection on the Labor Movement of Postwar Taiwan 1: Labor Policy, Laws and Regulations*. Taipei: Academia Historica.

Hong, Shi-cheng. 2006. *Taiwan Labor Movements*. Taipei: Huali Books.

Ko, Jyh-jer. 2003. *The Analysis and Investigation of Atypical Employment*. Taipei: Council of Labor Affairs.

Lan, Ke-jeng. 2001. "International Labor Mobility Policy: Taiwan's Experience in Introducing Foreign Workers." In *Labor Policy in the New Economic Century: Socio-Labor Part of Welfare White Paper*, ed. Chan Hou-sheng. Taipei: Welfare Foundation, pp. 25–65.

Lee, Joseph S. 2000. "Employment Relations in Taiwan." In *International and Comparative Employment Relations*, ed. G. Bamber et al. Taipei: Hwatai Publishing, pp. 325–56.

Lee, Joseph S., ed. 2003. *Who Has Stolen Our Jobs?* Taipei: Bookzone.

Lee, Yun-jie. 1999. *Political Economy of Labor Policy in Taiwan*, 2nd edition. Taipei: Shinning Culture Publishing.

Shen, Tzong-ruey. 2001. *State and Society: Analyzing the Experience of the Republic of China*. Taipei: Weber Publication.

Taiwan Labor Front. 1999. *New Nationalization Policy: Critics of Privatization in Taiwan*. Taipei: Business Weekly Publications.

Taiwan Labor Front. 2004. *Stand Up and Fight Together: 20 Years of the Taiwan Labor Front*. Taipei: Workers Publishing.

Wei, Ming. 2001. "Cross-Century Policy for Industrial Democracy." In *Labor Policy in the New Economic Century: Socio-Labor Part of Welfare White Paper*, ed. Chan Hou-sheng. Taipei: Welfare Foundation, pp. 107–34.

English

Chen Shyh-jer, Ko Jyh-jer and John Lawler. 2003. "Changing Patterns of Industrial Relations in Taiwan." *Industrial Relations* 42, no. 3: 315–40.

Huang, Chang-Ling. 2002. "The Politics of Reregulation: Globalization, Democratization, and the Taiwanese Labor Movement." *Developing Economies* 40, no. 3: 305–26.

Kamimura, Yasuhiro. 2006. "Welfare States in East Asia: Similar Conditions, Different Past and Divided Future." In *Managing Development: Globalization, Economic Restructuring and Social Policy*, ed. Junji Nakagawa. London: Routledge, pp. 306–32.

Regini, Marino. 2000. "The Dilemmas of Labour Market Regulation." In *Why Deregulate Labour Markets?*, ed. Gøsta Esping-Andersen and Marino Regini. Oxford: Oxford University Press, pp. 11–29.

Rhodes, Martin. 2001. "The Political Economy of Social Pacts: 'Competitive Corporatism' and European Welfare Reform." In *The New Politics of the Welfare State*, ed. Paul Pierson. New York: Oxford University Press, pp. 165–94.

Schmitter, Philippe C. 1979. "Still the Century of Corporatism?" In *Trends toward Corporatist Intermediation*, ed. Philippe C. Schmitter and Gerhard Lehmbruch. London: Sage, pp. 7–52.

Schmitter, Philippe C. 1982. "Reflections on Where the Theory of Neo-Corporatism Has Gone and Where the Praxis of Neo-Corporatism May Be Going." In *Patterns of Corporatist Policy-Making*, ed. Gerhard Lehmbruch and Philippe C. Schmitter. London: Sage, pp. 259–79.

Japanese

Kamimura, Yasuhiro. 2005. "Social Welfare as an Interface between Welfare State and Civil Society: A Comparison of Models in Taiwan and Singapore." In *Social Protection Systems in Newly Industrializing Countries in the 21st Century*, ed. Koichi Usami. Tokyo: Institute of Developing Economies, pp. 37–69.

6
Labor and Welfare for an Advanced Economy in the Republic of Korea: A Policy Mix of Universalism and Neoliberalism*

Jo-Seol Kim

Introduction

As is well known, in recent decades the welfare paradigm of the Republic of Korea (hereafter, Korea) has changed quite rapidly from a residual one formed as a privilege conferred by the authoritarian governments of the 1960s into a universal one following the winning of citizens' rights by the civil rights movement since the mid-1990s, a development that has come about as a result of the processes of democratization. At the same time, affected by the splitting of the labor movement into two since 1995, neoliberal economic reforms have been introduced in an attempt to enable Korea to recover from the IMF crisis and also as a means of moving the country towards industrial peace in the form of a social pact arrived at via tripartite negotiations initiated by the government.

Of its own, the policy mix of universal welfare and a flexible labor market is not surprising. However, its historical significance, real process and results are of crucial importance in any understanding of the nature of the Korean approach to the provision of a welfare state. In any discussion of Korean labor politics, we must take into account not only the policy mix between labor and welfare, but also employment and industrial relations.

---

*This chapter is based on two of my previous papers (Kim Jo-Seol 2006, 2007), which are the results of a joint research project headed by Mr Koichi Usami of IDE. I should like to express my gratitude to Mr Usami, other co-researchers and anonymous referees for useful suggestions and advice. However, all the mistakes are entirely my own responsibility.

We can interpret the combination and mutual relationship of these three key aspects as follows. Dating back to the 1960s, Korea's authoritarian government introduced some critical prescriptions, albeit only in name, to secure employment by fostering the growth of single unionism, whereas welfare was blatantly and severely restricted due to budget constraints and to the existing legal system which was carried over from the period of Japanese colonial rule. After the period of rapid growth, which lasted until the 1970s, the government during the 1980s made some minor changes aimed at securing the livelihoods of ordinary workers. Thus a minimum wage system was introduced as well as a national pension scheme and universal health insurance. At the same time, the maintenance of single unionism was somewhat intensified in an attempt to eliminate the new radical independent unions.

In the mid-1990s, the situation began to change conspicuously, and important developments occurred as a result of both external and internal pressures for reform. Contrary to what the government had expected in previous decades, an advanced society began to take shape. Having secured the membership of the UN in 1991, of the ILO in 1991, and of the OECD in 1996, and having been confronted by the unprecedentedly serious economic crisis of 1997, the government was forced to respond to citizens' petitions and accept proposals for universal welfare reform. At the same time, the government set about deregulating the labor market in an attempt to revive the economy, and started to promote industrial peace by abolishing single unionism, despite the presence of a radical second national center of union activity.

Applying Schmitter's corporatism framework (Schmitter 1984: 45) and focusing on whether interest organizations are dependent on, or independent of the state, we can divide the above process into three stages: first, the predominance until the 1970s of state corporatism or authoritarianism; second, the transition, or post-authoritarian, stage from the 1980s until the mid 1990s; and third, the neocorporatism that has prevailed since the mid-1990s.

The main purpose of this chapter is to analyze the development of the policy mix of labor (employment and industrial relations) and welfare throughout the above three stages, and to identify the causes and the reality of the current policy mix as a form of neocorporatism.

I should perhaps point out that owing to the limitations of space, the discussion of welfare has been kept to a minimum. A more detailed treatment can be found in my previous publications (Kim Jo-Seol 2002, 2003, 2005).

The first section will explain the focus of the present research and will provide a survey of previous studies by way of preliminary analysis. We will then proceed to depict the development of Korea's labor policy mix through the three aforementioned stages and will examine the flexible labor market policy of the 1990s, which is the most controversial aspect of Korean welfare, in the second section. In conclusion, the third section will explain the role of the major policy makers and especially the tripartite negotiation bodies in order to highlight the characteristics of Korean neocorporatism.

6.1 Scope of study and previous studies

6.1.1 Labor policy and economic background

Since the late 1990s, the liberalization of the South Korean labor market and the welfare shift to universalism have been developed simultaneously under conditions of low growth and high unemployment. As is shown in Figure 6.1, with the exception of 1980, annual economic growth was around 8 percent until the 1990s. However it has since

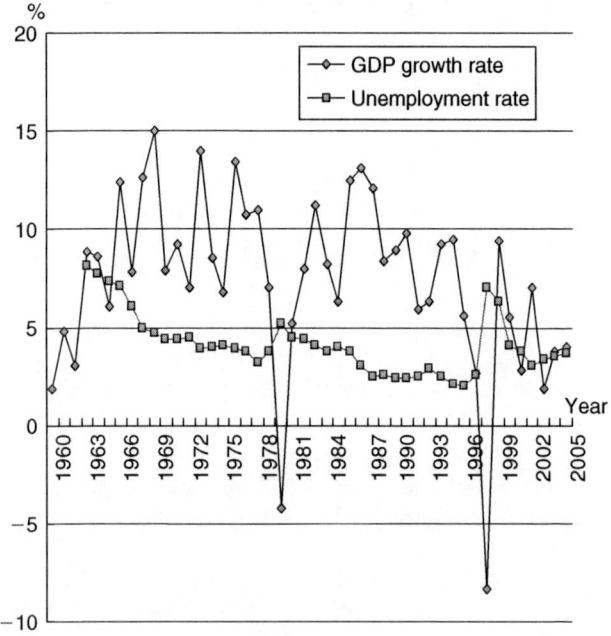

Figure 6.1 GDP growth rate and unemployment rate, 1960–2005
Source: National Statistical Agency, Republic of Korea.

dropped to around 4 percent, and unemployment has apparently risen. It must be noted that there has existed since the 1990s a large number of new employees with low levels of job security: the so-called non-standard workers, who will be mentioned in the next section.

Under the high rates of economic growth that obtained in Korea from the 1960s onwards, a restrictive welfare paradigm had been compensated for by an expanding labor market. Since the mid-1990s, however, a policy mix of a very different kind has been predominant, namely a combination of universal welfare with a flexible labor market. It is worth mentioning that the new flexible labor policy has followed the adoption of pro-employee measures that were introduced in the 1960s. The first aim of this chapter is to examine this transformation of the policy mix from a historical and political point of view.

What is important is that in addition to the promotion of a flexible labor market, a new policy-making institution in the form of the tripartite negotiation body also appeared. This body can be said to symbolize a departure from the authoritarian regime of the past, although it has been organized and led by the government in an attempt to establish "advanced" peaceful industrial relations in the context of the split of the labor movement in two since the mid-1990s. To understand the change, we have to focus on the labor politics that have been associated with the current policy reform.

For the purposes of our analysis, we divide the development of the policy mix into three main stages: (1) the state corporatism characteristic of the authoritarianism or developmentalism that predominated in Korea during the 1960s and 1970s, when the policy mix consisted of restrictive welfare, expanding employment and greatly strengthening the control of labor; (2) the phase that followed state corporatism, or the transition stage between the 1980s and the mid-1990s, a period of minor reforms by the government; and (3) the neocorporatism that has held sway since the mid-1990s. This has been a period of universal welfare promoted by the citizens' movement, flexible employment, and the deregulation of labor control by the tripartite body.

Whatever terms are used to describe these three stages, the existence of the stages is unanimously accepted (Tamura 2008). Tsujinaka (1994: 473), for example, recognized the 1980s as the decade of post-state corporatism, in which there emerged independent organizations that were distinctly different from the institutions of state corporatism.

McNamara (1999), analyzing the state-led development of the Korean economy, proposed "sectoral corporatism" (p. 142) as an alternative, while Im (1999) pointed out that there had already appeared "a neo-corporatist wage settlement" in 1993 (p. 85), but that "welfare is funded and provided by private companies" (p. 86). The situation has changed dramatically since this time.

Taking into account the nature and function of Korean policy makers, we emphasize the difference between the periods before and after the mid-1990s. However, it will be revealed that the third stage is still a fledgling one so far as social corporatism is concerned.

Finally, if we may mention welfare in passing, it was the newly emerging voluntary citizens' organizations such as the People's Solidarity for Participatory Democracy (PSPD) who pushed the National Assembly to make radical amendments to all the existing welfare legislation. The PSPD organized support for a Constitutional trial on livelihood standards in a 1994 civil rights case brought by an old couple in Seoul, and petitioned the National Assembly for a revision of the Livelihood Protection Act. This marked the start of a welfare revolution pioneered by the civil rights movement and led to the establishment of Productive Welfare by President Kim Dae-Jung (1998–2003) and Participatory Welfare by President Roh Moo-Hyun (2003–2008).

The active members of Korea's civil organizations are called *the 386 (sam-pal-yuk) generation*, because they were in their thirties when the first civil protests were organized. People belonging to this generation, born in the 1960s, had been protesting students during the democratization campaigns of the 1980s. They succeeded in making universal welfare a paradigm, not only indirectly by submitting petitions to the Assembly but also directly by being taken into the government or the presidential offices of the two former presidents.

Both Presidents Kim and Roh adopted, or were expected to adopt, a stance that was both pro-welfare and pro-labor. However, the labor politics in the third stage was more complicated than the welfare politics, and also more complicated in this stage than in the previous two stages, as will be shown in the third section.

6.1.2 Previous studies

Many studies have focused on the welfare paradigm shift and the recent Korean labor reforms, and several have dealt with both of these changes as a single theme. There is considerable controversy surrounding the nature of "Productive Welfare". It is undeniable that the government's ability to intervene in the economy has been weakened. On the other hand, Nam (2006) challenges the notion that Productive Welfare represents a move to neoliberalism because, as he points out, the government's role in welfare has increased due to the adoption of the new universal paradigm.

Cheon Moo-Gwon (2006: 126) stated clearly that in order to understand both the production regime and the welfare regime, a unified perspective is required and that social policies have been subordinate to economic policies in the case of the Korean "developmentalist regime". However, he does not investigate fully the dynamic aspects of labor and welfare, and this gives us the impression that his approach belongs to what may be termed development/economy centrism.

In respect of studies on welfare, contributors to the debate have drawn attention to the gap between ideas and reality (Kuhnle 2004) and to the significance of developmentalism (Holliday 2000; Kwon 2005). Other observers have examined the new regime itself (Takegawa and Kim 2005; Takegawa and Rhee 2006; and Yamaji 2007), but the liberal reforms relating to labor and the economy, which accompanied the universal shift in welfare legislation, are so confusing that they have been largely overlooked. The main area of scholarly controversy as regards the Korean welfare state and the regime (Kim Yeong-Myeon 2006) has surrounded the role of the government. One question that has attracted particular attention has been whether economic liberalism (non-intervention by the state) has been maintained or whether the role of the government has been strengthened.

Kim Seong-Won (2006) has argued that in order to have a meaningful discussion, it is essential to avoid the false dichotomy of "market" versus "state" or "large state" versus "small state" and that it is also important to explain "the simultaneous progress of economic liberalization and the making of the welfare state", because notions such as "small" and "large" government vary according to one's position and such evaluation, being highly subjective, is often less than useful.

In fact, international comparisons mainly on the basis of policy tend to lead us to an over-simple dichotomy in which Korea is portrayed as an exception among the other welfare-diminishing major developed countries. In that case, which conceptual framework is the more useful?

What helps us to understand the Korean dynamics of labor and welfare is to describe the historical process by which a welfare state is created.[1]

Tamai (2006) suggested that Japan's experience has been as follows. Widespread unemployment and poverty before World War II were followed by a second stage of full employment with social security policy arrangements during the postwar period of rapid economic growth. But, ironically, low economic growth has caused employment and welfare provision to fluctuate since the government's welfare declaration of 1973. In the Korean case, as mentioned earlier, the first stage – up to the 1970s – was characterized by full employment and restrictive welfare; the second by full employment and low welfare; and the third by unstable employment and universal welfare.

The differences between Japan and Korea tell us two things. First, political and economic factors are more decisive for labor and welfare than cultural homogeneity in matters such as paternalism within the family and the workplace. This implies that even in Asian countries, the Confucian model is more limited in terms of providing a methodology for the classification of welfare states than the analysis of economic and labor policies. The Asian welfare model nevertheless remains relevant to some extent, especially when applied to countries that are latecomers.

Second, taking into account that in Japan, welfare provision developed during periods of rapid growth and fluctuated during periods of lower growth, it is necessary to discover why welfare policies were built and how they have changed. The Korean case reminds us that, as a rule, welfare provision is a product of political economy. For this, reason, corporatism can be considered as the most effective concept for examining the complicated and interactive processes that led to the emergence of the Korean welfare state.

As regards the characteristics of the Korean welfare state, we must refer to Noguchi (2007), who suggests that "centralism" is the decisive factor in making Korea different from the other three welfare worlds postulated by Esping-Andersen (2001). Noguchi avoids the trap of the simplistic state-versus-market dichotomy by introducing a second axis of centralism-versus-decentralism and expects that Korea will come to resemble one of Esping-Andersen's models as a result of future reforms.

6.2 Development of the labor–welfare policy mix

6.2.1 Development of labor and welfare policy

First of all, let us consider the main changes in Korea's economy and society through the three stages shown in Table 6.1, which contains data that help us to understand the preconditions of labor and welfare policy.

With rapid industrialization, the employment rate increased very sharply from 40.1 percent in 1975 to 60.5 percent in 1990 and then, more slowly, to 66.4 percent in 2005. During the same period, the total share of employees working in self-owned enterprises and as unpaid family members – employees, in other words, who are not unionized – fell from 60 percent to around 40 percent. As regards vocational status, standard employment data for the period before the 1980s are unavailable, and our information is therefore limited to the last 25 years or so.

Table 6.1 Economic and social indicators

	1975 (*1974)	1990 (*1985)	2005 (*2004)
GDP annual growth rate (%)	13.4 (1976)	8.9	4.0
Unemployment (%)	4.1	2.4	3.7
Population (thousand persons)	31,466	43,411	48,138
No. of workers (thousand persons)	11,830	18,036	22,856
Workers' Status (%)			
Self-employed	33.9	28.0	27.0
Unpaid family workers	25.5	11.4	6.6
Employees	40.6	60.5	66.4
Employees' status (%)			
Regular employees	31.0	50.4	34.6
Temporary employees			22.1
Daily workers	9.6	10.2	9.7
Industrial structure (%)			
Agriculture, forestry and fishery	45.9	18.3	7.9
Mining and manufacturing	19.1	27.3	18.6
Services	35.0	54.4	73.5
Workers in manufacturing (thousand persons)	1,298*	2,438*	2,798*
Workers in establishments with over 300 employees (thousand persons/%)	815*/62.8*	1,070*/43.9*	678*/24.2*
Ratio of organized labor	23.0	21.5	13.0*
Average length of employment (years)	2.4	4.0	5.9
Per capita GNI (US dollar)	602	6,147	14,162*
Average monthly wage, all industry (won)	46,654	616,765	2,210,478

(*Continued*)

Table 6.1 Continued

	1975 (*1974)	1990 (*1985)	2005 (*2004)
A Monthly minimum wage (won): B	–	155,940	700,600
B/A (%)	–	25.3	31.7
Monthly minimum living cost (won)	Urban 3,500 Rural 2,900	Nation-wide 48,000	By family size One-person: 401,466
Monthly livelihood (won)	Home-care 1,010 Institutional 14,424	Home-care 39,000 Institutional 48,000	Two-persons: 668,504 Three-persons: 907,929 Four-persons: 1,136,332
Tax burden ratio to GNI (%)	15.5	18.6	19.5*
Government expenditure, by purpose (%):			
Economic development	32.4	26.6	26.0*
Health, social security and welfare	4.9	7.1	11.0*
National defense	22.9	16.1	16.9*
Ratio of population over 65	3.5	5.1	9.4
TFR	3.47	1.59	1.08
Average family size (person)	5.0	3.7	2.9

Notes: (1) * indicates values that are respectively those for 1974, 1985 and 2004.
(2) The minimum wage has been determined on an hourly basis since the system was enforced in 1988. The monthly wages in the table are calculated from the hourly ones (690 won in 1990 and 2,840 won for 2005) by multiplying by the standard monthly working hours, 226 hours, based on the legal weekly working hours, 44 hours.

Sources: National Statistical Agency, *Korea Statistical Yearbook*, various issues; Economic Planning Board, *Report on Mining and Manufacturing Survey*, 1974 and 1990; Ministry of Labor, *Labor Statistical Yearbook*, 2005; *White Paper on Labor*, 2005; Ministry of Welfare, *Statistical Yearbook of Health and Welfare*, various issues.

So far as the main industrial sectors are concerned, the mining and manufacturing sector's share of employees dropped after reaching a peak around 1990, while the service sector accounted for 73.5 percent of employment in 2005. At the same time, there has been a decline in the proportion of industrial workers employed by large manufacturing establishments with 300 workers and over, from 62.8 percent in 1974 to 24.2 percent in 2005, which means that slightly under three-quarters of manufacturing workers belong to small and medium-sized companies.

The shift to the service industry and to small and medium-sized companies has resulted in a decline in unionization since 1990, when the deregulation of unions had at last been achieved.

Considering the change in the average number of working years in Korea from 2.4 years in 1975 to 5.9 in 2005, or just half of the 11.3 years recorded for Japan in 1999, we can probably conclude that employment security such as life-time employment has been preserved, if only partly.

Needless to say, rapid economic growth was accompanied by an increase in income and wages. Generally speaking, it was in the 1970s that Korea escaped from poverty, in the 1980s that the country became a middle-level economy, and in the 1990s that it was confidently expected to reach advanced economy status.

In addition to these developments, we can see signs of fundamental social changes: the aging of the population (9.4 percent in 2005) being the fastest in the world, the total fertility rate having fallen sharply to the lowest recorded level (1.08) in the world in 2005,[2] and the shrinking of the family. As a result, the risk structure related to employment has largely changed substantially.

So far as the large company is concerned, we should note in passing that the decrease in the number of employees working in large enterprises does not necessarily mean the decline of the political, economic and social power of the *Chaebol*, the Korean family-based conglomerates, which played a key role in industrialization during the period of state corporatism. In fact, their loose management and system of mutual financial support within broad business groupings were the main cause of the IMF crisis (Ko, Yong-Soo 2000; Lee, Tae-Wang 2004), and because of this, liberal reforms of *chaebol* structure had to be introduced before the economy could recover.

We now turn to the development of the labor and welfare policy mix at each of the three main stages, using as background the data contained in Table 6.2. The important point that holds good throughout the course of a very complicated process is that the government has seen conciliatory industrial relations as being symbolic of an advanced

Table 6.2 Development of labor and welfare policy

1st Stage: State Corporatism (Until 1970s)	2nd Stage: Transitory Era (1980s and mid-1990s)	3rd Stage: Neo Corporatism (Since mid 1990s)
Political Situation		
1948 First Constitution 1961 Military Coup 1961–79 Pres. Park Chung-Hee (*) **1963–71 Third Republic** **1971–80 Fourth Republic** (Yushin Constitution/Regime)	**1980–87 Fifth Republic** 1980–87 Pres. Chun Doo-Hwan (*) **1988– Sixth Republic** 1988–93 Pres. Roh Tae-Woo	1993–98 Pres. Kim Yeong-Sam 1998–2003 Pres. Kim Dae-Jung 2003–08 Pres. Roh Moo-Hyun
Public Assistance and Social Insurance Policy		
Government-Led Restrictive Benefit for Absolute Poverty	Government-Led Restrictive Benefit with Worsened Relative Standards	Universal Minimum Security won by Civil Rights Led by Citizens and Assembly
1961 Livelihood Security Act 1963 Social Security Act	1981 Elderly Welfare Act 1982 Total Revision of Livelihood Protection Act (introduction of Education Allowance and incorporation of 'Self-protection' clause)	1994 Constitution legal case on Livelihood (Dismissed in 1997) 1995 Framework Act on Social Security 1997 Revision of Livelihood Protection Act (introduction of universalism) 1999 Declaration of Productive Welfare, National Livelihood Security Act (enforced in Oct. 2000)

Social Insurance

Introduction of Restrictive/ Occupational Pension and Health Insurance	Generalization of Public Insurance	Generalization of Pensions	Generalization of Pensions
1960 Officers Pension Act 1963 Military Pension, Industrial Accident Compensation Act 1977 Health Insurance Act	1988 National Pension 1989 Generalization of Health Insurance 1993 Enactment of Employment Insurance; enforced in Jul. 1995	1998 Generalization of Pensions 2001 Framing Act on Employees Welfare Pension Fund's 2004 Forecast of Pension Fund's Bankruptcy around 2040	

Employment and Wage

Labor Protection under an Expanding Labor Market	Minimum Wage and Labor Protection for an Advanced Economy		Liberalization of Labor Market under Low Growth and Globalization
1953 Labor Standards Act (applied to establishments with 300 employees or over) 1961 Revision of dismissal allowance in retirement pay 1961 Employment Security Act (revised in 1967, 1994) 1974 Introduction of 'Restriction of Dismissal' and 'Wage Claim Guarantee' 1974 Labor Standards Act, applied to establishments with 16 or over 1975 Labor Standards Act, applied to establishments with 5 or over	1980 Prohibition of Differentials of Wage Claim Guarantee within Enterprise 1988 Minimum Wage Act, Equal Employment Act 1991 The Aged Employment Act 1993 Employment Policy Act 1994 Total revision of Employment Security Act		Dec.1996-Mar.1997 The *'nalchigi'* (nonsense) revision of labor laws 1997 Revision of Labor laws Feb 1998 Legalization of M&A dismissal, Wage Claim Guarantee Act, Act of Dispatched-employee Security 1999 Equal Employment and Relief Act Mar. 2004 Limited-time Act of Youth Employment, until Aug. 2008 Dec. 2004 Employees Skills Development Act Jan. 2005 Employee Retirement Benefit Act Nov. 2006 Three Acts relating to Non-standard Employee Security (enacted in 2007)

(*Continued*)

Table 6.2 Continued

Collective Industrial Relations

Introduction of Restrictions on Trade Unions and Labor Disputes	Diversification of Labor Oppression against Independent Radical Unions	Bipolarization of Labor Power under Relaxation of Labor Oppression
1953 Free Foundation and Resister System of In-company Trade Union Unionization (until 1997), Banning of Political Activity, Single Unionism *de facto*, Labor–Management Council 1971 *De facto* Prohibition of Industrial Action 1973 Single Unionism	1980 Elimination of the Third Persons Act of Labor-Management Council 1987 Strengthened Single Unionism	1997 Plural Unionism of Upper /Industrial Association, Removal of Ban on Political Activities 1999 Legalization of Teachers' Unionization 2005 Legalization of Government Officers' Unionization 2006 Postponement of Company-level Pluralism until 2010

Major Background Events

Authoritarianism for tackling Poverty and Development	Democratization, Globalization and De-industrialization	Economic Maturing and Polarization under Economic Crisis and Aging of Population
1950–53 Korean War 1955 Assembly Resolution to enter ILO 1962 First Five-year Economic Development Plan 1963 Labor Bureau established within Ministry of Health and Social Affairs	1981 Promotion of offices to Ministry of Labor 1982 Korea becomes Official Observer at ILO 1982 Five-year Economic and Social Development Plan 1987 Great Workers Struggle, 'Declaration of Democracy'	1995 Establishment of Korean Confederation of Trade Unions (Legalized in 1999) 1996 Committee for Industrial Relations' Reformation Sep. 1996 Korea enters OECD. Nov. 1997 IMF Crisis Feb. 1998 Tripartite Social Pact

1988 Enforcement of Current 9th Constitution	1998 Abolition of Board of Finance and Economy
1991 Korea enters U.N. and I.L.O.	2000 Establishment of Korea Democratic Labor Party
1994 Recommendation to revise Labor Laws by OECD	2003 Roadmap for Advancing Industrial Relations
1994 Merger of Economic Planning Board into Board of Finance and Economy	Sep.2006 '9-11 Deal'/(Non-standard Employees laws, Another three years postponement of In-company Union-Pluralism and No-pay for union fulltime Officers, and so on)
	Nov. 2006 Revision of Labor Laws

*Presidents Park and Chun were appointed by direct election after the Constitutional Revision, and took office respectively in 1963 and 1981.

industrial state and/or society. The extent to which it has succeeded in establishing arrangements worthy of an advanced country will be discussed critically in the third section, which deals with the 1990s.

Let us begin by explaining developments under the state corporatism that held sway until the 1970s. During that period, the policy mix was characterized by restrictive welfare, by the security provided by a continuous expansion of employment and by the oppression of the labor movement (Choi 1988, 1991).

The oppression of the labor movement began with a legislative amendment of 1963, soon after the start of government-led industrialization, that introduced a variety of restrictive arrangements, including the permission system of *de facto* unionization, the prohibition of unions' political activities, and the compulsory establishment of a joint labor–management conference within each establishment. The first of Korea's labor acts, in 1953,[3] allowed unions to be formed freely in each establishment, but allowed the government to issue orders for union dissolution subject to the three major labor rights that were laid down in the first Constitution.

The first Labor Standards Act, passed in 1953, restricted employers' rights of dismissal, introduced dismissal allowances and set a minimum wage. Although in reality there were departures from these legal requirements, Korea's first modern labor law, as represented by this act, compared favorably with labor legislation in advanced countries at that time (Kim Yoo-Seong 2001: 132; Song 2001). The enlightened and protective nature of the legislation must be seen in the context of the National Assembly's resolution to join the ILO in 1955, which was in turn aimed at allowing Korea to compete successfully with the then favorable performance of the economy of the Democratic Peoples' Republic of Korea, or "North Korea".

One of the most important characteristics of Korean state corporatism was the gap between law and reality. In November 1970, by way of a public protest, Cheon Tai-il, a textile worker, set himself on fire, shouting "Keep the Labor Laws!" His suicide came after the rejection of his appeals for better labor conditions, and occurred when the existing over-moderate union and the labor office did not listen to him. Moreover the situation worsened during the period of the notorious *Yushin* (Restoration) Constitution (1972–1980) when, as is well known, not only labor disputes but also unionization itself were subject to strict limitations or were suppressed by Presidential orders.

In respect of restrictive welfare during the period of state corporatism, the reality was that in the 1950s, a minimum quantity (about 500 grams per day) of American relief grain was distributed to the absolute poor such as orphans, widows, the disabled and the elderly. In 1963, the Social Security Act declared that welfare provision should be suspended until such time as the state's budget allowed its resumption.

Compulsory forms of insurance, covering industrial accidents (since 1963) as well as health provision (since 1977), were mostly limited to the employees of large companies. On the other hand, progress was made during the early industrialization stage with the implementation of a food distribution scheme and the introduction of public insurance policies.

The assassination of President Park in 1979 marked the end of the authoritarian regime, and initiatives for improving social justice and economic equality came to the fore among Korea's major policy targets. For instance, the term "social development" was symbolically included in the title of the Five Year Plan introduced in 1982. Not to be underestimated, either, were the passing of the Minimum Wage Act and the National Pension Act in 1988 and the accomplishment of nationwide comprehensive health insurance in 1989. Even so, the basic concept and regime of welfare provision remained restrictive, and welfare was regarded by the authorities as a privilege rather than as a social right. What was improved by the revised Livelihood Protection Act of 1982 was an essentially minor matter, in the form of the introduction of the supplementary allowance for compulsory education and the inclusion of a 'Self-Protection' clause taken from another act that had been abolished. As I have pointed out elsewhere (Kim Jo-Seol 2005), while the number of the beneficiaries rose in the transition period, the relative standard of livelihood made possible by the average wage or income worsened. In fact, the livelihood standard, shown in Table 6.1, was less than one-third of the average wage even in 1994, and the gap became a major issue in the epoch-making Constitutional trial.

During the transition stage, restrictions on union activity were diversified rather than mitigated by means of introducing the notion of "Removal of the Third Person" in 1980, third persons in this case including professional unionists and radical students who entered workplaces as so-called "disguised employees". Moreover plural unionism within a single establishment was banned in 1987.

It was clear that during the transition stage, there was a pressing need for the government to revise the laws formed by previous authoritarian regimes, so that progress could be made towards the formation of a more balanced economy and society. However, there were few autonomous groups who were willing to become directly involved in the legislation process. As a result, the top-down revision that was carried out never radically attempted to eliminate the restrictions on labor and welfare imposed by former regimes.

So far as labor legislation was concerned, the most important episodes during the transition stage were the Declaration of Democratization in 1987 and the Great Workers Struggle during 1986 and 1987. These two events opened the way for the new political and economic developments that were introduced during the next stage.

In terms of the political power game, the newly emerged radical independent trade unions finally succeeded in organizing a second national center in 1995 and a workers' party in 2000. On the other hand, the increase in wages since the Great Struggle (Koo 2004: 212, 252–3; Baek 1996) has encouraged the spread of so-called non-standard employees.

Given these circumstances, the 1990s were expected to form the final stage in the formation of an advanced economy with high wages and, by world standards, peaceful industrial relations. In fact, the first civilian government set up an ad hoc tripartite negotiation body to deregulate Korea's notorious industrial relations provisions. However, the currency crisis in November 1997, otherwise known as the IMF crisis, interrupted this process.

Let us now move on to examine how this fledgling advanced society has dealt with the issues carried over from the previous era and how it has attempted to meet global standards and follow advice and instructions.

A list of the urgent and important issues affecting economy and labor during the early 1990s, some of which were related to the requirements for securing OECD membership, would include the liberalization of capital, the introduction of employment insurance, and a flexible labor market, to ensure higher competitiveness, but the most sensitive and difficult of the various measures was the relaxing of the crackdown on trade unions, a measure that was proposed despite the government's reluctance to allow the spread of independent radical unions.

Partly because of the IMF crisis, the flexible labor market policy has continued to assume importance, as will be made clear below, and was helped by the introduction of managerial dismissal in 1997.

However, while there has been some gradual deregulation, some critical issues have been postponed, despite the tripartite agreements that have been in place since 1996. The deregulation measures accomplished so far include the political activities of unions, vertical and regional union pluralism (in 1997), the unionization of teachers and public officials, and the legalization of the second national center (in 1999).

On the other hand, however, the provisions not yet tackled include company-based union pluralism and the introduction of long-duration customs dues to pay union full-time officials, a vital question in Korea not only for the two mutually conflicting union centers but also for companies.

In addition to the policy achievements, what is conspicuous in the third stage is the emergence in 1996 of the so-called tripartite negotiation body. Although details will be provided in the third section, the development of the *"nalchigi"* (nonsense) legislation in 1996 is worth mentioning as a symbolic incident that put an end to the government's implementation of measures by force.

The first tripartite negotiation body in Korea's history, the Presidential Commission for Industrial Relations' Reform, was set up in 1996 by the first civilian president, Kim Yeong-Sam (1993–96) and contained delegates from the second and as yet illegal national union center. The Commission agreed on a number of reforms, including the introduction of union pluralism and the provision of dismissal based on judicial precedents. When the government amended these items in the relevant legislation, the anti-government parties created a disturbance in the house (on December 10) to prevent the bill being forced through. The government passed the bill unilaterally at a plenary session from 6 a.m. on the 26th, expecting the existing national center's *ex post facto* approval (Song Gang-Jik 2001: 27–31).

Contrary to expectations, not only the new trade union center but also, surprisingly, the existing union center for the first time in its 40-year history called for a general strike, involving 556 enterprises and 160,000 unionists. Faced with this threat, the government decided not to enforce the act but to revise the bill in line with the agreements that had been reached within the Commission.

At the same time, the National Assembly started to revise the Livelihood Protection Act toward universalism in November 1996. This contrast in the treatment of welfare and labor in the third stage also will be mentioned later.

To sum up, the policy mix of expanding employment, suppression of labor movements and restrictive welfare was introduced during the period of state corporatism and was successively maintained throughout the 1980s. The policy mix then underwent a sharp reversal in the context of democratization, low rates of economic growth and globalization. Also relevant were unstable employment, the slow deregulation of trade unions and the development of universal welfare led by ordinary citizens.

6.2.2 Policy and reality of flexible employment

I will now deal with the policy and reality of the flexible labor market during the third stage.

First, we have to recognize that the deregulation of managerial dismissal was introduced under the insecure employment insurance legislation.

Employment insurance provision was enacted in 1993 and enforced in 1995 as the last of the four public insurance initiatives, the other three being industrial accidents insurance (1961), health insurance (1976) and national pensions (1988).

According to Kim and Seong (2005) and Yoo (2000), the establishment of employment insurance was discussed at the time when industrial accidents insurance was introduced. Later, in May 1967, the Cabinet issued the relevant resolution. Nevertheless, the attempt to hire the increasing *"Yongse-min"*, the workable unemployed poor, who made up the urban informal sector, was the responsibility of the Ministry of Health and the Social Affairs. Moreover, the relief works project carried out by the Labor Bureau was reduced in 1972 owing to a marked decrease in the unemployment rate (Ahn 1982: 188).

When the Korean unemployment rate rose sharply to 7.5 percent in 1980, the introduction of employment insurance was proposed by the Korea Development Institute (Park Jong-Gi 1981), a highly influential think-tank, and was discussed formally within the newly established Ministry of Labor. However, the outcome was a decision to impose the national pension and the minimum wage legislation before the employment insurance bill because of the strength of negative opinion against allowances for the unemployed, who were widely regarded as idle. After agreement had been reached within the government in 1991, the Korea Labor Institute was asked to carry out the practical research needed as a preliminary step for drawing up concrete plans.

When the act was enacted in July 1993 alongside the Framework Act on Employment Policy, it was scheduled to be applied compulsorily to all establishments with thirty employees or more from 1995. It took very little time to broaden the terms of the legislation to include nearly all establishments in October 1998 (see Figure 6.2), the move having been hastened by the first Social Pact to recover from the damage caused to the economy by the IMF crisis. While the government reported that coverage reached around 80 percent of establishments and 64 percent of the workers who had to be insured, Song and Hong (2006: 151) pointed out that the number of the insured was in fact half of all wage earners (Table 6.3).

Park Chan-Yong (1998: 134) estimated that the recipients would be no more than 10 percent of the one and half million unemployed in 1998, which was much less than the 43.5 percent registered in Germany and 27.8 percent in Japan. Subsequently, the urgent reduction of the prerequisites for payment soon resulted in an improvement in the ratio

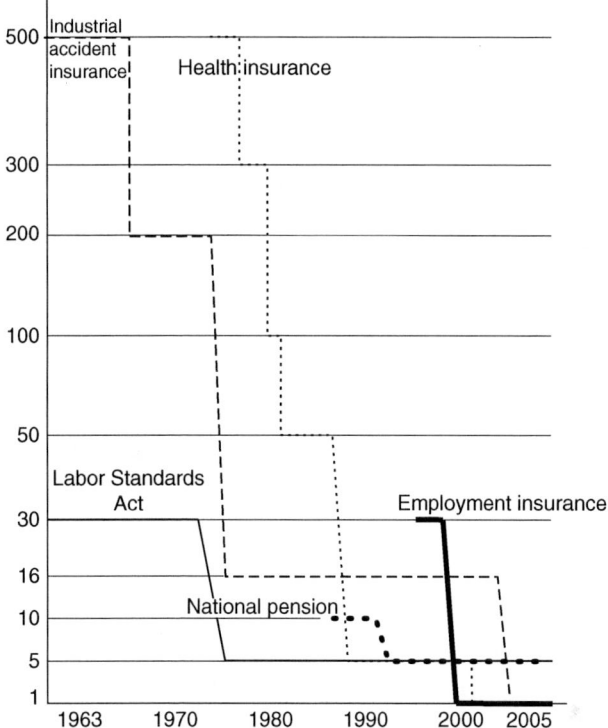

Figure 6.2 Mandatory establishment size for labor standards act and social security

Note: Besides mandatory standards for the manufacturing sector, each scheme has particular provisions for other occupations. The employment insurance also legally covers employers, while health insurance and the national pension are also compulsorily applied in the case of the self-employed. A voluntary contract by non-mandatory workers is available for all schemes.
Source: Yoon (2006: 175) and the Ministry of Labor.

of recipients to 27.7 percent of the unemployed in 1998 to over 70 percent in 2004, as shown in Table 6.4.

Now let us turn to the text of the managerial dismissal clause, which had been the most important means of protecting employees during the economic crisis.

Ever since the first enactment of the legislation in 1953, the Labor Standards Act included the article of "Restriction of Dismissal etc" ("No employer shall dismiss, lay off, suspend, or transfer a worker, or reduce wages

Table 6.3 Applicability and actual coverage of social insurance (as of May 2005)

	Public pension[1]	Health insurance	Employment insurance[2]	Industrial accident insurance[2]
Applicability: number (thousands)	Workers over 18 years old: 22,956	All nationals: 48,294	Wage earners: 15,401	Wage earners: 15,401
Insured (thousands)	16,903	46,000	7,759	10,697
coverage (%)	73.6	96.0	50.3	69.4
Establishments (2004)	–	96.0	1,002,000	1,039,000
coverage (%)	–	–	80.1	83.0

Notes: (1) The national pension, the government officials' mutual aid pension and the private school teachers/workers mutual aid pension are included, while the military pension is excluded.
(2) The self-employed are implied separate category.

Source: Song and Hong (2006: 151) and White Paper on Labor (2005: 219) for the mandatory establishment.

Table 6.4 Performance of employment insurance

	Employees, in thousands	(A) Unemployed persons, in thousands (Unemployment rate, %)	No. of those Designated as Unemployed	(B) Recipients of Unemployment Allowance, in thousands	B/A (%)	The insured, in thousands (% of Coverage)
1998	19,938	1490 (7.0)	2,480,448	412.6	27.7	5,267 (63.1)
2004	22,557	831 (3.5)	3,781,280	589.6	71.0	7,577 (72.7)

Source: Ministry of Labor, White Paper on Labor (2005) and Statistical Yearbook of Labor (2005).

or take other punitive measures without justifiable reasons") and also the article relating to Dismissal Allowance (Retirement Payment, from 1963).

According to Kim Yoo-Seong (2001: 347–73), after the arguments on legal niceties in the academic world, the Supreme Court suggested the four prerequisites to justify managerial dismissal in 1989: (1) urgent managerial need; (2) the employer having made efforts to avoid dismissal; (3) the establishment of criteria to choose the worker to be dismissed; and (4) negotiation procedures on dismissal.

The critical process to relax restrictions on dismissal went through two steps during 1996 and 1998 (see Table 6.5).

Table 6.5 Revision of dismissal for managerial reasons

Revision in 1997	Now in force since February 1998 by the Tripartite Agreement
Article 31 (Employment Adjustment for Managerial Reasons) (1) Dismissal of a worker by an employer for managerial reasons shall be based on urgent managerial needs.	Article 31 (Restriction of Dismissal for Managerial Reasons) (1) Dismissal of a worker by an employer for managerial reasons shall be based on urgent managerial needs. In such cases as transfer, acquisition and merger that are aimed at avoiding financial difficulties, it shall be deemed that an urgent managerial need exists.
(2) In the case of paragraph (1), an employer shall make every effort to avoid dismissal of workers and shall select workers to be dismissed by establishing rational and fair criteria for dismissal. (3) (4): Omitted –	(2) In the case of paragraph (1), an employer shall make every effort to avoid dismissal of workers and shall select workers to be dismissed by establishing rational and fair criteria for dismissal. In such cases, there shall be no discrimination on the basis on gender. (3), (4) and (5): Omitted Article 31-2 [NEW] Preferential Re-employment, etc.
Article 32 (Advance Notice of Dismissal): [Revised in 1974]	Article 32 (Advance Notice of Dismissal) [Partly revised in 1999]
Article 33 (Application for Remedy for Unfair Dismissal)	Article 33 (Application for Remedy for Unfair Dismissal)

Note: The article numbers in the current act are those that were introduced after the wholesale amendments that were carried out in 2007: 31 for 24, 31-2 for 25, 32 for 26, 33 for 28. However the provisions of the articles remained unchanged.
Source: Ministry of Labor. The English text is available on the 'Legislation' page of its website at http://english.molab.go.kr/english/Legislation. See Nihon Rōdō Kenkyū kikō (2001: 238–9, 282) for a commentary.

Regarding the first step in 1997, as a result of the withdrawal of the "*nalchigi*" (nonsense) legislation, the initial managerial dismissal clause was confined to the four principles mentioned above.

During the second step, namely the Social Pact of the Tripartite Commission in February 1998, the reasonable scope of managerial dismissal was widened to include cases of mergers and acquisitions simply by adding the introductory proviso "In such cases".

In return for the easing of managerial dismissal, the Pact decided to add Article 31-2 (Preferential Re-employment) and also attempted to utilize and refine the wage credit guarantee and retirement payment arrangements, whose origins date back to the1960s, in order to protect the workers (Song and Hong 2006: 289).

The details of the latter two refinements are as follows.

In the case of retirement payment (see Table 6.6), the 1961 Labor Standards Act stated that the employer should pay to workers at retirement, or at the voluntary cessation of employment, or following a discharge for disciplinary reasons, an amount equivalent to 30 days or more of the average wage (including bonuses, etc.) for each year of consecutive service to the firm. As of 1987 the penalty for failing to implement this provision was imprisonment for up to three years or a fine not exceeding ten million won. The severity of this penalty was exceeded only by that accompanying the legislation applying to compulsory saving and unjustifiable dismissal. A minor amendment was made in 1980, and 1997 saw the introduction of payment in the form of lump sums and retirement insurance. The relevant articles were transferred into the Retirement Benefit Security Act of 2005. As mentioned earlier, "retirement payment" in fact fulfilled the role of unemployment insurance, because lifetime employment was not rooted in the overall labor system (Bang 1998: 22–3).

The wage claim guarantee was introduced in 1974, during the oil crisis, and an improved version appeared in the form of the Wage Claim Guarantee Act of 1998, which ordered the Minister of Labor to establish the Wage Claim Guarantee Fund. The Fund collects a charge up to 0.2 percent of the total wage from the employers and in the event of bankruptcy of the firm, pays the workers an amount equivalent to three months of unpaid wages as well as retirement payments.

The birth of this provision may be related to a temporary one-year suspension of the National Welfare Pension Act in 1974. The suspension became indefinite (which meant in effect that the act was abolished) in 1975. After that, not only because the initial article had never been executed in fact but also because there were many court cases relating to the tax-priority principle and the mortgage priority system during the 1980s,

Table 6.6 Development of provisions of retirement benefit

Date of Revision	Provision in Labor Standards Act	Size of establishments affected • No. of the workers affected
Dec. 1961	Article 28 (Retirement Benefit) An employer shall set up a retirement benefit scheme that makes it possible to pay workers who retire a sum equivalent to 30 days or more of average wages for each year of their consecutive service as retirement pay, but this shall not apply to workers whose consecutive service period is less than one year.	From 4 Dec. 1961 to 27 Apr. 1975: with more than 30 workers • 452,951 workers in 1966 • 945,675 workers in 1970
Dec. 1974	Article 28 (Retirement Benefit): [Unchanged] Article 30-2 (Preferential Reinforcement for Claim of Wages): [New: Omitted]	From 28 Apr. 1975 to 31 Dec. 1987: with more than 16 workers • 1,448,099 workers in 1975 • 2,841,317 workers in 1980 • 3,583,457 workers in 1985
Dec. 1980	Article 28 (Retirement Benefit System) (1): [Same as the former Article 28] (2) Prohibition of Differentiation System within Same Business:[New] Clause 2 of Article 30: Preferential Reinforcement for Claim of Wages: [Unchanged]	From 1 Jan. 1988 to 28 Mar. 1989: with 10 workers over
Dec. 1997	Article 34 (Retirement Benefit System) (1)(2): Same as the former (3) Put-off Payment before Retirement is available: [New] (4) Retirement Insurance and Retirement Pay Trustee system: [New] Article 37 (Preferential Reinforcement for Claim of Wages)	Since 29 March 1989: with more than 5 workers • 5,365,613 workers in 1990 • 6,167,596 workers in 1995 • 7,255,721 workers in 1999
Jan. 2005	Article 34 (Retirement Benefit System): With regard to the retirement benefits paid by employers to retiring workers, conditions prescribed by the employee under the Retirement Benefit Security Act shall apply.[1] Article 37 (Preferential Reinforcement for Claim of Wages)	

Note: [1] The act was newly enforced at the same time as the amendment in January 2005.
Source: The Provisions are from Kim Soo-Bok (2006) and So-Peop-jeon, various issues. The mandatory applications are from Yoon (2006: 206), and the applied numbers are from Park and Rhee (2002: 30).

the three-month rule was finally adopted for wages by an amendment of 1989 and for the retirement benefit by the Constitutional judge in 1997.

In very broad terms, the new Fund system can be regarded as an inter-business mutual support system, or in other words a way in which funds can be redistributed from profitable companies to bankrupt ones.

Thus, the government has taken advantage of legislation such as the retirement benefit and the wage claim guarantee to prepare the way for the introduction of a flexible labor market during the third stage. Furthermore, urgent measures have been taken to set up a new scheme for the "limited-time" livelihood recipient, who will not be fully covered by these various labor-related measures in the process of the radical welfare reform being undertaken by the Special Committee for Unemployment and Economic Restructuring within the Assembly in 1998 (Ministry of Labor 2001: 265). The unemployment rate declined between 1998 and 2002, and provided grounds for hope among government officials. However, the expectation of a long-term improvement turned out to be too optimistic. Unemployment again worsened after 2003 and did not rebound, even after the economic recovery that got under way in 2004 (Cheon et al. 2005a, b). With the worsening of the unemployment situation, it has become widely recognized that a modern informal sector (otherwise known as the working poor), typically consisting of a large number of non-standard workers, has emerged due to policy of promoting flexibility in the labor market (Nam, Ryu and Choi 2005; Cheon, Kim and Sin 2006; Cheong et al. 2005).

Let us now examine the reality of these non-standard workers.

In Korea, where it was hoped that lifetime employment would take root from the 1960s onwards, the legalization of dismissals through mergers and acquisitions in 1998 caused an expansion in the number of non-standard workers, even among male employees, a development that was widely attributed to the business reforms introduced after the IMF crisis (Park Tae-gyeon 2003; Oh 2006; Mukōyama 2005; Yokota 2000; Lee 2004).

The positive opinion of Ka and Yang (2004), who find merit in the existence of non-standard labor, remains very much a minority view.

Whereas the two kinds of non-standard labor (flexi-time workers and dispatch workers) were defined (for the first time ever) in the Labor Standards Act of 1997, Yokota (2003) has pointed out three types of classification based on labor contracts and working patterns: time-limited labor in which the workers do not expect their contracts to be renewed (in fact they have no clear contract period), fixed-term labor, and abnormal labor in special occupations such as dispatching and call-center work.

It has turned out that the existing way in which the labor statistics are organized by status, and in which regular workers (originally full-time and permanent labor), and temporary and daily workers (typically hired in construction work day-by-day) are distinguished, does not fit Yokota's classification, and, more importantly, under the official system of classification, short-time or part-time employees are easily slipped into the unemployed category (Kang, Cheon and Lee 1999: 90–3). As shown in Table 6.7, an additional survey in August 2005 found that the number of non-standard employees who are at the same time classified as temporary or daily amounted to as much as three million or 20 percent of the total workforce. Although they in fact work as non-standard employees, the government has not officially identified them as non-standard but as "unstable and vulnerable employees" in accordance with the agreement of the tripartite committee.

With the issue of the definition and the number of the non-standard employees unresolved, the bills to provide security for non-standard employees which were sent to the Assembly in 2004 finally came to an abortive end as a result of strong objections from the Democratic Labor Party and the *Min-nochong* in February and April 2006 (Kim Jo-Seol 2007: 42–3). The reasons for their forcible blocking of the legislation were twofold. First, the bills excluded other categories of non-standards, and, second, the introduction of one- or two-year contract terms, when applied to these employees, would have forced them out of work and on to the street. However, regarding the latter point, the employers, too, opposed the proposals because non-standards would have to be treated as standards immediately after the expiry of their formal contracts.

Table 6.7 Cross-classification by status and type of employment in the supplementary survey of August 2005

Type of employment Status	Standard/direct employment	Non-standard/ indirect employment	Total (Thousands) (%)
Regular employees	6,414 (42.9)	1,512 (10.1)	7,926 (53.0)
Temporary employees Daily workers	3,073 (20.5)	3,970 (26.5)	7,034 (47.0)
Total	9,786 (63.4)	5,483 (36.6)	14,968 (100.0)

Source: Kim, Jo-Seol (2006: 87). (Originally from the website of the Ministry of Labor, at http://molab.news.go.kr/molab/index.html – last accessed on January 31, 2006).

The power balance that affected labor policy in those days will be discussed in the next section and at this point, suffice it to point out that the bills were slightly amended at the tripartite committee (with the exclusion of the *Min-nochen*) on September 11, 2006 and then passed through the Assembly after only 20 minutes of discussion. The minutes of the discussion record 18 declarations of "House in disorder" and one of "Unable to hear". The 2006 legislation for dispatching, fixed-term and short-term employees prescribed the application of contract terms of two years, with a fine of thirty million won payable by any employer violating the law. Moreover the legislation prohibits any discrimination against non-standard workers, controls abuses in the way they are hired, and imposes and penalties on any illegal industrial action.

Whether the new measures will succeed in promoting conversions from non-standard to standard employment, and whether the legislation will bring about equality of treatment between the two categories without encouraging evasion of the regulations, very much remains to be seen.

To summarize our discussion so far, first we showed how the flexible labor market system has been legalized since the beginning of employment insurance in 1995. We have noted several refinements of the legislation pertaining to employment security, and we have pointed out that in 2006, and in the context of growing unemployment and the expansion of the number of non-standard employees, the Assembly succeeded in legalizing the two-years-contract rule and introduced a ban on discrimination against dispatchers and fixed-term employees by means of the tripartite negotiation.

6.3 Characteristics and possibilities of modern Korean neocorporatism

In order to make clear the features and functions of Korean neocorporatism, we will now examine the emergence of the policy makers, and will then discuss the concrete processes and arguments that have occurred during the period since 1996.

6.3.1 Labor and welfare policy makers

First let us trace the emergence of the policy makers: the government bureaus, the employers' organizations, the trade unions and the civil protest movement.

The governmental bureaus provided the laws and the policy recommendations until the third stage, when the National Assembly and other bodies emerged as policy makers. Labor and employment policy was taken over by a small department in the Ministry of Social Affairs[4] from 1948 until the establishment of the Labor Agency in 1963. Two offices were involved: the Industrial Policy Office whose brief in the early days was to control the left-wing labor movement and the Unemployment Measurement Office, which was concerned with measures to maintain job security. It was after the upgrade of these offices to Ministry status in 1981 that labor policy went into full swing, securing for Korea observer membership of the ILO in 1982, setting up the Standing Committee on labor within the National Assembly in 1988, and establishing the Korean Labor Institute (KLI).[5]

As for welfare, the various successive names given to the livelihood office rather than the Ministry itself (see footnote 4) are revealing, despite the status of the institution: *"wonho"* (support or assistance) from 1948 to 1961; *"kuho"* (relief and protection) from 1961 to 1970, *"boho"* (security or protection) from 1970 to 2000; and *"sengfal-bojang"* (security of lovelihood) following the welfare paradigm shift in 2000. The Korea Institute of Health and Social Affairs (KIHASA) was brought into being in 1981, through the merger of the Institute of Family Planning (established in 1971) and the Institute of Health Development (established in 1976), and given the name of the Institute of Population and Health.

Until the KLI and the KIHASA began to publish a wealth of research papers and policy suggestions in the 1990s, labor and welfare matters had come under the aegis of economic development, as has already been mentioned, and were handled by the Korea Development Institute (established in 1971) and by the Economic Planning Board (established in 1962 and later merged into the Board of Finance and Economy), whose chairperson was also vice prime minister.

Regarding the employers' organizations, the five major bodies have engaged in closer cooperation with each other since they set up the Private Committee for National Competitiveness in 1993.

The largest two of these, the Federation of Korean Industries founded in 1961 and the Korea Employers Federation organized in 1970, have sent representatives to the central tripartite negotiation, starting in 1996.

The former, with a membership of 421 enterprises, played a very important role in the execution of development policy under the authoritarian Park regime. It established the Korean Economic Research Center in 1981 and has recently entered the culture war by publishing materials opposing left-wing arguments, as shown by its editing high-school textbooks of economics in cooperation with the Ministry of Education and Human Resources. Significantly, these textbooks included no reference to workers' rights in their analysis of capitalist society and they were strongly criticized and rejected by the Korean Teachers and Education Workers' Union, which since being legalized in 1999, is one of the ultra-left members of the second national center.

The latter has been a particularly active agent in the maintenance of industrial peace since 1996.

The other major three organizations are as follows. The Korean Chamber of Commerce, whose origin dates back to 1884, was officially established by a special law in 1948.[6] The Korean International Trade Association was set up by 106 trading companies in 1946; and the Korea Federation of Small and Medium Business, was founded by a special law in 1961.

The business world has generally shown steady and strong collusion with the government, with the exception of the economic system reforms insisted on by the IMF during the time of President Kim Dae-Jung. However, we should note the fact that for a long period, the cooperative industrial relationship between employers and the state has aimed consistently at building an advanced system through legal methods, as was shown in the previous section. Examples include company-level single unionization from the 1970s onwards and the current reinforcement of compulsory in-house labor–management consultation (Kim Soo-bok 1998; Lee and Lee 2005).

Despite these efforts, such was the new strength of opinion within organized labor against the existing economic order that by the 1990s, there was no way to avoid legalizing second unions and allowing their entry into advanced society (Koo 2001, 2004; Kong 2000; Yoo 2005). This was the main reason why the government set up the first tripartite committee in 1996.

Let us now take a close look at a third party involved in the formulation of Korean labor policy.

The first national center, the Federation of Korean Trade Unions, *Han-nochong* or just *Nochong* in the Korean abbreviation, was an important partner of the authoritarian regime as the one and only legal union recognized by the government, a position it had held since its foundation in 1961. Moreover, as is well known, the chairperson of *Han-nochong*'s predecessor, a *de facto* subordinate organization of the government party in the 1950s, served as the first minister in 1955. *Han-nochong*, in a word, can be described as one of the most moderate trade unions in the world, and apart from a brief period from the end of 1996 to early 1997, when it was sorely provoked by the government's recklessness, it has never called for a general strike. *Han-nochong* tried to establish its own political party, first in the 1960s and again in the

1980s. Encouraged by the gradual liberation of political activity by the unions from 1997 onward, it established the Democratic Social Party in 2002, but the party later collapsed because of disunity (Yoo 2005: 493–502). Instead, it enjoys such a good relationship with the Conservative Party (the governmental party, except from 1998 to 2008) that it was subsidized by the right and its leaders entered the political world with the backing of the Conservatives. It is perhaps worth mentioning that the chairperson of *Han-nochong* declared his support for Kim Dae-Jung, a prominent candidate from the opposition party in the 1997 Presidential election, albeit at the risk of losing his personal status.

If *Han-nochong* were the only national center, the tripartite negotiation would have easily succeeded in liberalizing labor control. But the IMF crisis and also the emergence of a new radical national center made the situation more complicated, a development that will be dealt with below.

The new radical national center, the Korean Congress of Trade Unions, or *Min-nochong*, was established in 1995 and legalized in 1999 after the pluralism of unions was made possible by the 1997 law. No sooner had the union's political activities been permitted, but it established a new party, named People's Victory, and for the first time in the country's history, took part in a presidential election, in 1997. In 2000, the party was reorganized into the current Korean Democratic Labor Party (*Min-no-dang*). As of 2000, some 40 percent of its membership came from *Min-nocheong*. The KDLP, despite being such a newcomer, nevertheless won 10 seats out of the total of 299 in the National Assembly elections of 2004.[7]

As shown in Table 6.8, *Min-nochong* contains 20 percent of the unions in Korea, and accounts for more than 40 percent of total union membership. This is no mean achievement, considering that it is impossible to organize a vertical or regional branch in a company in which there is already an existing union. Moreover, as a result of *Min-nochong*'s combativeness, there have been more than 200 labor disputes since 2000. For example, the Hyundai Motor Workers' Union, one of *Min-Nochong*'s largest members, and founded by a mere 34 members in 1987, has been involved in labor disputes every year except 1994.[8]

In October 2006, just after the 9–11 Agreement, the police announced that they had arrested some leading members of a North Korean spy group within the DLP. They are a part of the 386 generation and the leader has American citizenship. The incident was a very strong setback for the DLP, and delivered a strong blow to *Min-Nochong*'s illegal disputes.

The then moderate executives of the two national centers agreed to merge the two units into one in 2006, when it was reported that the

Table 6.8 Labor unions and labor disputes

	1996 [1997]	2000	2005
No. of unions	6,424	5,698	5,971
Of which			
Vertical unions	27	46	44
Local unions	6,397	5,652	5,927
No. of unionists, in thousands	1,598	1,526	1,506
(Unionization ratio: %)	(13.3)	(12.0)	(10.3)
Share of *Han-Nocheon* and *Min-Nochen*			
In terms of no. of unions (%) (See note 1)	–	–	H60.7: M20.4
In terms of union members (%) (See note 1)	–	–	H51.2: M42.7
No. of applications for mediation	731	1,036	891
No. of labor disputes (see note 2)	85 [78]	250	287
By *Han-Nocheon*	[30]	32	39
By *Min-Nocheon*	[48]	208	244
No. of Participants I disputes (1,000 persons)	79	178	118
No. of lost work days (1,000 days)	892	1,893	1,199
No. of illegal labor disputes	13	67	17

Notes: (1) Because of the existence of non-affiliated independent unions, the total of the two largest unions does not come to 100.
(2) The data in the [ ] are as of 1997.
Source: Ministry of Labor, *White Paper on Labor* (2005).

newly emerged *Min-Nochong* had exceeded *Han-Nochong* in terms of union numbers. (This seemed an unrealistic suggestion as the two units were as unlikely to mix as oil and water.) Unfortunately, the integration plan was turned down by less moderate executives after the ones who made the proposal resigned over incidents such as accepting bribes for job placement. The two then resorted to a slanging match, using abusive terms such as "Yellow Union" for *Han-nochong* and "Underworld Body" for *Min-Nochong*.

The emergence of the new national center in 1995 was one of the main reasons that led the government to organize the tripartite negotiation body in the following year, a development that symbolized the beginning of a new sophisticated stage designed to lead the country into an advanced society.

6.3.2 Korean neocorporatism for a welfare state: from the first negotiation in 1996 to the '9–11 Agreement' of 2006

We will now discuss the development and inner workings of the tripartite negotiation bodies since 1996 and will then go on to compare Korean labor politics to welfare ones in order to identify the main features of neocorporatism in Korea.

Let us start by tracing the evolution of the government-led negotiation bodies over the three periods shown in Table 6.9. As has already been mentioned, the first presidential advisory body, introduced in 1996 and named the Presidential Commission on the Reform of Industrial Relations (hereafter, the Reform Commission), prepared the way for a comprehensive revision of the labor laws after repealing the government's forcible intervention in 1997. The second body, the Korea Tripartite Commission, was organized in an attempt to overcome the economic crisis, by President-elect Kim Dae-Jung in January 1998 and then legalized in May 1999. After the Grand Tripartite Agreement on the Roadmap for Industrial Relations Reforms that was published on September 11, 2006, the Commission was reorganized into the Economic and Social Development Tripartite Commission under new legislation in January 2007.

Regardless of differences in their legal status, the three bodies have shared three points in common: (1) though each of them has differed from the others in terms of composition, all of them were set up and controlled by the leadership of the government; (2) in each of the three bodies, third parties, such as governmental or neutral delegations, were given a majority membership in order to strengthen the arbitration function not only between labor and management but also between the two union federations; (3) the membership of each body has been appointed by the government; (4) the main aim of each body has been industrial relations reform under titles such as "normalization", "advancement", or "industrial peace" and each has attempted to resolve issues, such as pluralism, that form part of the authoritarian legacy; (5) all three bodies have supported the creation of a flexible labor market, albeit one that provides for some security of employment; and (6) each body has experienced the incomplete participation of *Min-Nochong* as a result of its decision to reject the first-phase version of the Commission.

Although the bodies share many similarities, each one has shown unique features according to the circumstances of its development and its internal composition.

Table 6.9 Three phases in the development of tripartite negotiation

Name of body		Membership composition	Major achievements
The Presidential Commission on Reform of Industrial Relations (ad-hoc): May 1996–1997		Five from labor and management, ten from universities and public-interest groups	Dec. 1996 '*nalchigi*' (poor and haste) Revision: failed Mar. 1997 Revision of Acts
The Commission of Labor Unions, Management and Government	First Phase (ad hoc): Jan.–Jun. 1998		Feb. 1998: the Grand Tripartite Agreement to overcome the crisis
	Second Phase (standing): Jun.1998–Sep.1999		Dismissal issue at Hyundai Motors
	* Third Phase: Sep. 1999–Dec. 2006	Less than 20 in total: one chairperson, one standing member, members from labor, management, govern-ment and public-interests	Sep. 2006: Roadmap for Advancement Dec. 2006: Revision of acts according to the Roadmap
* (Fourth phase) The Economic and Social Development Commission of Labor Unions, Management and Government: since Jan. 2007		Ten: one chairperson, one standing member, two each from labor, management, government and public-interest groups	

* The Act of the Tripartite Commission was enforced in May 1999. Despite of the new name given after the act's revision in 2006, the Commission itself regards the current Commission from 2007 as the fourth phase Commission.
Source: Kimiya (2001); Economic and Social Development Commission (2007); the Commission's website homepage at http://www.lmg.go.kr/eng/index.asp Last accessed February 9, 2009.

The membership of the first Reform Commission consisted of five delegates from the employees' side, five from the employers' side, ten from academic institutions and another ten neutral members. The most remarkable feature of the membership was the inclusion of two delegates from the newly founded and illegal *Min-Nochong* who joined formally together with three delegates from *Han-Nochong*. Thanks to the balanced composition of the committee, it succeeded in reaching agreements without much delay. Moreover, the committee intervened strongly whenever the government violated the regulations. As a result, the first commission can be praised for demonstrating the constructive possibilities of the new consulting mechanism on labor issues.

The unexpected economic crisis, however, disrupted the desired functioning of the following commission, whose development underwent three phases. According to Kimiya (2001), in the first phase, and while it still had only ad hoc status (from January to June 1998), the commission in February 1998 persuaded *Min-Nochong* to agree to "the Great Social Pact", which included greater transparency in management and the establishment of a social security safety net. The most important outcome of the second phase (from June 1998 to September 1999) was the resolution of the managerial dismissal of workers by Hyundai Motors, even though this was by law originally a matter for the Labor Committee. The most undesirable incident was the total withdrawal of *Min-nochong* in protest over the dismissal provision and, more than that, over the suspension of the legalization of the teachers' union, which meant that by the same token, *Min-Nochong* itself was suspended, in February 1999, just a few months before the commission's legalization.

The third phase (from September 1999 to the end of 2006) was the most impartial in the history of the membership of the commission, which eventually ended up with just one member from labor (needless to say, *Han-nochong*), two from management, eight from government (the Ministries of Labor, Industry and Resources, Economy and Finance, Banking Control and Budget) and another eight from neutral parties as well as a chairperson and a standing member: The act that established the commission stipulated that the membership should consist of one chairperson, one standing member, together with members from labor, management, the government and the public interests and that it should be less than twenty in total.

In its third phase, the commission, whose standing status by law remained unchanged, recorded no activities until 2003 (Nihon Rōdō Kenkyō Kikō 2001: 155), when President Roh took office at a time of fragile economic recovery with higher unemployment and an increasing number of non-standard workers. The Roh government sent the "Reform Proposal for the Advancement of Industrial Relations Laws and Systems", sometimes known as "the Roadmap" or "the Advancement Proposal", to the commission in September 2003.

Even though the commission could have agreed on the reform plans, the bill would have been turned down by the National Assembly after the general election of 2004, when for the first time the Democratic Labor Party won ten seats. In fact, it took two years to pass the non-standard workers' bills since they were not submitted until November 2004.

When *Han-Nochong* fully re-joined the commission in February 2006, the Roh government again pushed the commission for intensive discussions, in March. In the event, *Han-Nochong* agreed to the Roadmap in August with two employer organizations, the Korea Chamber and the Employers Federation.[9] The Roadmap was soon authorized and published by the commission on September 11, 2006, and then, as stated in the previous section, the relating bills in line with the Roadmap were enacted despite DLP members' attempts to block the legislation in November and they were passed at the end of the year.

The essence of the Roadmap was, briefly, a mixture of containment of *Min-nochong* and the introduction of a more flexible employment system followed by a measure of employment security. The major contents are: (1) the postponement of company-based union pluralism until 2010; (2) the postponement of the application of the no-pay rule to full-time union officials; (3) allowing firms to hire 'substitute workers' during a legal strike; (4) the abolition of the compulsory arbitration system for essential public services instead of enlarging the scope of its application, and as regards employment; (5) the shortening of the advanced notification of dismissal to a range of 30 to 50 working days from 60 working days; (6) compensation for unfair dismissal, and the abolition of the criminal penalty against unfair dismissal; and (7) the requirement for employment contracts and dismissal notifications to be in written form.

Min-Nochong and the DLP have bitterly criticized the Roadmap as "the 9-11 Deal" and have so far rejected joining what they consider to be an "unfairly-composed" commission.

Let us now briefly consider the third commission, "Economic and Social Development Commission of Labor Unions, Management and the Government" established in January 2007. The new commission, in which the regional commissions and the subcommittees by agenda (now six) and industry (now two) take part, has been strengthened in structure so that it can effectively take leadership on all-round labor issues.

The Plenary Committee for deliberation and decision consists of a chairperson, a standing member, and two members each from labor, management, government and the public interest; ten members in total. Whereas the number of the labor-and-management members has to be four out of ten by law, the current composition is just two among the total, and the total, curiously, becomes 11 because of *Min-nochong*'s absence. To sum up, how can we evaluate the commission since 1996 from the corporatism point of view?

First, we can regard the commission as discharging a social dialogue function appropriate for an advanced citizens' society, especially when compared to the authoritarian stage, in which workers were required to "keep the labor laws." The commission has also moved beyond the transition stage, when the workers' rights to unity and to take industrial actions were still limited.

Second, although it is true that the commission played an important role in introducing laws and provisions designed to promote a flexible labor market, it is impossible to be sure whether the flexibility could have been prevented without the commission. What we have to take into account is the fact that employment security policies have also been introduced.

Third, judging from the composition and operation of the commission, it could be said that "tripartite" is a misnomer. Besides the chair and standing member, the commission is made up of four groups: labor, management, government and public interest. Therefore the term quadripartite might be more appropriate. When we consider that the two members of labor represent two separate and conflicting bodies and moreover when we consider that the public interest figures are appointed by the government, perhaps it is more accurate to say that the commission is composed not of three or four parts but of two and a half.

At the present stage, the commission resembles an administrative bureau typical of current Korean neocorporatism but with a serious division in the representation of labor. A true evaluation of the commission must wait until the full execution of union pluralism in 2010.

Finally, I should like to mention, if only briefly, another three points. First, even within official employment policy, there has been an interaction of security and mobility. All that we can say with confidence is that flexibility and security, including universal welfare, proceeded simultaneously. To judge which is the main or leading factor requires further research. Moreover, both the tripartite commission in labor and the citizens' movement in welfare can be regarded as new policy makers in the third stage and as symbols of Korean neocorporatism. Finally, despite the differences in status between the authorized body in labor and voluntary organizations in welfare, both have relied on legislation as a method to realize the formation of an advanced society.

Conclusion

Why and how did the Korean government abolish security of employment in the 1990s in the form of social dialogue, while at the same time introducing a universal welfare paradigm? And what does it mean in terms of social development?

In order to answer these questions, this chapter has analyzed the development of the policy mix of labor, or, in other words, of employment and industrial relations, and welfare through three main sections and we have examined the process of reform under the government-led tripartite negotiation bodies in the 1990s as an exemplar of Korean neocorporatism. It is also worth mentioning that in the case of Korea, globalization, such as membership of the UN, the ILO and the OECD, and also the IMF crisis, has affected policy trends as well as the economic situation in general.

In the context of a flexible labor market for global competition, what will come after Korean neocorporatism very much depends on the labor politics that will follow the introduction of full union pluralism in 2010.

Notes

1. Takegawa (2007: 146–51) observed, while discussing the methodology of international comparison, that the choice of the times to be compared is of critical importance: should we compare different performances at the same time or different stages in the same process of creating a welfare state?
2. Over fifty years have passed since the Ministry of Health and Social Affairs was established in 1955 (the Ministry of Health and Social Welfare from 1995; now the Ministry of Health, Welfare and Family, from February 2008), and during that time, birth control policy has switched completely, from how to decrease the population to how to increase it.
3. The enforcement of the four major labor acts, namely the Labor Standards Act, the Labor Committee Act, the Trade Union Act and the Labor Relations Act (the last two of which were merged into one in 1997), was postponed by the Korean War after 1949 and was finally achieved following Korea's largest labor dispute, led by the left wing at the Chosun Bangjik (Spinning) Company in 1952.
4. Often mentioned as a symbolic episode of state corporatism is the fact that the influential chairperson of the single national labor center, Mr Cheon Jin-han, was appointed as the first Minister of Social Affairs in 1948. The ministry's name was changed to Health and Social Affairs (1955–1994), then to Health and Welfare (2000–2008) and finally to Health, Welfare and Family (since February 2008).
5. Later, in 1997, the Korea Research Institute for Vocational Education and Training was established with the task of implementing the arrangements for employment insurance and for the new Employment Framework Act.

6. Until 2006, the law required all commercial and industrial enterprises with a certain sales tax of over a certain volume to become members of the Chamber through its 71 local branches.
7. The members of the Labor Party have so much knowledge of labor that, according to the media, even the Conservative Party's representatives have hired no less than 30 LP supporters as advisers or secretaries even though aware of their LP affiliation (*Chosun Ilbo*, 4 Dec. 2006).
8. The company announced that the financial damage caused by the disputes amounted to a total of 164 billion won for 2006, and decided to take legal action for damages caused by the illegal disputes of 2007, in response to which the union took another action. A member of the same group, Hyundai Heavy Industry, appealed, arguing that the union had been cooperative and had instigated no labor dispute for 12 years (*Chosun Ilbo*, 6 February 2007).
9. http://english.molab.go.kr/english/labor/Industrial_Reform.jsp. The agreement among the three bodies in August may have been done behind closed doors according to the media, and, in fact, there was no formal session in the short history of the Commission (http://www.lmg.go.kr/committee/committee03_2006.asp; As is the same in its Korean text)(Last accessed on 21 August 2008).

References

Japanese

Ahn, Chun-Sik. 1982. *Shūshin Koyōsei no Nikkan Hikaku* [Comparative Study of Lifetime Employment in Japan and Korea]. Tokyo: Ronsō-sha.

Baek, Pil-Gyu. 1996. *Kankoku Rōshi Kankei no Shin-Kōzō: Amerika-gata kara Nihon-gata e* [The New Structure of Labor–Management Relations in Korea: from the American Type to the Japanese Type]. Tokyo: Nihon-keizai-hyōron-sha.

Cheong, Moo-Gwon. (Odagawa Hanako tr.) 2006. "Kankoku no Kaihatsushugi Fukushi Reejimu" [The Korean Developmental Regime of Welfare]. *Shakai Seisaku Gakkai* 2006: 113–33.

Hōsei University [Hōsei Daigaku], Ohara Shakai Kagaku Kenkyūsho. 1998. *Gendai no Kankoku Rōshi Kankei* [Modern Industrial Relations in South Korea]. Tokyo: Ochanomizu Shobō.

Inagami, Tsuyoshi et al. 1994. *Neo-corporatism no Kokusai Hikaku Kenkyū* [International Comparative Study of Neo-corporatism]. Tokyo: Nihon Rōdō Kenkyū Kikō.

Ishizaki, Nao. 2003. "Kankoku no Safety-net" [The Safety-net in South Korea]. Hitotsubashi University and Teranishi 2003: 55–101.

Kankoku Shakai Kagaku-in. (Yeon-Ja Kim ed./tr.) 2002. *Kankoku no Shakai Fukushi* [South Korea's Social Welfare]. Tokyo: Shinkan-sha.

Kim, Jo-Seol. 2002. "Kankoku-gata 'Fukushi-kokka' e no Seiji-shakai Rikigaku" [Social and Political Dynamics for the Formation of a Korean 'Welfare State']. *Chōsen-Shōgakkai Gakujutu Ronbun-shū* 24: 49–74. Tokyo: Chōsen Syōgakkai.

Kim, Jo-Seol. 2003. "Kankoku-gata 'Fukushi-kokka' no Shidō" [The Starting-up of a 'Korean Welfare State']. Usami ed. 2003: 85–134.

Kim, Jo-Seol. 2004a. "IMF Taisei to 'Kankoku-gata Fukushi Kokka'" [Korean Welfare State under the IMF Framework]. *Kaigai Shakai-Hoshō Kenkyū* 146: 43–53. Tokyo: Shakai Hoshō Jinkō Mondai Kenkyū-sho.

Kim, Jo-Seol. 2004b. "Shakai Hoshō Seido no Kakuritsu" [The Establishment of a Social Security System]. In *Henbō-suru Kankoku Keizai* [The Changing Korean Economy], ed. Park Il: pp. 183–200. Kyōto: Sekai Shisō-sha.

Kim, Jo-Seol. 2005. "Kankoku/Kōteki Fujo no Kyūgo/Hogo kara Fuhen-teki Saitei-seikatsu-hoshō e no Tenkan" [Transition from the Protection of State Aid to the Universal Guarantee of a Minimum Livelihood in the Republic of Korea]. Usami ed. pp. 73–124.

Kim, Jo-Seol. 2007. "Rensai Shiryō 3 : Shinkō-kōgyō-koku ni okeru Koyō to Shakai Hoshō" [Research Materials Series 3: Employment and Social Security in the Newly Industrializing Economies]. *Ajia-keizai* 48, no. 1: 32–51.

Kim, Seong-Won. 2006. "Kankoku Fukushi Kokka Ronsō" [Controversy over the Korean Welfare State]. In *Kōhatsu Fukushi Kokka-ron* [On the Late Developing Welfare State], ed. Noguchi. 2006: 107–23. Tōkyō Daigaku Shuppan-kai.

Kim, Yeong-Myeong ed. (Kankoku Shakai Hoshō Kenkyū-kai tr.) 2006. *Kankoku Fukushi Kokka Seikaku Ronsō* [Controversy over the Characteristics of the Korean Welfare State]. Chiba: Ryūtsū Keizai Daigaku Shuppan-kai.

Kim, Yu-Seong. 2001. *Kankoku Rōdō-hō no Tenkai* [Development of Korean Labor Laws]. Tokyo: Shinzansha-shuppan.

Kimiya, Masahi. 2001. "Kankoku ni okeru Keizai Kiki to Rōshi Kankei Reejimu no 'Tenkan'" [Economic Crisis and the 'Turning' of Industrial Relations in South Korea]. In *Kankoku Keizai no Kaibō* [A Dissection of the Korean Economy], ed. Matumoto Koji and Tamio Hattori. Tokyo: Bunshin-dō, pp. 213–35.

Ko, Yong-Soo. 2000. *Kankoku no Keizai Shisutemu* [The Korean Economic System]. Tokyo: Tōyō-keizai-shinpō-sha.

Koo, Hae-Gun. (Ko Yong-Soo tr.) 2004. *Kankoku no Rōdōsha* [Korean Workers]. Tokyo: Tōyō Keizai Shinpō-sha.

Lee, Tae-Wang. 2004. *Hyundai Shisutemu no Kenkyū* [A Study of the Hyundai System]. Tokyo: Chūō Keizai-sha.

Mukōyama, Hidehiko. 2005. "Kankoku Rōdō Shijō no KōzōHenka" [Structural Change in the South Korean Labor Market]. *Kan-Taiheiyō Business Jōhō, RIM.* vol. 5(18): 7–29. Tokyo: Nihon Sōken.

Nam, Chang-Sub. (Kim Yeong-Ja tr.) 2002. "Kankoku no Fukushi Seido to sono Seikaku" [Korea's Welfare System and its Characteristics]. Kankoku Shakai Kagaku-in, pp. 9–35.

Nam, Chang-Sub. (Kim Jo-Seol tr.) 2006. "Kankoku Fukushi Kokka no Ruikeika ni kan-suru Hihan-teki Kenkyū" [Critical Study of Systematic Classifications of the Korean Welfare State]. ed Kim Yeong-Meong, pp. 203–40.

Nihon Rōdō Kenkyū Kikō, ed. 2001. *Kankoku no Rōdō-hō Kaikaku to Rōshi kankei* (Revision of the Labor Laws and Industrial Relations in South Korea). Tokyo: Nihon Rōdō Kenkyū Kikō.

Noguchi, Sadahisa, ed. 2007. *Fukushi Kokka no Keisei-Saihen to Shakai Fukushi Seisaku* [Formation and Reorganization of the Welfare State and Social Welfare Policy]. Tokyo: Chūō Hōki.

Oh, Hak-Ju. 2006. "Nikkan Rōshi-kankei no Hikaku: Hi-seiki-shoku wo Chushin-ni [Comparative study of the labor–management relations between Japan and Korea: on the non-regular worker]. Mimeo of presentation for the seminar held at Ohara Shakai Mondai Kenkyusho, Hosei University on February 23, 2005.

Park, Jong-Nyul. (Yoon Yong-Taek tr.) 1998. "Kankoku Rōdō-hō no Kadai" [Issues concerning South Korean Labor Laws]. In *Nikkan ni okeru Rippō no Shin-tenkai*

[New Developments in Legislation in Japan and South Korea], ed. Atsumi Tōyō and Takeshi Kojima. Tokyo; Chūō Daigaku Shuppan-bu, pp. 103–19.

Park, Tae-Gyeon. 2003. *Naze Kankoku no Ginkō wa Yomigaetta kanoka* [Why South Korea's Banks have Recovered]. Tokyo: Diamond-sha.

Schmitter, Philippe C. and Gerhard Lehmbruch. (Yamaguchi Yasusi et al. trs.) 1984. *Gendai Koporatizumu* [Modern Corporatism]. Tokyo: Bokutaku-sha.

Shakai Seisaku Gakkai ed. 2006. *Higashi Ajia ni okeru Shakai Seisaku-gaku no Tenkai* [Developments in the Study of Social Policy in East Asia]. Kyoto: Hōritsu Bunka-sha.

Son, Chang-Hee. 1985. *Kankoku no Rūshi Kankei* [Korea's Industrial Relations]. Tokyo: Nihon Rōdō Kenkyū-Kikō.

Song, Chang-Hee. 1995. *Kankoku no Rōshi-kankei* [Industrial Relations in South Korea]. Tokyo: Nihon Rōdō Kenkyū Kikō.

Song, Gang-Jik. 2001. *Kankoku no Rōdō-hō* [Korea's Labor Laws]. Tokyo: Yūyū-sha.

Takegawa, Shōgo and Hyegyeon Rhee, eds. 2005. *Fukushi Reejimu no Nikkan-hikaku* [Comparison of the South Korean and Japanese Welfare Regimes]. Tokyo: Tokyo Daigaku Shuppan Kai.

Takegawa, Syogo and Yeong-Myeong Kim ed. 2005. *Kankoku no Fukushi-kokka, Nihon no Fukushi-kokka* [Korean Welfare State, Japanese Welfare State]. Tokyo: Toshin-dō.

Tamai, Kingo. 2006. "Nihon ni okeru Shakai-seisaku no Tenkai to Tokushitu" [Development and Characteristics of Social Policy in Japan]. Tokyo: Shakai Seisaku Gakkai, pp. 25–46.

Tamura, Toshiyuki. 2008. *Kankoku Keiken no Seiji-keizaigaku* [Political Economy of South Korea's Experience]. Tokyo: Seizan-sha.

Tsujinaka, Yutaka. 1994. "Hikaku Koruporachizumu no Kiso-teki Sūryō Bunseki" [A Basic Numerical Analysis of Comparative Corporatism]. Inagami et al., pp. 423–37.

Usami, Kōichi (ed.) 2003. *Shinkō Fukushi Kokka-ron* [A Theoretical Approach to Newly-emerging Welfare States]. Chiba: Institute of Developing Economies.

Usami, Kōichi. 2005. *Shinkō Kōgyōkoku no Shakai Fukushi* [Social Welfare in the Newly Industrializing Countries]. Chiba: Institute of Developing Economies.

Usami, Kōichi, and Kumiko Makino, eds. 2007. *Shinkō Kōgyōkoku ni okeru Kōyō to Shakai Hoshō* [Labor and Social Security in the Newly Industrializing Countries]. Chiba: Institute of Developing Economies.

Yamaji, Kumiko. 2007. "Book Review: *Fukushi Rejimu no Nikkan Hikaku* (Takegawa and Lee, 2006)". *Asia Kenkyū* 53, no. 1: 84–9.

Yang, Jae-jin. 2006. "Kankoku ni okeru Shinjiyū-shugi to Rōdō Shijō" [Neo-liberalism and the Labor Market in South Korea]. Takegawa and Lee 2006, pp. 207–27.

Yokota, Nobuko. 2000. "1987-nen igō no Kankoku Rōdō Shijō no Kōzō Henka to Rōshi kankei" [Structural Change in the Labor Market and Industrial Relations since 1987 in South Korea]. Yamaguchi University, *Tōa Keizai Kenkyū* 58, no. 3: 1–31.

Yokota, Nobuko. 2003. "Kankoku ni okeru Rōdō Shijō no Jūnan-ka to Hiseikishoku Rōdōsha no Kibo no Kakudai" [Flexibility of the Labor Market and the Expansion in the Number of Non-standard Workers in South Korea]. Hōsei University, *Ohara Shakai Mondai Kenkyū-sho Zasshi*, no. 535 (June 2003): 36–54.

Yoon, Jo-Deok (Park Kwan-Jun tr.). 2006. "Kankoku ni okeru Shakai Seisaku no Kanōsei" [Possibilities for Social Policy in South Korea]. Tokyo: Shakai Seisaku Gakki, pp. 2–60.

Korean

Bang, Ha-Nam. 1998. *Hanguk Kieob wui Taejik-kum Jedo Yeongu* [Research on the Retirement Lump Sum System of Korean Companies]. Seoul: Korea Labor Institute.

Chamyeo Bokji Kihoik-dan [Project Team for Participatory Welfare], Ministry of Health and Welfare and Korea Institute of Heath and Social Affairs. 2004. *Chamyeo Bokji 5-geyeon Kyehoik* [Five-year Plan for Participatory Welfare]. Seoul: Korea Institute of Heath and Social Affairs.

Cheon, Byeon-Yoo, Hye-Won Kim and Dong-Gyun Shin. 2006. *Nodong Sijang wui Yangguk-hwa wa Cheongcek Kwaje* [Polarization of the Labor Market and Policy Issues]. Seoul: Korea Labor Institute.

Cheon, Byeon-Yoo, Hye-Won Kim and Dong-Gyun Shin. 2005a. *Koyong eop-nun Seonjang e teahan Taeoon Chellyak Yeongu* [Critical Research on the Strategy of Pursuing Economic Growth without Employment]. Seoul: Korea Labor Institute.

Cheon, Byeon-Yoo, Hye-Won Kim and Dong-Gyun Shin. 2005b. *Koyong eop-nun Seonjang e teahan Taeoon Chellyak Yeongu* [Critical Research on the Strategy of Pursuing Economic Growth without Employment]. Seoul: Korea Labor Institute.

Cheong, Gwan-Soo. 2000. *Hanguk Tosi Kullo-ja Kagye e taehan Yeongu* [Research on the Income and Expenditure of Urban Wage Earners' Households]. Seoul: Korea Development Institute.

Cheong, Jang-Ho, Hwang Deok-Soo, Lee Byeong-Hee and Chan-Im Park. 2005. *Hanguk wui Kunlo Binkon Yeongu* [Research on the Working Poor in South Korea]. Seoul: Korea Labor Institute.

Choi, Jang-Jip. 1988. *Hanguk wui Nodon Undong gwa Kukka* [Labor Movement and State in South Korea]. Seoul: Yeolum-Sa.

Im, Yeon-Jae and Lee Jung-Ga. 2003. *Kieop Nyeongum wui Jibae Kujo Siltae e kwanhan Sogo* [A Study of the Dominant Structure of Corporate Pensions]. Seoul: Korea Development Institute.

Ka, Jae-San, and Byeon-man Yang. 2004. *Bi-jeongyu-jik* [Non-standard or Flying Work]. Seoul: Joins H.R.

Kang, Sun-Hee, Cheon Jae-Sik and Kye-O Lee. 1998. *Sileob Tonggye wui Kaeseon Bangbeop* [Method for the Revision of Unemployment Statistics]. Seoul: Korea Labor Institute.

Kim, Hyeong-Bae and Ji-Sun Park. 2004. *Kunlo-ja Gaenyeom wui Byeonchang gwa Kwanryeon Beob wui Cheokyong* [Changes in the Concept of the Worker and Application of Related Laws]. Seoul: Korea Labor Institute.

Kim, In-Chun et al. 2005. *Segyehwa wa Nodong Kaehyeok* [Globalization and Labor Reform]. Seoul: Beaksan Seodang.

Kim, Seong-Jung and Je-Hwan Seong. 2005. *Hanguk wui Koyong Cheongchek* [Employment Policy of South Korea]. Seoul: Korea Labor Institute.

Kim, Soo-Bok. 1998. *Kunloja Chamye mit Hyeokryeok Chunjin e kwanhan Beobryul* [The Acts to Promote Workers' Participation and Cooperation]. Seoul: Chungang Kyeongje-sa.

Kim, Soo-Bok. 2006. *Kunro-Kijun-Beob (rev.)* [The Labor Standards Act]. Seoul: Chungang Kyeongje-sa.
Kim, Soo-Geon and Ju-Ho Lee. 1995. "Nosa Kwangye wa Inryeok Kaebal Cheongchek" [Industrial Relations and Human Resource Development Policy]. In *Hanguk Kyeonje Ban-segi* (A Half-century of Change in the Korean Economy), ch. 9. Seoul: Korea Development Institute, pp. 524–65.
Kong, Deok-Soo. 2000. *Hanguk wui Nodong Chohap kwa Nodong Cheongchi* [Trade Unions and Labor Politics in South Korea]. Seouk: Kyeonjin-sa.
Koo, Hae-Gun. (Shin Gwan-yeong tr.) 2002. *Hanguk Nodon Kyegub wui Kyeongseong.* [The Formation of the Korean Working Class]. Seoul: Changjak-kwa-pipyong.
Kyeonje Kujo Chojeong Chamun Hoeui [Council for Economic Structural Adjustment]. 1988. *Kyeonje Seonjin-hwa lul uihan Kibon Kusang* [Basic Plan for Economic Advancement]. Seoul: Council of Economic Structural Adjustment.
Lee, Ho-Gun. 2005. "Hanguk Nodon Sijan wui Yunan-hwa wa Bi-Jeongyu Kunro" [The Flexible Labor Market and Non-standard Work in Korea]. Kim In-Chun et al., pp. 259–319.
Lee, Ju-Hee and Lee Sung-Hyeop. 2005. *Kyeongyeong Chamye wui Siltae wa Kwaje* [Actual Situation and Problems of Workers' Participation]. Seoul: Korea Labor Institute.
Lee, Yong-Ha and Jin-Su Kim. 1998. *Kukmin Nyeongum Minyeon-wa wui Hosang* [The False Image of Privatizing National Pensions]. Seoul: National Pension Administration Corporation.
Nam Jae-Ryang, Ryu Gun-Gwan and Hyomi Choi. 2005. *Koyong Bulan-Kyechun wui Sinltae mit Koyong Cheonchek Kwaje* [The Actual Situation as regards Unstable Employees and Employment Policy Issues]. Seoul: Korea Labor Institute.
Nodon beob Pyeonram [Handbook of Labor Laws]. 2005. Seoul: Chunang Kyeonje-sa.
Nodon-bu [Ministry of Labor]. *Nodong-Baekseo* [White Paper on Labor]. various issues.
Nodon-bu [Ministry of Labor]. 2001. *Sileob Taechek Beakseo 1998–2000* [White Paper on Measures against Unemployment 1998–2000].
Nodon-bu [Ministry of Labor]. 2003. *Kukmin wui Jeongbu (1998–2002) Sileob Taechek Beakseo* [White Paper on Measures against Unemployment during the Years of the Kim Dae-Jung Government 1998–2002].
Nodon-bu [Ministry of Labor]. *Nodong Tongye Nyeonkam* [Yearbook of Labor Statistics]. Various issues.
Nodon-bu [Ministry of Labor]. *Koyong Boheom Baekseo* [White Paper on Employment Insurance]. Various issues.
Noh-Sa Kwangye Kaehyeok Uiwon-hoi [Committee on Industrial Relations Reform]. 1996. *Ingum Taejik-kum-jedo, Nodong Johab wui Hwaldong* [Wages, the Retirement Lump Sum System and the Activities of Trade Unions]. Seoul: Committee on Industrial Relations' Reform.
No-sa-jeon Uiwon-hoi [The Tripartite Committee]. 2007. *Nosajeon Uiwon-hoi Hwaldong Bogo-seo 2006* [Report on the Tripartite Committee's Activities, 2006]. Seoul: Tripartite Committee.
Park, Jong-Gi et al. 1981. *Hanguk Sahoi Bojang Jedo Kaeseon ul uihan Yeongu Bogo-seo* [Research Report for the Improvement of the Korean Social Security System]. Seoul: Korea Development Institute.

Park, Chan-Yong. 1998. *Sahoi Bojang Palceon Mokpyo Seolceon gwa Cheongcek Kwaje* [Target-setting and Policy Issues for the Development of Social Security]. Seoul: Korea Institute for Health and Social Affairs.
Park, Hong-Min, and Gyeong-Hee Lee. 2002. *Kieop Neongum Sijang Hwalseon-hwa wa Boboheom hoisa Taeung Ceolyak* [Activation of the Company Pension Market and the Strategy of the Insurance Companies]. Seoul: Insurance Development Institute.
Salm wui Jil Hyangsang Kihoik-dan [Project Team for the Improvement of the Quality of Life] in the Secretary Section to the President. 2002. *Sengsan-cheok Bokji wui Seongkwa wa Jeonman Toron-hoi Jaryo-Jip* [Discussion Materials on Results and Prospects of Productive Welfare].
Song, Ho-Gun, and Gyheong-Jun Hong. 2006. *Bokji Kukka wui Taedong* [The Rise of the Welfare State]. Seoul: Nanam Chulpan.
Yeo, Yu-Jin, Kim Mi-Geon, Kim Ta-Hwa, Yang Si-Hyeon and Hyeon-Soo Choi. 2005. *Bingon gwa Bul-gyundun wui Donghyang mit Yoin Bungae* [Trends in Poverty and Inequality: a Factor Analysis]. Seoul: Korea Institute of Health and Social Affairs.
Yoo, Beom-Sang. 2005. *Hanguk wui Nodong Undong Inyeom* [Principles of the Korean Labor Movement]. Seoul: Korea Labor Institute.
Yoon, Neong-Seon et al. 1986. "Nodong Cheonchek" [Labor Policy]. In *Hanguk Kyeonje Cheonchek 40 Nyeonsa* [A Forty Years' History of Korean Economic Policy], ch. 9. Seoul: Federation of Korean Industries, pp. 827–909.
Yoon, Uk-Hyeon (ed.). 2006. *Sae Nodong-beop Haeseol* [Handbook of the New Labor Laws]. Seoul: Hanguk Kyeonje Sinmun.

English

Choi, Jang Jip. 1991. *Labor and the Authoritarian State: Labor Unions in South Korean Manufacturing Industries, 1961–1980*. Seoul: Korea University Press.
Ginsburg, Tom. 2004. *Legal Reform in Korea*. London and New York: Routledge Curzon.
Holliday, Ian. 2000. "Productivist Welfare Capitalism: Social Policy in East Asia." *Political Studies* 48: 706–23.
Im, Hyung-Baeg. 1999. "From Affiliation to Association." McNamara, pp. 75–94.
Kim, Jo-Seol. 2004. "Formation and Development of the Welfare State in the Republic of Korea." *Developing Economies* 42, no. 2: 146–75.
Kim, Jo-Seol. 2007. "The New Strategies of Welfare and Labour for the Aging Society in the ROK". Presented for *the International Symposium on Social Policy in Asia* (pp. 21–34) on February 9–10, 2007 organized by the Public Economics Group, School of International and Public Policy and Graduate School of Economics, Hitotsubashi University, in Tokyo.
Kim, Soh-Yeong. 2004. "Korean labor law reform." Ginsburg, pp. 134–47.
Koo, Hagen. 2001. *Korean Workers*. Ithaca and London: Cornell University Press.
Kuhnle, Stein. 2004. "Productive Welfare in Korea." In Mishra et al. 2004.
Kwon, Huck-ju, ed. 2005. *Transforming the Developmental Welfare State in Asia*. New York: Palgrave Macmillan (UNRISD).
Lee, Byoung-Hoon. 2004. "Social Dialogue and Union Involvement in Korea." *Korea Journal of Political Economy* 2: 163–80.

Lee, Jae-Hyup. 2004. "Controlling Foreign Migrant Workers in Korea." Ginsburg 2004: pp. 148–68.
McNamara, Daniel I. ed. 1999. *Corporatism and Korean Capitalism*. London and New York: Routledge.
Martin, J.P., Peter Tergeist and Raymond Torres. 2004. "Reforming the Korean Labor Market and Social Safety Net." In *The Korean Economy*, ed. Charles Harvie, Hyun-Hoon Lee and Jung-Gun Oh. Cheltenham: Edward Elgar Publishing Limited, pp. 78–119.
Mishra, Ramesh, Stein Kuhnle, Neil Gilbert and Kyunbae Chung. 2004. *Modernizing the Korean Welfare State: Towards the Productive Welfare Model*. New Brunswick and London: Transaction Publishers.
Organization for Economic Cooperation and Development (OECD). 2000. *Pushing Ahead with Reform in Korea: Labour Market and Social Safety-net Policies*. Paris: OECD.
Shin, Dong-Myeon. 2003. *Social and Economic Policies in Korea*. London and New York: Routledge Curzon.
Yi, Ilcheong, and Byeong-hee Lee. 2005. "Development Strategies and Unemployment Policies in Korea." ed. Kwon. pp. 143–69.
Yoo, Kil-Sang. 2000. *The Employment Insurance System in Korea*, 2nd edition. Seoul: Korea Labor Institute.

URLs

The Assembly of the Republic of Korea www.assembly.go.kr/index.jsp.
The Reference System of the Assembly Record www.likms.assembly.go.kr/record/index.html.
The Ministry of Labor, the Republic of Korea www.molab.go.kr/.
The Ministry of Health and Welfare www.mohw.go.kr/index.jsp.
The Tripartite Committee www.img.go.kr.
The Democratic Labor Party www.kdlp.org/.
Korean Confederation of Trade Unions www.nodong.org/.
Federation of Korean Trade Unions www.fktu.or.kr/.

Index

Abascal, Carlos 24
African National Congress 73
Amín, Raúl 60
Argentina 47–72
   Association of Banks of Argentina (ADEBA) 52
   Association of Banks of the Republic of Argentina (ABRA) 52
   Bankruptcy Law 55
   Center of Argentine Workers (CTA) 51
   competitive corporatism 49, 50–7, 67–8
   Economic Emergency Law 50
   GDP 63
   General Confederation of Labour (CGT) 51
   Industrial Accident Law 55
   industrial relations 57–9
   labor contracts 58, 64
   Labor Liberalization Law 55
   labor market and deregulation 63–4
   labor reforms 57–9, 61–3
   Macro-Agreement on Employment, Productivity, and Social Equity 54, 55, 68
   medical insurance 59–60
   Menem regime 50–7
   National Reform Law 50
   neoliberal reform 48–50
   pension reform 53–4, 59–60
   Small and Medium-Sized Companies Law 55
   social security reform 59–60, 61–3, 64–6
   Stock Exchange of Buenos Aires 52
   unemployment insurance 64–6
   unemployment rate 2, 63–4, 65
Argentine Chamber of Commerce 52
Argentine Chamber of Construction 52
Argentine Industrial Union 52
Argentine Rural Society 52
Argentine Union of Construction 52
Australia, unemployment rate 2
authoritarianism *see* state corporatism

Bair Jeng-sharn 162
bargaining councils 78, 83
Brazil, unemployment rate 2

Cafiero, Antonio 51
Caro Figueroa, José Armando 52, 54, 55, 56, 60, 62
Cavallo, Domingo 50, 52, 54
Chan, Anita 101
Chang Kai 102
Chen Chieh 158
Cheon Moo-Gwon 181
Cheon Tai-il 190
China 98–141
   All China Federation of Industry and Commerce (ACFIC) 123
   All China Federation of Trade Unions (ACFTU) 103, 117–22
   Blue Book of Chinese Employment 104
   CED/CEDA 122–6
   dangzheng fenkai 103
   employers' associations 122–6
   employment 106–11
      increase of 109
      job vacancies 110
   GDP 106, 107
   General Chamber of Commerce 148–9
   gonghui 102
   gongren fuli-hui 119
   hexie shehui 98
   irregular employment 105

Labor Contract Law 98, 125, 134
labor disputes 98, 99, 106–11
labor laws 111–17
labor reforms 111–17
Labor and Social Security Inspection Agencies 115
labor surplus 107
lianyi-hui 119
migrant workers 108–9
  shortage of (*ming-gong huang*) 105
  social welfare reform 126–35
  unstable working conditions 111
  women 129
Minimum Wage Provision regarding Companies 113
minimum wage standards 114
National Labor Congress 157
neocorporatism 102–3
one-child policy 105–6
People's Liberation Army 103
Provision on Collective Labor Contracts 116
Provisional Regulation on Job Placement Service 113
Provisions on Collection of Social Insurance Premium 113
Regulations on Labor Protection Inspection 115
social corporatism 102
social security reform 1
state corporatism 102
Tiananmen Square Massacre 103, 113
tongxiang-hui 119
Trade Union Law 116, 117
  2001 Amendment 119
Transitional Provision on Pay Management of the Seasonal-workers in the Construction Industry 115
tripartite relations 100, 117–18
Unemployment Insurance Provisions 113
unemployment rate 2, 63
  young people 135
unionization 117–22
welfare policy 6
welfare reform 100
  migrant workers 126–35
  unemployed 126–35
Wailai Renshi Zonghe Baoxian 128
Work-related Injury Insurance Provisions 113
xiongdi-hui 119
yuangong julebu 119
Chinese Communist Party 103
Chinese Federation of Labor 149, 157
Chinese General Labour League 157
Chinese National Association of Industry and Commerce 149
Chinese National Federation of Industries 148
Chinese National Federation of Labor 157
Chinese People's Political Consultative Conference 123
Chuang Chueh-an 164
class mobilization 145
competitive corporatism 49, 50–7, 61, 67–8
core workers 82
corporatism 9–11, 14
  classification of 19
  as cognitive tool 143–6
  competitive 11, 49, 50–7, 61, 67–8
  control 145
  decline of 14
  definition of 19, 49
  fictitious 41
  neocorporatism *see* neocorporatism
  representation 145
  sectoral 179
  social *see* social corporatism
  state *see* state corporatism

delegative democracy 48
democratization 12
Deng Xiaoping 112
deregulation of labor markets 5, 63–4
developmentalism 181
distributional regime 81
Duharde, Eduardo 67

Economic Commission for Latin America and the Caribbean (ECLAC) 8
employers' associations, China 122–6
employment
  China 106–11
    increase in 109
    job vacancies 110
  flexible *see* flexible employment
  informal 7–9
  Korea 201
    non-standard workers 179, 192, 200–1
  Mexico
    flexible 29–35
    formal sector 33
    informal sector 33
  non-standard 8–9, 179, 192, 200–1
  short-term 43
  Taiwan 169
    by size of establishment 156
    female 168
    method of applying for 156
  unstable 2–3
employment liberalization, Mexico 29–35

fictitious corporatism 41
flexibility
  functional 9, 170
  labor *see* labor flexibility
  organizational 61
  quantitative 61
  temporal 61, 171
  wages 9, 61, 170
flexible employment 7–8, 62
  China 105
  Korea 193–202
  Mexico 29–35
foreign workers 168, 173
  see also migrant workers
formal sector employment, Mexico 33
France, unemployment rate 2
functional flexibility 9, 170

González, Erman 67
gross domestic product (GDP)
  Argentina 63
  China 106, 107
  Korea 178

Ho Tsai-feng 157, 158
Hong Kong, unemployment rate 2
Hong Shi-cheng 145
Hsieh Chuang-chih 164
Hu Jintao 98, 106, 133
Huang Chang-ling 145
Huang Ching-hsien 157, 162
Huang Mei-ling 166
Huang Mengfu 123
Huang Shui-chuan 162

import-substitution industrialization 18, 51
industrial relations, Argentina 57–9
informal sector employment 7–9
  Mexico 33
insurance
  employment 194, 196
  medical 59–60
  social 196
  unemployment
    Argentina 64–6
    exclusions from 66
    South Africa 84, 88

Japan
  unemployment rate 2
  welfare model 181–2

Kang Xiaoguang 101
Kim Dae-Jung 180, 204, 205, 207
Kim Seong-Won 181
Kim Yeong-Sam 193
Koo Chen-fu 149
Korea 176–219
  centralism 182
  chaebols 185
  Declaration of Democratization 192
  developmentalism 181
  economic situation 178–80

Index

economic and social indicators 183–4
employment 201
  non-standard workers 179, 192, 200–1
employment insurance 194, 196
Federation of Korean Industries 203
flexible employment 193–202
Framework Act on Employment Policy 194
GDP 178
Great Workers Struggle 192
Han-nochong (Federation of Korean Trade Unions) 204–5, 206, 209–10
Hyundai Automobile union 205
labor policy 178–80
  development of 186–9
  dismissal for managerial reasons 197
  mandatory establishment size 195
Labor Standards Act 190, 195–6, 212
Livelihood Protection Act 191, 193
Min-no-dang (Korean Democratic Labor Party) 205
Min-nochong (Korean Congress of Trade Unions) 201, 205, 206–9, 210, 211
Minimum Wage Act 191
nalchigi (nonsense) legislation 187, 193, 198, 208
National Pension Act 191
National Welfare Pension Act 198
neocorporatism 12, 177, 179, 202–11
People's Solidarity for Participatory Democracy (PSPD) 180
policy makers 202–6
Presidential Commission for Industrial Relations Reform 193, 207
productive welfare 180
Removal of Third Person 191
retirement benefit 199

sam-pal-yuk (386) generation 180
sectoral corporatism 179
social insurance 196
Social Security Act 191
social security reform 1
state corporatism 177, 179
tripartite relations 179, 193, 207–11
unemployment rate 2, 178, 194
unionization 190
  "disguised employees" 191
  labor disputes 206
United Nations membership 177
Wage Claim Guarantee Fund 198
welfare policy 6, 182–3
  development of 182–93
  productive welfare 180
Yongse-min 194
Yushin Constitution 190
Korean Congress of Trade Unions (*Min-nochong*) 201, 205, 206–9, 210, 211
Korean Democratic Labor Party (*Min-no-dang*) 205
Korea Development Institute 194, 203
Korea Employers Federation 203
Korea Federation of Small and Medium Business 204
Korea Institute of Health and Social Affairs (KIHASA) 203
Korea Research Institute for Vocational Education and Training 212
Korea Tripartite Commission 207
Korean Chamber of Commerce 204
Korean Democratic Labor Party 205
Korean Economic Research Center 203
Korean International Trade Association 204
Korean Labor Institute 203
Korean Teachers and Education Workers' Union 204

labor contracts, Argentina 58, 64
labor disputes
  China 98, 99, 106–11
  Korea 206
labor flexibility
  Argentina 57–9
  Mexico 31–5
  Taiwan 167–71
labor laws
  China 111–17
  Mexico 21–9
    Central Decision Panel 24
    factors preventing
      approval 25–8
    Federal Labor Law 22
    state–labor relationship 28–9
  South Africa 83
    Basic Conditions of Employment
      Act (BCEA) 83
    Industrial Conciliation Act
      (ICA) 83
    Labour Relations Act (LRA) 83
    reforms 85–7
labor market
  deregulation of 5, 63–4
  entry into 62
  South Africa 77–82
    insiders and outsiders 81
labor reforms
  Argentina 57–9, 61–3
  China 111–17
  Mexico 29–35
  South Africa 85–92
labor surplus, China 107
labor unions *see* unionization
Latin America
  social security reform 1
  tripartite negotiations 49
  welfare policy 6
  see also individual countries
Lee Teng-hui 142
Lin Hui-kuan 157, 158, 162, 164
Lu Tien-lin 158

Malaysia, unemployment rate 2
Mandela, Nelson 73
Menem, Carlos 47, 48, 53
Menem regime 50–7, 67

Mexican Council of Businessmen
    (CMHN) 20
Mexican Employers' Confederation
    (COPARMEX) 20, 22, 24, 31,
    42
Mexican Institute of Social Security
    (IMSS) 20, 32–3
  number of affiliated workers 34
  reforms 35–7
Mexican Telephone Workers'
    Union 21
Mexican Workers Front 25, 27
Mexico 18–46
  Agreement for Stability,
    Competitiveness and
    Employment 30
  Business Coordinating Council 20
  compensation schemes 39–40
  Conciliation and Arbitration
    Boards 23
  Confederation of Mexican
    Workers 19
  Democratic Revolutionary
    Party 23
  Economic Solidarity Pact 30
  employment
    flexible 29–35
    formal sector 33
    informal sector 33
  employment liberalization 29–35
  Federation of Public Goods
    and Services Unions
    (FESEBES) 21, 26
  Federation of Public Service
    Workers 19, 38
  Institute of Social Security
    for Federal State Workers
    (ISSSTE) 36
  Institutional Revolutionary Party
    (PRI) system 18–21
  Integral Quality and
    Modernization Program
    (CIMO) 40
  Labor Conciliation and Arbitration
    Boards (JCAS) 20, 23, 27
  Labor Congress 19
  labor flexibility 31–5
  labor law reform 21–9
    Central Decision Panel 24

factors preventing
    approval   25–8
Federal Labor Law   22
state–labor relationship   28–9
labor reforms   29–35
May First Inter-union Coordination
    Group (CIPM)   27
Minimum Wage Commission   26
National Action Party   22
National Agreement for the
    Promotion of Quality and
    Productivity (ANEPC)   30
National Chamber of the
    Manufacturing Industry
    (CANACINTRA)   20
National Confederation of
    Chambers of Commerce
    (CONCANACO)   20
National Confederation of Labor
    (CNT)   27
National Minimum Wage
    Commission (CNSM)   20
National Service for Employment,
    Study and Training
    (SNECA)   40
National Social Insurance Workers'
    Union (SNTSS)   37–8
National Social Security Workers'
    Union   21
National Teachers Union   19, 38
National Workers' Assembly
    (ANT)   27
National Workers' Housing Fund
    Institute (INFONAVIT)   20
National Workers' Union
    (UNT)   21, 27, 38
official/corporate unionism   21
Pact for Stabilization and
    Economic Growth   30
pension reform   35–7
    state–labor relationship   37–9
Retirement Savings System
    (SAR)   36
state–labor relationship   18–21
strikes   42
Training Grants Program for
    the Unemployed
    (PROBECAT)   40
unemployment rate   2, 32

Workers' Housing Fund Institute
    (INFONAVIT)   36, 37
Workers' Union of the Mexican
    National Autonomous
    University   21, 27
migrant workers   105, 108–9
    shortage of (*ming-gong huang*)   105
    social welfare reform   126–35
    unstable working conditions   111
    women   129
minimum wage standards,
    China   114
Mo Rong   104–5

National Economic Development
    and Labor Council
    (NEDLAC)   11
neocorporatism
    China   102–3
    Korea   12, 177, 179, 202–11
    Taiwan   144, 161–7
    see also social corporatism
new risk   9, 14
New Zealand, unemployment rate   2
newly industrializing
    countries   11–12
    social security provision   3–4
    welfare policy   6
    see also individual countries
non-core workers   82
non-standard employment   8–9
    South Africa   79
        limits of reforms   88–92
        social security legislation   82–5
non-standard workers   179, 192,
    200–1
North American Free Trade
    Agreement (NAFTA)   22
numerical flexibility   9

organizational flexibility   61

Park Chang-Yong   194
pension reform
    Argentina   53–4, 59–60
    Mexico   35–7
        state–labor relationship   37–9
People's Republic of China *see* China

pluralism 142, 144, 152–60
productive welfare 180

quantitative flexibility 61

Republic of Korea *see* Korea
risk structure 9
Roh Moo-Hyun 180

Schmitter, Philippe C. 19
sectoral corporatism 179
Shen Tzong-ruey 146
Shih Chao-hsien 164
short-term employment 43
Singapore, unemployment rate 2
single-issue movements 145
social corporatism 10, 19, 49, 144, 172
  adverse factors 145, 165–7
  China 102
  Taiwan 142
social democratization 147
social security provision 1–2
  newly industrializing countries 3–4
  problems of 4–5
  South Africa 82–5
    expansion of 87–8
    non-standard employment 84–5
  Taiwan 171
social security reform
  Argentina 59–60, 61–3, 64–6
  China 1
  Korea 1
  Latin America 1
  South Africa 85–92
  Taiwan 1
social welfare *see* welfare
South Africa 73–97
  Accelerated and Shared Growth Initiative for South Africa (ASGISA) 78
  apartheid 73
  bargaining councils 78, 83
  Basic Conditions of Employment Act 13, 87
  Business Unity South Africa (BUSA) 75
  Child Support Grant 87
  civics 73
  Compensation for Occupational Injuries and Diseases 84
  Confederation of Associations of Private Employment Sector (CAPES) 79
  Congress of South African Trade Unions (COSATU) 73–4, 75, 86
  Disability Grant 87
  Employment Equity Act 87
  employment relations 77–82
  Federation of Unions of South Africa (FEDUSA) 75
  Growth, Employment and Redistribution (GEAR) strategy 75, 85
  labor laws 83
    Basic Conditions of Employment Act (BCEA) 83
    Industrial Conciliation Act (ICA) 83
    Labour Relations Act (LRA) 83, 85–6
    reforms 85–7
  labor market 77–82
    insiders and outsiders 81
  National Council of Trade Unions (NACTU) 75
  National Economic Development and Labor Council (NEDLAC) 15, 74–5, 76, 80–1, 86
  non-standard employment 79
    limits of reforms 88–92
    social security legislation 82–5
  Old Age Grant 87
  Quarterly Labour Force Survey (QLFS) 79
  Skills Development Act 87
  social security provision 82–5
    expansion of 87–8
    non-standard employment 84–5
  social security reform 85–92

Unemployment Insurance Fund
(UIF) 84, 88
unemployment rate 2, 78
welfare policy 6
workers' rights 85–7
South African Communist
Party 74
state corporatism 19, 49, 144
China 102
Korea 177, 179
legacy of 146–52
Taiwan 142, 146–52
Sun Chunlan 121

Taiwan 142–75
company benefits 153
Confederation of Trade
Unions 154
Conference on Sustaining Taiwan's
Economic Development
(COSTED) 161, 163–5, 167,
173
democratization 152–60
Economic Development Advisory
Council (EDAC) 161–3
economic organizations 148–9
employees' welfare council
benefits 153
Employees' Welfare Funds
Act 151
employment 169
by size of establishment 156
female 168
method of applying for 156
flexibilization 167–71
foreign workers 168, 173
Gender Equality in Employment
Act 168
independent labor movement
152–7
industrial relations
enterprise level 150–2
national level 146–50
Kaohsiung Incident 142
Labor Pension Act 165
Labor Standards Act 151,
165
neocorporatism 144, 161–7
pluralism 152–60

Protective Act for Mass
Redundancy of
Employees 165
social corporatism 142, 144
adverse factors 145, 165–7
social democratization 147
social security provision 171
social security reform 1
state corporatism 146–52
strikes 154
Three Principles of the
People 146–7
unemployment rate 2, 169
unionization 149–52
organization of 157–60
rate of 155, 160
Taiwan Confederation of
Labor 157
Taiwan Confederation of Trade
Unions 157, 158, 159, 166
Taiwan Labor Legal Assistance
Association 152
temporal flexibility 9, 61, 171
Tiananmen Square Massacre 103,
113
totalitarianism 146
trade unions *see* unionization
tripartite relations
China 100, 117–18
Korea 179, 193, 207–11
Latin America 49
Taiwan 142–75
Turkey, unemployment rate 2

Ubaldini, Saul 60
unemployment insurance
Argentina 64–6
China 126–35
exclusions from 66
South Africa 84, 88
unemployment rate 1–2
Argentina 2, 63–4, 65
China 2
young people 135
Korea 2, 178, 194
Mexico 2, 32
South Africa 2, 78
Taiwan 2, 169
see also individual countries

Unger, Jonathan 101
unionization 149–52
  China 117–22
  Korea 190
    "disguised employees" 191
    labor disputes 206
  Mexico 21
  Taiwan 149–52
    organization of 157–60
    rate of 155, 160
United Kingdom, unemployment rate 2
unstable employment 2–3
USA, unemployment rate 2

wage flexibility 9, 61, 170
Wang Zhongyu 122
welfare policy 5–6
  China 6
  Korea 6, 182–3
    development of 182–93
    productive welfare 180
  Latin America 6
  newly industrializing countries 6
  South Africa 6
welfare reform 100
  China 100, 126–35
    migrant workers 126–35
    unemployed 126–35
    Wailai Renshi Zonghe Baoxian 128
  migrant workers 126–35
  unemployment insurance *see* unemployment insurance
welfare regime 81
Wen Jiabao 98, 106
West Germany, former, unemployment rate 2
White, Gordon 101
Wiarda, Howard J. 19
women
  employment 168
  migrant workers 129
Wu Ching-pin 164
Wu Hai-rui 157

Xing Xiaobo 104

Yang Peng-fei 102
Yang Yiyong 104

Zhang Qixin 126
Zheng Bingwen 101